Tc
(

Bad Blood

Lyndon B. Johnson, Robert F. Kennedy, and the Tumultuous 1960s

Jeffrey K. Smith

AuthorHouse™
1663 Liberty Drive
Bloomington, IN 47403
www.authorhouse.com
Phone: 1-800-839-8640

First published by AuthorHouse   11/23/2010

ISBN: 978-1-4520-8442-8 (sc)
ISBN: 978-1-4520-8443-5 (hc)
ISBN: 978-1-4520-8444-2 (e)

Library of Congress Control Number: 2010917757

Printed in the United States of America

Any people depicted in stock imagery provided by Thinkstock are models,
and such images are being used for illustrative purposes only.
Certain stock imagery © Thinkstock.

This book is printed on acid-free paper.

Because of the dynamic nature of the Internet, any Web addresses or links contained in
this book may have changed since publication and may no longer be valid. The views
expressed in this work are solely those of the author and do not necessarily reflect the
views of the publisher, and the publisher hereby disclaims any responsibility for them.

PROLOGUE

Political feuds have long been a colorful component of American history. The origins of the feuds have sometimes been ideological, other times personal. Some have arisen from simple misunderstandings.

John Adams and Thomas Jefferson literally ceased communicating for years after the bitter 1800 presidential election. Years later, with the help of an intermediary, the two founding fathers finally reconciled.

The acerbic Andrew Jackson engaged in a number of bitter disputes with rivals, escalating to the point of violence. Jackson spent a good portion of his life with a bullet imbedded in his upper body, courtesy of an opponent's dueling pistol.

Theodore Roosevelt designated William Howard Taft to be his successor, and then helped elect the rotund Ohioan to the presidency. Before Taft could complete his four-year term, Roosevelt grew disenchanted with his former Vice-President, and helped create the formidable *Bull Moose* Party, dooming his successor's chances for reelection.

The tumultuous decade of the 1960s began with promise and hope, when John F. Kennedy (JFK) became the youngest elected President of the United States. Kennedy promised youthful, energetic leadership, as the country headed into the latter half of the twentieth century, christening his presidency as the *New Frontier*. After a thousand days, an assassin's bullets shattered the dreams of an idealistic generation.

After the shocking murder of President Kennedy, the Civil Rights movement and the Vietnam War dominated the headlines, leading to turmoil at home and abroad. In 1968, the back-to-back assassinations of Martin Luther King and Robert F. Kennedy further traumatized an already disillusioned society. A decade that began with hope, ended with sadness and uncertainty.

Following the assassination of John F. Kennedy on November 22, 1963, Lyndon Baines Johnson (LBJ) was catapulted into the presidency. Emerging from political exile, Johnson readily assumed the leadership role, and consolidated his power base.

LBJ's political resurrection led to a dramatic decline in the power and influence of Robert Francis Kennedy (RFK). As Attorney General and brother to the President of the United States, RFK earned the unofficial title of the "second most powerful man in the country." As his brother's closest confidant, the younger Kennedy participated in both domestic and foreign policy decision-making at a level far beyond that of any Attorney General before him. When his brother was assassinated, RFK's idyllic life unraveled.

During the Kennedy Administration, Lyndon Johnson and Robert Kennedy had never enjoyed a cordial relationship. President Kennedy had managed to function as peacekeeper of sorts, preventing the animosity between his brother and the Vice-President from fracturing the *New Frontier*. After JFK's murder, the war of words and political machinations between the two long time enemies escalated to bitter, unrestricted warfare.

The new President launched his own vision, the *Great Society,* and the idealistic days of the *New Frontier* became a sad memory for Kennedy loyalists. In the eyes of Robert Kennedy, Johnson was the usurper of his slain brother's hopes and dreams.

When the mounting cost of the Vietnam War imperiled Lyndon Johnson's domestic programs, proving the idealistic goal of *guns and butter* was unsustainable, Robert Kennedy made his move to reclaim the presidency. By the end of 1968, both men would be losers.

Driven, and sometimes blinded, by ego, ambition, and self-righteousness, Lyndon Johnson and Robert Kennedy engaged in an epic duel that significantly influenced the course of history.

Bad Blood: Lyndon B. Johnson, Robert F. Kennedy, and the Tumultuous 1960s chronicles the personal and political feud between two powerful and controversial twentieth century icons.

Chapter 1

The Loyalists and the Realists

In the early evening hours of November 22, 1963, *Air Force One* made its final approach to Andrews Air Force Base, just outside Washington D.C. Shortly before 6:00 p.m., darkness had descended upon the nation's capitol, and the waiting crowd was mournfully silent.

A distinguished group of Congressional leaders, Supreme Court Justices, the Secretary of the Defense, White House aides, and an assortment of military leaders stared into the distant skies, hoping to catch a glimpse of the approaching aircraft. Nearly *3000* private citizens were congregated outside the fence surrounding the air base, not yet willing to accept the reality of the day's tragic events. An eerie gray hearse, surrounded by a spit and polished military honor guard, caught the eye of television cameras.

The gleaming silver, blue, and white *Boeing 707*, Aircraft number *2600*, was nearing the end of a 1300 mile flight from Dallas. Colonel Jim Swindal, who had piloted President John F. Kennedy thousands of miles over the past three years, was bringing his Commander-in-Chief home for the final time. Cruising at an altitude of 41,000 feet, Air Force One had flown well above a series of thunderstorms and tornadoes that were ravaging the Deep South. The flight had taken only two hours, at the breakneck speed of 635 miles per hour (at one point, Swindal was instructed to slow down, so that the presidential jet would not land before all the dignitaries arrived at Andrews).

In the aircraft's stateroom, an airborne version of the Oval Office, Lyndon Johnson stretched his six feet three inch frame, and prepared to meet the welcoming party at the terminal. He had been President for less than three hours, and the casket of his predecessor, sitting in the tail section of the plane, served as a grim reminder of the day's horrific events.

Three years earlier, Lyndon Johnson had been one of the most powerful men in America. As Senate Majority Leader, LBJ had exercised unprecedented power over the legislative process. When his own bid for the presidency had ended in defeat, Johnson agreed to serve as John F. Kennedy's running mate. When Kennedy defeated his Republican opponent, Richard M. Nixon, in the 1960 presidential election, LBJ became the Vice-President.

Harboring high hopes for a prominent role in the Kennedy Administration, Johnson quickly found himself marginalized. Attorney General Robert Kennedy, who also happened to be the President's younger brother, became the *number two man* in the executive branch. LBJ was the odd man out, as RFK assumed the role as his brother's primary domestic and foreign affairs adviser.

President Kennedy treated his Vice-President with respect, and recognized the sacrifice LBJ had made by relinquishing his powerful position in Congress. At the same time, JFK refused to be upstaged by the proud Texan, and Johnson was relegated to the sidelines for the first time in his political career.

Unlike his older brother, Robert Kennedy neither liked nor respected Lyndon Johnson, and did nothing to encourage or facilitate his participation in the *New Frontier*. The Attorney General's animosity was no secret to Johnson: "Bobby hates me."

The Vice-President was also aware that RFK regularly poked fun at him, nicknaming LBJ and his wife, Lady Bird, *Uncle Cornpone and Mrs. Pork Chop*. Angry and demoralized, Lyndon Johnson held Robert Kennedy personally responsible for his personal and political humiliation.

While he craved a return to power, LBJ had grown sadly accustomed to his diminished role as Kennedy's Vice-President. At the start of this November day, Johnson was mired in political exile. In less than ten seconds, a sniper's bullets changed the course of history, and Lyndon Johnson suddenly became the thirty-sixth President of the United States.

The new President realized he would need to tread a fine line between exercising his newfound powers and displaying an appropriate degree of sensitivity toward the Kennedy family. During the flight from Dallas, LBJ called President Kennedy's mother, Rose, and offered his condolences. He also asked the newly widowed, former First Lady to remain in the aircraft's more comfortable stateroom, but Jacqueline Kennedy, still wearing the dress stained with her husband's blood and brain matter, chose to remain in the tail section next to the coffin.

Earlier in the day, Johnson had phoned Robert Kennedy to offer his sympathies and to inform the Attorney General that he wished to be sworn into office before departing Dallas. Constitutionally, LBJ became President when John F. Kennedy was pronounced dead, but Johnson (and several of his advisers) believed that a swearing in ceremony was necessary to formalize the transfer of power. Stunned by the death of his brother, RFK spoke briefly with the new President, but offered no opinion on the exact timing and location for the oath of office recitation. Since the Attorney General did not voice opposition to the plan, Johnson disingenuously interpreted RFK's silence as tacit approval to proceed with the swearing in ceremony, before departing Texas.

The hearse transporting President Kennedy's body from Parkland Hospital reached Dallas's Love Field prior to the arrival of Judge Sarah Hughes, who had been summoned to administer the oath of office to the new President. Once the casket was aboard Air Force One, President Kennedy's closest aides assumed that their departure would be immediate. When forced to wait a half hour for the arrival of Judge Hughes, the Kennedy staffers were puzzled and angered.

Lyndon Johnson, fully aware that he was skirting the truth, told Kennedy aide, Kenneth O'Donnell: "Bobby wants me to be sworn in down here."

While puzzled by LBJ's explanation, O'Donnell accepted it at face value, and assumed that his close friend, Robert Kennedy, had sound reasons for giving Johnson such advice.

O'Donnell fumed when Johnson insisted that Jacqueline Kennedy join him for the swearing in ceremony. Shell shocked and blood stained, the widowed First Lady nevertheless stood beside the new President as he recited the formal oath of office.

During the flight from Dallas to Washington D.C., Johnson also asked O'Donnell to join him for a discussion about the tragic events of the day, and to make plans for the future. Shocked and angry, O'Donnell refused to leave the side of his fallen leader, maintaining vigil over the casket, alongside Jackie Kennedy.

The new President did manage to capture the ear of one of Kennedy's closest aides, David Powers: "You fellows can't leave me now. I don't know a single soul north of the Mason-Dixon Line. I want all of you to remain on board with me."

Johnson was convinced that his decision concerning the oath of office had been correct, but also knew there would be hell to pay, when Bobby Kennedy learned that the plane had been delayed to await the arrival of Judge Hughes. JFK's presidential aides were already dividing into camps— the *Realists,* who felt that they served the office of the President, rather than a single individual, and the *Loyalists,* who were not yet prepared to say goodbye to the *New Frontier.*

The Kennedy loyalists were clustered in the tail section of Air Force One, comforting Jackie and consuming copious amounts of alcohol. The new President realized that he was being ignored by his predecessor's closest advisors: "I thought they were just wine heads. They were just drinkers—just one drink after another coming to them, trying to drown out their sorrow, and we were not drinking, of course."

LBJ adviser, Jack Valenti, was more generous in his assessment, believing that the Kennedy faithful were simply traumatized: "What I saw in O'Brien and O'Donnell and those guys, was such numbing grief; such an avalanche of doom flowed over them. Here you are—you're next to the President—you're the most powerful men in the world, and suddenly, your leader is struck down. And, where are you? I didn't see hostility—I just saw dumb, mute grief."

Johnson was certain that Bobby Kennedy would exploit the anger and resentment of the loyalists, and try to undermine his presidential authority. LBJ's paranoia and animosity toward RFK, led him to believe that the Attorney General might set up a *shadow government* of sorts, plotting to regain his brother's lost office.

Nevertheless, LBJ was determined to show sensitivity to the Kennedy family. He planned to give the loyalists an opportunity to grieve and come to terms with their anger. In time, he would do his best to win over the hearts and minds of the people who had so faithfully served his predecessor.

The new President tried not to appear unduly opportunistic. When the Secret Service recommended that he spend the night in the White House, where he could be more easily protected, Johnson refused.

"It would be presumptuous on my part. I won't do it," LBJ replied, and ordered the Secret Service to find a way to secure his private residence (*The Elms*).

Johnson knew RFK and the remaining Kennedy loyalists would find plenty of reasons to criticize him, without his providing extra ammunition.

The Attorney General sat alone in the back of a canvas covered military truck, awaiting the arrival of his brother's body. Two days earlier, Robert Kennedy had celebrated his thirty-eighth birthday, enjoying a position of power rarely afforded to someone his age. At midday, he had been the *second most powerful man* in the entire country. Five hours later, he was *merely* the Attorney General, serving under a new President that he had long despised. RFK had lost a brother, a President, and a huge piece of his own identity.

During the lunch hour, RFK had been entertaining the U.S. Attorney from New York (and his assistant) at his home, when the poolside telephone extension rang. FBI Director, J. Edgar Hoover, matter-of-factly informed the Attorney General that the President had been shot. While he hastily dressed and prepared to depart for Dallas, RFK received word from the White House Situation Room that his brother was dead. For the remainder of the afternoon, the Attorney General struggled to control his grief, while comforting his wife, children, and friends.

During the drive to the Pentagon, where he would be transported by helicopter to Andrews Air Force Base, RFK masked his grief by focusing on his long time nemesis: "People just don't realize how conservative Lyndon really is. There are going be a lot of changes."

In the semi-darkness of the military vehicle, the wiry five feet eight inch tall RFK avoided the television cameras, microphones, and consoling words of the D.C. dignitaries gathered to greet Air Force One. Bobby only wanted to talk to one person—his sister-in-law, Jacqueline Kennedy. Together, the stunned brother and widow would somehow find a way deal with the pain of their mutual loss.

Illness and death were not strangers to Robert Kennedy. His older brother, Joe, had been killed during a World War II bombing raid in Europe, and his older sister, Kathleen, had perished in a plane crash. Bobby's father, Joseph P. Kennedy, Sr. was paralyzed and aphasic after suffering a stroke, two years earlier. Another sister, Rosemary, was institutionalized as a result of mental retardation and a botched frontal lobotomy. His brother Jack, had long suffered from *Addison's disease*, a form of chronic adrenal insufficiency, and lived with constant, unremitting pain caused by a degenerative spinal condition (the adrenal deficiency was potentially fatal, and, on at least two occasions, JFK had lingered near death, receiving the last rites of the Catholic Church).

In spite of his precarious health, Jack Kennedy had been tanned, handsome, and youthful, and Bobby had never given any serious thoughts to his brother meeting a violent death. After all, RFK had been the one making enemies, in an unprecedented wave of indictments and prosecutions of Mafia leaders.

"I always thought they might get one of us, but not Jack—I figured it would be me," RFK mournfully reflected.

Emotionally devastated, RFK warded off the nighttime chill and wistfully remembered the last time he had waited for President Kennedy to return to Washington, just over a year ago, during the height of the *Cuban Missile Crisis*. The resolution of this international conflict, which had pushed the world to the brink of nuclear destruction, was a triumph for the Kennedy Administration.

Now, RFK was certain his life would never be the same.

Lyndon Johnson studied the index card containing a brief statement he planned to make in front of the reporters, microphones, and television cameras assembled at Andrews Air Force Base. It would be LBJ's first media appearance as President, and he was determined to maintain a solemn and dignified image: "I want the world to know, that while the leader has fallen, the nation isn't prostrate."

LBJ had also planned to escort the blood stained former First Lady from the rear of plane, acutely aware that television cameras would see Jacqueline Kennedy on his arm, as they jointly supervised the unloading of his predecessor's coffin. The painful image would let the world know that the man might die, but the presidency would not perish. The new President and the young widow would stand together in grief—dignified, but defiant.

Air Force One touched down at 5:58 p.m. EST. Colonel Swindal's landing had been so smooth that many of the passengers were not aware they were on the ground, until the aircraft began to slowly taxi toward the terminal.

Robert Kennedy had made arrangements to board the jet without delay. The aircraft had barely come to a full stop, when the Attorney General ran up a portable walkway, as it was being rolled into place. When the door nearest the cockpit was opened, RFK began elbowing his way down Air Force One's center aisle, hell bent on locating his sister-in-law.

Lyndon Johnson was surprised to the see the Attorney General heading his way, and wondered how RFK had been able to board the plane so quickly. In spite of his inherent dislike and mistrust of the younger Kennedy, the new President was determined to be dignified and sympathetic.

"Bob," Johnson said, holding out his hand to greet the grieving brother.

RFK never paused to make eye contact, or even acknowledge LBJ's presence.

"Where is Jackie? I want to see Jackie," Kennedy repeated, as he continued to rush toward the rear of the aircraft.

In the frantic hustle of RFK's mad dash to find his sister-in-law, Johnson was literally shoved to the side. LBJ was astonished at his Attorney General's brashness: "He ran, so that he would not have to pause and recognize the new President."

Johnson knew that RFK had seen him, and had spitefully ignored him at the first available opportunity. While he realized the deceased President's younger brother was in a state of shock and consumed by grief, he would never forget RFK's rudeness and blatant insubordination.

On Friday evening, November 22, 1963, the *bad blood* between Lyndon Johnson and Robert Kennedy grew from a trickle into a bold stream.

Chapter 2

The Johnson treatment

By the end of 1959, Lyndon Johnson had reached the pinnacle of power in America's legislative branch of government. As Senate Majority Leader, he influenced the outcome of every major piece of legislation enacted into law. As a new decade approached, the fifty-one year old Texan had his eye on the ultimate prize—the White House. LBJ had little reason to doubt that his powerful personality and political adroitness would take him all the way to the top.

Lyndon Baines Johnson was born on August 27, 1908 in Blanco County, Texas, on the banks of the Pedernales River. This eastern portion of south central Texas was known as the *Hill Country*, and the while undulating topography was far from mountainous, it was not at all like the pancake flatness of most of the state.

Fourteen miles to the east, Johnson City, was the nearest town to LBJ's rustic birthplace. Located fifty miles east of Austin, Johnson City was home to some 300 residents, but, in the early twentieth century, lacked paved roads, electricity, natural gas, indoor toilets, or rail lines. Telephones and automobiles were also scarce commodities among the Hill Country residents.

Born and year and a half after his parent's marriage, Johnson was named for one of his father's lawyer friends, whose last name was *Linden*. By the estimate of the midwife who delivered him, Lyndon weighed in at a whopping eleven pounds, and was the first of his parent's five children.

Lyndon's father, Sam Ealey Johnson, was a rancher and state legislator, who passed along his love of the land and a passion for politics to his oldest son. Lyndon's mother, the former Rebekah Baines, was a cultured woman and a graduate of Baylor College. Having earned a degree in literature, she dreamed of one day writing a novel.

Instead, Rebekah resigned herself to the less refined and physically demanding life of a rancher's wife. Nonetheless, she stressed the importance of education, and often read to her young children from Tennyson and Longfellow. At age two, Lyndon could already recite long passages of poetry.

The Johnson family was not impoverished, but a rancher's life in the Texas hill country was far from privileged. At an early age, Lyndon grew determined to improve his financial and social standing.

The Johnson's oldest child was precocious and restless, as his mother later recalled: "Lyndon, from his earliest days, possessed a highly inquisitive mind. He was never content to play quietly in the yard. He must take his toys apart to see what made them go, or he must set out to conquer that new, unexpected world beyond the gate, or up the lane."

Lyndon idealized his mother, and adopted a protective and nurturing attitude towards her. He knew that Rebekah was self-conscious of her red, swollen hands—the byproducts of pumping and toting well water from the outdoor pump, plucking chickens, scrubbing floors, and hand washing laundry. Young Lyndon tried to comfort her: "Oh, Mamma, when I get big, I'm going to see that you don't have to do any of this hard work, so you can have pretty white hands."

Lyndon grew to understand that his father was not particularly interested in improving his wife's social position or standard of living: "My Mother soon discovered my Daddy was not a man to discuss higher things. To her mind, his life was vulgar and ignorant. His idea of pleasure was to sit up half the night with his friends, drinking beer, telling stories, and playing dominoes."

Throughout his political career, Lyndon Johnson often reflected on his mother's backbreaking physical labor, and became an outspoken advocate of rural electrification to improve the quality of life for farmers and ranchers. He also made good on a childhood promise—after his father's death in 1948, Lyndon purchased a house for Rebekah, just outside Austin, where she could permanently escape the rigors of ranch life.

Lyndon learned to control and manipulate his siblings. His younger brother, Sam Houston Johnson, remembered it well: "Lyndon somehow did fewer chores than the rest of us. He was like the foreman—you might say the boss."

Lyndon regularly delegated hog slopping, wood gathering, and egg gathering chores to his younger brothers and sisters. He would sometimes organize contests between the others to see who could stack the most firewood on the rear porch, and then take full credit for the labors of his siblings.

"I used to think it was because he was older. I now think it was because, well, to put it one way, he was smarter," Sam Houston later surmised.

Industrious and inquisitive, Lyndon eventually discovered a way to make money, while indulging his burgeoning interest in current affairs. Shining shoes in a local barbershop, LBJ listened and learned as the men discussed politics.

When under duress, Lyndon was prone to histrionics—a characteristic that persisted into his adult life. After falling out of the barn loft and fracturing his leg, Johnson wailed loudly before and after the family doctor arrived.

"How are you, Lyndon?" the physician inquired, as the boy dramatically writhed in pain.

"Oh, I'm killed! I'm killed!" Lyndon cried.

When the doctor suggested that he be given a "shot" for pain, LBJ's hysterics escalated: "Oh, please doctor, don't shoot me! I want to live awhile longer!"

Six feet tall and towering over his peers, Lyndon showed little interest in spending time with children his own age, preferring to hang out with older kids. He also developed more mature interests, such as scouring the *Congressional Record*, in order to expand his political knowledge.

Later in life, Johnson reflected on his particular interest in presidential history: "...I had great respect for Jefferson, because he believed in the land…Then, I loved Jackson, because he was a guy that didn't let 'em tread on him…And, Wilson; I devoured him, because everything he wrote or said, I memorized nearly, because he was President during the time I was six to fourteen."

By the time he was in high school, Lyndon had begun to distinguish himself in dress and manner. While other young men dressed in jeans or khaki pants, Johnson wore white shirts and neckties to school.

With a strong emotional attachment to his mother, Lyndon gained a reputation as a *Mama's boy*. Lyndon's relationship with Sam Ealey was tumultuous, with frequent and noisy conflicts between father and son. The outspoken, elder Johnson did not appreciate his older son's attention seeking ways, to the point of publicly rebuking Lyndon and resorting to harsh physical discipline.

Lyndon had difficulty fully respecting his father (who, in addition to ranching, traded in cotton futures and bought and sold real estate, but invariably seemed to lose more money than he earned): "…When he had too much to drink, he'd lose control of himself. He used bad language. He squandered the little money we had on cotton and real estate markets. Sometimes, he'd be lucky and make a lot of money, but more often, he lost out."

A competition, of sorts, arose between father and son to win the affections of Rebekah Johnson. Rebekah knew how to manipulate her oldest son, and if Lyndon displeased her, she would simply withhold all affection. The aptly named *Johnson Freeze* would be modeled by LBJ during his adult years to deal with those people who betrayed his loyalty or otherwise angered him.

The love of politics helped maintain a fragile bond between Lyndon and his father. At age ten, LBJ accompanied Sam Ealey to the legislative session in Austin. Inside the state capitol building, young Lyndon sat in the gallery and watched the lawmakers in action. He also roamed the halls of the statehouse, running errands for legislators, and learned how various politicians operated; differentiating the *followers* from the *leaders*.

Sam Ealey Johnson differed from many Texas legislators of his time, supporting such liberal causes as women's suffrage, anti-Prohibition, and immigration rights. He also opposed the Ku Klux Klan, at a time when the racist organization exercised considerable influence across the South. Because of his opposition to the Klan, Sam Ealey endured death threats from the white sheeted vigilantes. Lyndon Johnson later attributed his own lack of bigotry to the example set by his father.

LBJ remembered the unmitigated joy of accompanying his father on campaign swings: "Families all along the way opened up their homes to us. If it was hot outside, we were invited in for big servings of homemade ice cream. If it was cold, we were given hot tea. Christ, sometimes I wished it could go on forever!"

Not surprisingly, Lyndon Johnson was president of his graduating high school class—an accomplishment lessened by the fact that there were only *six* students in his class. After graduation, Lyndon stubbornly resisted the idea of obtaining a college education (in direct opposition to his mother's long-standing dreams for her first born). Instead, in 1925, Lyndon and several of his friends pooled their money and purchased a *Model T* Ford. While the decrepit vehicle lacked a roof and a windshield, it did provide the young men with a means to escape rural Texas, and the enthusiastic group packed their meager belongings and headed west. With just twenty-five dollars in his pocket, LBJ left Texas, dreaming of future riches.

After ten days on the highway, the young Texans arrived in California, the presumed *land of opportunity*. Lyndon worked at a variety of jobs (car washer, elevator operator, cook, garage mechanic, and grape picker). He also found employment as a clerk for his cousin, Tom Martin, who was an attorney. Filing court papers and running errands for Martin, Johnson briefly considered studying law by apprenticeship, but abandoned that notion, after learning, absent a college degree, he would have to wait three years before taking the California bar exam. After a year or so, LBJ had grew homesick, and managed to finagle a ride back to Texas.

Lyndon subsequently took a job on a road gang, driving a tractor, wielding a pick axe, and operating a mule-drawn dirt scraper. After working six days a week for six months (earning $92.50 per month), he approached his mother: "All right, I'm sick of working just with my hands, and I'm ready to try and make it with my brain."

After enrolling at Southwest Texas State University, Johnson learned that his high school education was not fully accredited (Johnson City public schools ended after eleven grades, and Lyndon did not meet the university's admission criteria). He was forced to attend *sub-college* for six weeks to gain academic eligibility. After watching her son struggle with plane geometry, Rebekah helped him study, until he passed his mathematics exam.

"I made seventy, and seventy was passing, and I never had a damned bit of use for plane geometry before, and I never have, since," LBJ later recalled.

Located in San Marcos, just thirty miles from LBJ's hometown, Southwest Texas State Teacher's College boasted only ten classroom buildings and fifty-six faculty members. Johnson's academic record was mediocre—eleven A's, twenty-two B's, fourteen C's, four D's, and a single F. The failing grade was in physical education, which LBJ considered a waste of time. Johnson found social sciences, particularly history and civics, more to his liking. He also joined a debate team, and excelled in verbal sparring matches.

Ever ambitious, Lyndon worked as a clerk in the college administration building, cultivating a relationship with the university President. He also developed a reputation as an aggressive and opinionated student, earning the nickname *Bull.* While some credited the origin of the nickname to LBJ's forceful, intrusive nature, others believed that it was a reflection of his tendency to pontificate and exaggerate the truth (equivalent to spreading verbal bovine manure). For better or worse, by the time he graduated college with a degree in history and education, everyone on campus knew *Bull Johnson.*

"You either liked him or you didn't," a college instructor recalled.

LBJ cut his political teeth at San Marcos. After he was blackballed by the *Black Stars,* a campus social fraternity that favored athletes, Johnson joined a competing organization. The newly founded *White Stars,* benefiting from LBJ's political guile and inside connections to the university President's office, gradually moved into positions of campus power. With Johnson's active support, a *White Star* was elected senior class President.

Johnson accompanied the college president to Austin to help him lobby the state legislature on behalf of the university. Ambitious and resourceful, LBJ was already plotting his future in politics.

During his sophomore year, President Evans secured an off campus job for Johnson, to help him pay for the remainder of his college. LBJ was hired as a teacher and principal at Welhausen Elementary School in Cotulla, Texas (near the Mexican border) at a salary of $125.00 per month. While completing his one year teaching assignment, Johnson was able to earn credit hours through special extension courses, which allowed him to graduate college in just three years.

Two hundred miles from Johnson City, Cotulla was home to 3000 people, *seventy-five* percent of whom were Hispanic day laborers and farmers. Anti-Mexican prejudice was an unfortunate way of life in that portion of Texas, with segregated public facilities and private accommodations. LBJ recalled that Mexicans were treated "just worse than you'd treat a dog."

The entire student body at Welhausen Elementary School consisted of Mexican-Americans, who had long felt the twin shames of poverty and racial prejudice. As a young teacher, LBJ approached his job with enthusiasm and vigor, insisting that his students learn to speak proper English and use it exclusively in the classroom. LBJ strived to improve their fledgling academic skills, and even took time to teach the school's elderly janitor how to read and write.

With no additional salary or funding to support extracurricular activities, Lyndon organized sports and debate teams. He spent his own money (half of one month's salary) to purchase bats, balls, and gloves for student athletics. When necessary, he transported his students to and from school functions. In later years, Johnson often cited the source of his benevolent inspiration: "My mother's philosophy was the belief that the strong must care for the weak."

"My students were poor and they often came to class without breakfast, hungry. They knew, even in their youth, the pain of injustice. They never seemed to know why people disliked them, but they knew it was so, because I saw it in their eyes…" Johnson recalled.

Lyndon Johnson grew to despise poverty and bigotry, as seen through the eyes of his Cotulla school children.

After completing the school term in Cotulla, Johnson returned to San Marcos to complete his degree. The new graduate then accepted a high school teaching job in Houston. After fifteen months, LBJ received a job offer that seemed too good to be true, when Fourteenth District Congressman, Richard M. Kleberg, offered the fledgling teacher a position as his Legislative Secretary. LBJ was soon on his way to Washington D.C. to embark on career in politics.

As a congressional office manager, Lyndon Johnson more than earned this salary of *$3900.00* per year. LBJ was a firm taskmaster, insisting that constituency mail be answered immediately. He was also meticulous, insisting that his staff re-type letters if they were not perfect. Johnson also kept the Congressman abreast of pending legislation. Kleberg, on the other hand, preferred spending time on the golf course rather than in the halls of Congress.

Johnson loved everything about Capitol Hill: "…There was the smell of power. It's got an odor, you know?"

LBJ paid twenty dollars per month to rent a room in the Dodge Hotel, where some twenty other congressional aides resided. The young

Texan quickly acquainted himself with his fellow lodgers. With one common bathroom on the floor, Johnson took four showers and brushed his teeth five times on the very first day, to meet as many legislative aides as possible.

Johnson became adept at navigating the massive federal government bureaucracy. He was determined to respond to the needs of Kleberg's constituents in a timely manner. On occasion, LBJ would impersonate Congressman Kleberg over the telephone in order to expedite his requests to governmental agencies.

LBJ's efforts on behalf of Kleberg knew no bounds. When the Congressman had an affair, Johnson helped him reconcile with his wife. At the same time, LBJ exerted considerable pressure on his boss to support populist legislation—when Kleberg initially refused to support the *Agriculture Agreement Act (AAA),* Johnson threatened to resign.

LBJ took on a second job as a doorkeeper to the House of Representatives. In short order, he struck up acquaintanceships with the lawmakers during his trips from the door to the House floor.

LBJ achieved wider personal recognition, when he was elected Speaker of the *Little Congress;* a shadow legislative body, comprised of various legislative aides. As Speaker, Lyndon Johnson savored his first opportunity to exercise political leadership.

Outspoken, but always accommodating, LBJ soon caught the eye of prominent Washington insiders, including President Franklin D. Roosevelt. With the famed FDR now in his corner, Johnson had gained a powerful political ally.

Lyndon Johnson was seen as a *man on a mission,* who cared little for anything other than politics. He hated the solitude of movie theaters, and would talk about politics between pitches at baseball games.

For a brief while, LBJ enrolled in law school night classes, but found the lectures boring and a distraction from his true love—politics. While he devoured the *New York Times, Wall Street Journal,* and *Congressional Record* on a daily basis, books bored him, and he soon abandoned his law school studies.

In September of 1934, Lyndon Johnson met his future wife. Claudia Alta Taylor, an attractive, polished, demure, twenty-one year old college graduate, bore the improbable name of *Lady Bird* (a black nursemaid had once proclaimed to the world that she "was as purdy as a ladybird", bestowing her with a lasting nickname). The couple met when Lady Bird traveled to Washington D.C. after graduating from the University of Texas (with twin degrees in journalism and history). Two weeks later, Lyndon and Lady Bird encountered each other a second time, when Johnson returned to Texas on congressional business for Kleberg.

"He was very, very good-looking. Lots of hair, quite black and wavy, and the most outspoken, straightforward, and determined young man I'd ever met," Lady Bird remembered.

At their second meeting Lady Bird was stunned when Lyndon proposed to her. When she took LBJ to meet her father, Mr. Taylor offered a definitive assessment: "You've been bringing home a lot of boys. This one looks like a man."

The couple married before the year ended (on November 17, 1934). Lady Bird later described their *ten* week, whirlwind courtship: "I felt like a moth drawn to a flame."

Lady Bird proved to be a calming influence on her new husband, and her congeniality and talent for organization were perfect compliments to LBJ's inexhaustible political ambition. At the same time, she stoically endured the humiliation of her husband's numerous, often flagrant, infidelities: "Everybody in the country loves Lyndon, and half the country are women."

"Ours was a compelling love. Lyndon bullied me, coaxed me, at times ridiculed me, but he made me more than I would have been. I offered him some peace and quiet, and maybe a little bit of judgment," Lady Bird explained.

Over the course of their *thirty-eight* year marriage, Lady Bird suffered three miscarriages (including a life-threatening tubal pregnancy in 1945). Eventually, she gave birth to two daughters—Lynda Bird and Luci Baines Johnson.

LBJ continued to expand his connections with a growing list of Washington power brokers, and his hard work on behalf of Congressman Kleberg drew rave reviews. President Roosevelt eventually offered Johnson an opportunity to direct the *National Youth Administration (NYA)* in Texas.

Before leaving for his home state, Johnson boldly declared: "When I come (back) to Washington, I'm coming back as a Congressman."

As the head of a high profile *New Deal* program designed to provide jobs for young people, LBJ was the youngest NYA Director in the United States. From this position, Johnson was also able to provide service to his fellow Texans during the height of the *Great Depression,* while building a statewide constituency.

Johnson put considerable energy into expanding the Texas NYA, and by the end of the first year, the program had grown from *four* to *twelve* districts, with a *four-fold* increase in staff members.

Six months into Johnson's NYA directorship, *18,000* young Texans were employed in secondary, vocational, and college work study programs. Over *100* permanent roadside parks were constructed by Texas NYA workers. LBJ, who was described as a "steam engine in pants," earned statewide recognition.

When the Congressman James P. Buchanan, a twenty year veteran of the Tenth Congressional District, died suddenly in 1937, LBJ capitalized on the unexpected opportunity, and announced his plans to run for the vacant seat. Lady Bird's father advanced *10,000* dollars of her future inheritance to help fund LBJ's maiden campaign. In the special election, Johnson faced a formidable challenge, with *eight* other candidates seeking Buchanan's seat. LBJ brought his characteristic energy and determination to the congressional race, telling Lady Bird: "Don't ever let me be in the house when there's daylight, and keep the screen locked until dark."

LBJ promised unwavering support for President Roosevelt's policies, and vowed to bring rural electrification to Texas. Forty-eight hours before Election Day, LBJ collapsed, and was rushed to the hospital for an emergency appendectomy. From his sick bed, the twenty-nine year old Johnson learned that he had been elected to Congress by a *two* to *one* margin (he won *twenty-eight* percent of the vote distributed among the *nine* candidates).

As the newly elected Congressman prepared to depart Texas for Washington D.C., he took heed of his father's advice: "Son, measure each vote you can by this standard—is the vote in the benefit of the people? What does this do for human beings? How have I helped the lame and halt (crippled) and the ignorant and diseased?"

Congressman Johnson fulfilled his campaign promises, securing funding for construction of dams and expansion of electrical service to previously darkened areas of Texas, cementing his popularity among rural voters. During a presidential visit to Texas, Franklin Roosevelt publicly declared that Johnson was "my boy;" a rare accolade for a freshman lawmaker. With FDR's recommendation, LBJ secured a coveted position on the House Naval Affairs Committee, where he helped steer a *forty-six million* dollar naval air station project to Corpus Christi.

LBJ found other ways to expand his power and influence. During the 1940 congressional elections, he volunteered for the labor intensive position of *Campaign Manager* for the House of Representatives. In this role, Johnson controlled the distribution of campaign donations to incumbent Congressmen. The vast sums of money were derived from private contributors, including wealthy Texas oilmen. Recipients of the coveted funds became permanently indebted to LBJ.

Johnson cultivated a close relationship with his fellow Texan—the legendary Sam Rayburn. Rayburn, who had known LBJ's father while the two served together in the state legislature, had been elected to Congress in 1913. Rayburn's influence increased with the passing years, and he was eventually elected Speaker of the House. A divorcee with no children, Rayburn occupied a lonely existence away from the halls of Congress, and Lyndon Johnson worked to fill the void. *Mister Sam* was soon a regular meal time guest in the Johnson household. LBJ was boldly affectionate with his mentor, often leaning down to kiss the diminutive Rayburn's bald head.

After three years, Johnson grew "terribly restless and unhappy" in the House of Representatives. Opportunities for advancement in the House were governed by seniority, and LBJ was simply too impatient to wait his turn. In April of 1941, Texas Senator, Morris Sheppard, died unexpectedly from a cerebral hemorrhage, providing LBJ with a golden opportunity for career advancement.

In the Special Election to fill Sheppard's vacancy, Johnson waged a hard fought campaign against incumbent Governor, William L. "Pappy" O'Daniel. Adopting *Roosevelt and Unity* as his campaign theme, LBJ held a *5000* vote advantage on Election Night (with *ninety-six* percent of the ballots tabulated). However, a day later, when the remaining ballots were tallied, O'Daniel emerged with a narrow victory (*1311* out of *576,000* votes cast). Johnson was certain that his opponent had committed ballot box fraud, but was also aware his own campaign had done much of the same, and did not contest the election.

Because the senatorial race had been a Special Election, LBJ was not forced to give up his seat in the House of Representatives. Nonetheless, Johnson was devastated by the defeat: "I felt terribly rejected, and I began to think about leaving politics and going home to make money. In the end, I just couldn't bear to leave Washington, where at least I still had my House seat. Besides, with all those war clouds hanging over Europe, I felt someone with all my training and preparedness was bound to be an important figure."

The 1941 election loss taught LBJ valuable lessons about logistics and ideology. In future campaigns, Johnson operatives would not report vote totals in select precincts until the last minute, such that illegal ballots could be added to ensure victory. Johnson was also aware that he had "gotten a little too far out in front" of the conservative Texas voters, and soon tempered his liberalism and unbridled devotion to Franklin Roosevelt. Moreover, LBJ learned that big money oil and business interests, who helped bankroll political campaigns, favored more conservative ideology.

Unwilling to risk the loss of his Congressional seat, Johnson chose not to challenge O'Daniel for the Senate in the 1942 regular election. World War II soon provided a traumatic interlude in LBJ's political career.

The day after the Japanese attacked Pearl Harbor on December 7, 1941, LBJ sent President Roosevelt a cable: "As a member of the Naval Reserve of the United States Navy, I hereby urgently request my Commander-in-Chief to assign me immediately to active duty with the fleet."

Johnson became the first Congressman to enlist in the armed forces. While LBJ served in the military, Lady Bird ran his Congressional office with remarkable efficiency, proving her worth as the perfect political spouse, which enabled her husband to pursue his ambition of becoming a war hero.

Lieutenant Commander Johnson, who had no prior military nautical training, was assigned to work in the office of Undersecretary of Navy, James V. Forrestal. Johnson was given the task of overseeing Naval training programs and shipbuilding in Texas and on the West Coast.

While he performed his administrative duties with diligence, LBJ longed to see combat action. In April of 1942, FDR granted LBJ's wish by dispatching him to the South Pacific to meet with Supreme Allied Commander, General Douglas MacArthur. Roosevelt hoped Johnson could at least partially pacify the outspoken MacArthur, who was unhappy with the amount of manpower and materials that were being diverted to the European Theater of war. For a month, LBJ hopped between Australia, New Zealand, and their neighboring islands.

Johnson developed a close enough relationship with MacArthur to soothe some of the General's unhappiness. He also convinced MacArthur to let him to fly on an actual combat mission. Serving as an observer on a *B-26* medium range bomber, Johnson earned a *Silver Star,* after the aircraft came under heavy attack from Japanese fighter planes. Many skeptics believed Johnson, who was FDR's protégé, had received the medal for political reasons, rather than actual combat bravery (however, the dangerous of the bombing raid is indisputable—the entire crew of the bomber LBJ was originally supposed to board was killed during the same mission).

Twelve months after Johnson enlisted; President Roosevelt issued a special order recalling Congressmen and Senators from active duty to Capitol Hill. With an established record of military service and a citation for bravery, LBJ was officially a war hero—a priceless recognition for politicians seeking higher office.

Paving his way toward financial security, Johnson purchased Austin radio station *KTCB* for 17,000 dollars. To avoid the appearance of a conflict of interest between an elected official and the *Federal Communications Commission (FCC),* Lady Bird Johnson was listed as the sole purchaser of the station. LBJ, however, used his considerable clout to obtain a lucrative contract with *CBS,* which vastly expanded *KTCB's* listening audience.

Lady Bird demonstrated excellent business acumen while managing the radio station, and transformed into a profitable enterprise. At the same time, LBJ exercised iron fisted control, and would not allow *KTCB's* disc jockeys to become media personalities. He also advised his female employees on their manner of dress, hairstyles, choice of mates, and timing of pregnancies.

Within twenty years, the radio station's assets would be worth *seven million* dollars. LBJ later expanded his media holdings into television, while judiciously investing in land and bank securities.

While serving in the House of Representatives, Johnson supported populist causes. He voted for the *Employment Act of 1945,* which provided federal aid to public works projects, and also supported the *Hill-Burton Act,* to assist states with construction of new hospitals.

In the arena of foreign policy, LBJ supported the *Truman Doctrine* and *Marshall Plan,* whereby the United States helped rebuild war shattered Europe. Fearful of the consequences of nuclear holocaust, Johnson supported an unsuccessful proposal to place atomic energy under international control: "We are here to make a choice between the quick and the dead."

Johnson was devastated by the sudden death of Franklin Roosevelt in April of 1945, weeping when he heard the news. Loyally supporting FDR's successor, LBJ endorsed Harry Truman's denunciation of the nationwide railroad strike, and concurred with the President's threat to draft the strikers into the Army. Johnson stubbornly refused to allow his radio station to unionize, and his pro-management views earned disdain from organized labor.

While he was considerably more progressive than the majority of white Southerners on the issue of Civil Rights, Congressman Johnson was unwilling to entirely abandon the time honored concept of States' Rights. On separate occasions, LBJ voted against anti-lynching and anti-poll tax proposals.

Johnson continued to feel constrained in the House of Representatives, and longed to be a bigger fish in a smaller pond. In 1946, LBJ's close advisor, John Connally, suggested that the Congressman run for Governor of Texas. Johnson quickly replied that he had "no interest in the 'ticky' little things Governors did," believing that his political future was in Washington D.C.

In 1948, forty-year old Lyndon Johnson launched a second bid for the United States Senate. Texas Governor, Coke Stevenson, emerged as LBJ's most formidable opponent (after the incumbent Senator, "Pappy" O'Daniel decided not to seek reelection). With boundless energy and manic enthusiasm, Johnson barnstormed Texas in a helicopter. The aircraft, known as the *Johnson City Windmill,* circled over towns, large and small, captivating local citizens, many of whom had never seen a helicopter.

While the whirlybird hovered overhead, a voice boomed down from its public address system: "This is Lyndon Johnson, your next United States Senator, and I'll land in just a minute. I want to shake hands with all of you."

Once on the ground, LBJ emerged from the helicopter and tossed his white Stetson into the crowd. A campaign worker was assigned to catch the hat and quietly return it to the helicopter, so Johnson could repeat the act in the next town. If the aide failed to deliver the hat before the aircraft departed, he was forced to drive at breakneck speeds to the site of the next campaign rally; the frugal candidate was unwilling to permanently relinquish his expensive hat.

Because of the oppressive heat, the helicopter's doors were left open, coating its passengers with dust during take offs and landings, forcing LBJ to take several showers each day. Throughout the summer of 1948, Johnson campaigned tirelessly, with only four hours of sleep per night.

LBJ's Senate campaign was nearly ended, when he was hospitalized for kidney stones. The physicians in Dallas recommended surgery, which would have required a five to six week recovery, sounding a death knell to his candidacy. Instead, LBJ flew to the Mayo Clinic, where urologists were able to crush the stones through a less invasive transurethral procedure.

Johnson's campaign centered on populist pledges—federal funding for hospitals, old age pensions, and education. To counter the spread of global Communism, he advocated increased defense spending. LBJ also supported President Truman's Civil Rights proposals, assuring black and Hispanic voters that government jobs and social programs would eventually promote racial equality.

On Saturday July 24, 1948, Texans went to their polling places to vote in the Democratic Senatorial Primary. Coke Stevenson led the balloting, winning *forty* percent of the popular vote. LBJ finished second, earning *thirty-four* percent, and forced a run-off election. For the next five weeks, both candidates fought *tooth and nail,* crisscrossing Texas.

Both campaigns engaged in flagrant voter fraud, with LBJ ultimately winning by a mere *eighty-seven* out of *900,000* votes cast (a recount of votes, six days after the election, showed that in a single precinct, LBJ's vote totals had increased from *765 to 965,* providing him with his narrow margin of victory). In Jim Wells County, *203* extra ballots were discovered in one voting box (*202* of those were marked for Johnson, with names listed in alphabetical order, straight from the voter registration list).

Coke Stevenson, accused the Johnson campaign of *ballot stuffing,* and appealed the election results to state authorities. On September 13, 1948, the Texas Democratic Executive Committee met in Fort Worth, and by a vote of *twenty-nine* to *twenty-eight,* certified LBJ as the winner. Stevenson then carried his protest as far as the United States Supreme Court, where Johnson's attorney, and future Supreme Court Justice, Abe Fortas, convinced the high court that it had no jurisdiction over vote counting in Texas, allowing LBJ to emerge victorious. The 1948 Senate campaign endowed LBJ with a humorous and lasting nickname—*Landslide Lyndon.*

A few weeks after his victory in the Senate race, Johnson regaled listeners with an amusing tale about his triumph in the run-off election. According to LBJ, a man had encountered a Mexican boy crying on the street curb in Jim Wells County. He inquired if the boy was sick or hungry. After the child answered no, the concerned Texan asked: "What's the matter? Why are you crying?"

"Well, yesterday, my Papa, he's been dead four years. Yesterday, he came back and voted for Lyndon Johnson, but didn't come by to say hello to me!" the boy wailed.

In January of 1949, Johnson joined a distinguished freshman Senate class, including Hubert Humphrey (Minnesota), Paul Douglas (Illinois) and Russell Long (Louisiana— son of the legendary Huey P. Long). In the House of Representatives, a future President of the United States, Michigan's Gerald Ford, was sworn into office.

Senator Johnson, vowed to meet personally with any of his *seven and a half* million constituents, and organized his office staff into around the clock shifts. Each day, LBJ's office hosted *seventy* visitors and answered *650* letters and *750* phone calls. The Senator worked as hard as his staffers, arriving at his office in the early morning hours and remained there until late at night.

Historian, Arthur Schlesinger, Jr. remembering an interview with the Texas Senator, expressed amazement at LBJ's encyclopedic knowledge of his colleagues: "…Johnson went over every member of the Senate—his drinking habits, his sex habits, his intellectual capacity, reliability, and how you manage him."

LBJ carefully cultivated relationships with senior statesmen; mostly notably, Speaker of the House, Sam Rayburn, and legendary Georgia Senator, Richard Russell. Like Rayburn, Russell was older, unmarried, and childless, and treated Johnson like a son, using his considerable influence to promote the young Texan's career. LBJ became Russell's protégé, maneuvering his Senate floor desk adjacent to the Georgian's. Russell, a frequent guest at Johnson's home, was called *Uncle Dick* by LBJ's young daughters. As the second highest ranking Senate Democrat, Russell arranged for Johnson to be appointed to the prestigious *Armed Services Committee*.

His close association with Russell also allowed Johnson to stay out of the *Southern Caucus*—a group of *twenty-two* Deep South Democratic Senators, who were marked as ardent Segregationists (a death knell for future presidential aspirations). Russell, whose opposition to racial integration had cost him the 1952 Democratic Presidential nomination, vicariously promoted LBJ's ascendency to power, believing that the young Texan could develop broader national appeal, and become the first Southerner elected President since the Civil War. With Richard Russell's guiding hand, Johnson was elected as the youngest *Party Whip* in American history.

In 1953, once again aided by Russell's active support, Lyndon Johnson was elected *Senate Minority Leader*; a rare occurrence for someone with only *three* years seniority. Among Johnson's newfound supporters was first term Massachusetts Senator, John F. Kennedy. After meeting Kennedy for the first time, LBJ offered an understated and oft repeated assessment: "He's a nice kid and probably has some future in politics."

When the Democrats reclaimed control of the Senate in 1954, Lyndon Johnson became the *Majority Leader,* just *six* years after his election to that legislative body. At age forty-six, LBJ was the youngest Senate Majority Leader in American history, and now held the most important leadership post in Congress. For the remainder of the decade, Johnson would boldly exercise his legislative powers.

As Majority Leader, Johnson remained a Populist and supported the *1955 Public Housing Bill,* and also led the fight to establish tax credits for heads of households. LBJ insisted that Senate debate be held to a minimum, believing that excessive deliberation damaged legislative proposals. In Johnson's eyes, the President was responsible for developing legislation, and the role of Congress was to react and modify those proposals.

With Dwight Eisenhower as the Republican President, LBJ stressed that the Democratic controlled Congress must find ways to cooperate with the Commander-in-Chief. Johnson reminded his colleagues of Sam Rayburn's familiar adage: "Any jackass can kick a barn down, but it takes a carpenter to build it."

In workaholic fashion, LBJ arose at half past six, breakfasting on coffee and cigarettes, as he read the previous day's *Congressional Record.* At 7:30 a.m., he departed his home in a chauffeur driven limousine, devouring the *Washington Post, Baltimore Sun,* and *New York Times* during the drive to Capitol Hill. His days were filled with phone calls, personal visits with colleagues and constituents, committee meetings, and floor votes. Johnson wolfed down fat-laden, Southern-style lunches and remained at his post until 10:00 p.m. Upon returning home, he enjoyed a late dinner, accompanied by liberal amounts of alcohol. LBJ's weight soon escalated to *225* pounds, and his aides estimated that he was consuming a *fifth* of *Cutty Sark* scotch per day.

On July 2, 1955, at the age of forty-seven, Johnson suffered a near fatal heart attack. Transported by ambulance to the hospital, LBJ's blood pressure plummeted, and he went into shock. The combined effects of genetics, poor diet, liberal alcohol consumption, heavy cigarette smoking, and a non-stop, sleep-deprived lifestyle left LBJ vulnerable to coronary artery disease. After spending six weeks in Bethesda Naval Hospital, he was allowed to return home for a three month recuperation period, with instructions to improve his diet, decrease his alcohol use, exercise more, and curtail his cigarette smoking.

"Will I ever be able to smoke again?" Johnson carefully questioned his cardiologist.

When told no, LBJ loudly moaned: "I'd rather have my pecker cut off."

While heeding the advice of his physicians, LBJ lapsed into a prolonged depression, accompanied by angry outbursts directed at his office staff and wife. Alarmed by Lyndon's near death experience, Lady Bird questioned her husband's physicians about his future. LBJ's cardiologist assured her that the Senator should not abandon his career: "I remember telling her that I didn't think he should retire from politics—that I thought if he were sitting on the porch at the LBJ Ranch whittling toothpicks, he'd have to whittle more toothpicks than anybody else in the country. Politics had been his life—it was what he knew, what he liked, and I told her that we had no evidence that continuing on working with a degree of consideration would not shorten his life a bit."

In January of 1956, Johnson returned to Capitol Hill, and soon regained his reckless swagger. He did, however, heed his doctors' advice, arriving at the office later each morning (ten o'clock), reducing his alcohol consumption, and eliminating cigarettes. With an improved diet and increased exercise, LBJ dropped his weight to a respectable 187 pounds.

At the same time, Johnson could not resist the occasional impulse toward recklessness. Influential Washington D.C. attorney and one-time aide to President Truman, Clark Clifford, vividly recalled a visit to the LBJ Ranch, soon after Johnson's heart attack. Speeding down a hill toward a lake in his Cadillac convertible, the Senate Majority Leader shocked his travel companions.

"The brakes have failed!" LBJ shouted.

The open convertible plunged into the lake, and water began seeping into the floorboards. Clifford and his wife crawled onto the seats, preparing to jump out of the sinking vehicle.

"Clark, what's the matter? Are you afraid you're going to get wet?" Johnson asked, before pushing a dashboard button that converted the automobile into an amphibious vehicle.

A bemused LBJ maneuvered the craft onto shore, and then regaled his guests with a list of previous visitors who had abandoned the sinking ship.

In spite of his health issues, LBJ continued to dominate the legislative scene in Washington. He convinced veteran Senators to relax seniority rules, such that the Majority Leader could provide younger lawmakers with choice committee assignments, thereby earning their gratitude and loyalty.

Johnson also developed a strong working relationship with President Eisenhower. LBJ shunned partisanship, explaining his concept of effective government: "...We have a solemn responsibility to cooperate with the President and produce a program that is neither his blueprint nor our blueprint, but a combination of the two. It is the politician's task to pass legislation—not to sit around saying principled things."

Johnson became a dedicated advocate of *non-partisan Nationalism:* "So long as men try to resolve their differences by negotiation—so long as they follow the prophet Isaiah to 'come now let us reason,' there is always a chance."

LBJ was credited for establishment of the *National Aeronautics and Space Administration (NASA).* In the tense months after the Soviets launched the world's first orbiting satellite *(Sputnik),* and leapt ahead of the United States in the *Space Race,* Johnson became a dedicated advocate of space exploration. LBJ believed the American space program should be controlled by a more innovative civilian agency, rather than the military.

"Control of space means control of the world," Johnson boldly declared.

LBJ was an eyewitness to America's early failed efforts to reach outer space. After a *Vanguard* rocket fell back to its Cape Canaveral launch pad and exploded, Johnson openly despaired: "How long, how long, oh God? How long will it take us to catch up with the Russians?"

Perhaps Johnson's greatest triumph was passage of the *Civil Rights Act of 1957;* the first such legislation to gain full Congressional approval since the days of Reconstruction. The powerful Majority Leader astutely found a middle ground between Southern Segregationists and Northern Liberals to pass what later became known as *Lyndon Johnson's Bill:* "I knew that if I failed to produce on this one, my leadership would be broken into a hundred pieces—everything I had built up over the years would be completely undone."

LBJ linked Civil Rights to his traditional Populist message: "What the man in the street wants is not a big debate on fundamental issues. He wants a little medical care, a rug on the floor, a picture on the wall, a little music in the house, and a place to take Molly and the grandchildren when he retires."

The broad shouldered, jug eared Lyndon Johnson roamed the halls of Congress with a Texan's swagger, and his booming voice and unmistakable laugh echoed from the walls and marbled floors of the Capitol building. LBJ's encyclopedic memory for names and faces and his innate talent for judging the strengths and weaknesses of his fellow law makers enabled him to orchestrate the outcome of crucial Senate votes.

While exhibiting an aura of bravado, in reality, LBJ hated being alone, fearing that he might become incapacitated by a second heart attack. When Lady Bird traveled back to Texas, Johnson insisted that his aides spend the night with him, and sleep in an adjoining bedroom (the doors had to be left open, in the event Johnson became ill and cried out).

A control fanatic, LBJ dominated all conversations; if a topic was introduced that did not interest him, the Majority Leader would abruptly change the subject, or simply walk away. A colorful storyteller and expert mimic, Johnson insisted on being the center of attention.

In LBJ's world, politics were his job and sole avocation. Reading, writing, hunting, fishing, and golfing paled in comparison to the satisfaction he derived from dominating the legislative process.

LBJ used his powerful physical appearance to capture the full attention of individuals within his immediate circle. The towering Texan would grasp the unsuspecting conversant by his arm and shoulder, lowering his face just inches away from his captive's nose, literally overwhelming the listener. The so-called *Johnson Treatment* led one journalist to complain that he had been "pawed over by a Saint Bernard."

LBJ's long time aide and future Texas Governor, John Connally, described his mentor's powerful personality: "There is no adjective in the dictionary to describe him. He was cruel and kind, generous and greedy, sensitive and insensitive, crafty and naïve, ruthless and thoughtful, simple in many ways, yet extremely complex, caring and totally not caring. He could overwhelm people with kindness and turn around and be cruel and petty towards those same people. He knew how to use people in politics the way nobody else could that I know of. As a matter of fact, it would take every adjective in the dictionary to describe him."

Senator Hubert Humphrey, who would later serve as Johnson's Vice-President, was a frequent recipient of the Johnson Treatment: "It is true that Johnson could be very rough. He didn't spend a lot of time trying to figure out whether he was going to hurt your feelings, but after he got you all bruised up, he put his arms around you and gave you a bear hug, and told you that you were the greatest man that ever lived—and, he'd get you almost to believe it, for a half an hour or so."

LBJ was subject to wild mood swings, cycling from melancholia into elation. With his mercurial temperament, narcissism, and histrionics, LBJ was unpredictable, formidable, and intimidating. He was also the most influential lawmaker of his generation.

Chapter 3

I don't care if anyone here likes me

In late 1959, Robert F. Kennedy eyed the future with anxious hope. Having just resigned his position as Chief Counsel to the Senate *Rackets Committee*, RFK was squarely focused on 1960 presidential election. The younger Kennedy had never orchestrated a national campaign, but knew that hard work and careful preparation would be the keys to propelling his charismatic brother into the presidency.

Robert Francis Kennedy was born on November 20, 1925 in Brookline, Massachusetts, the seventh of nine children born to Joseph and Rose Kennedy. In contrast to the hardscrabble upbringing of Lyndon Johnson, Robert Kennedy grew up surrounded by wealth and privilege.

RFK's father, Joseph Patrick Kennedy, amassed a fortune through banking, shipbuilding, stock market trading, commodity speculation, real estate investments, movie making, and whiskey importation. At age twenty-five, Joe Kennedy had become the youngest bank president in America. The elder Kennedy's business acumen was legendary, but also tainted, as he was rumored to have used insider information to improve his performance on Wall Street. Just prior to the stock market crash of 1928 that heralded the *Great Depression*, Joe Kennedy sold his interests in equities, averting financial disaster.

When asked by a young would-be entrepreneur about the key to success in the business world, Joseph Kennedy offered simple instructions: "Never meet anybody after two for lunch. Meet in the morning, because you're sharper. Never have long lunches—they're not only boring, but dangerous because of the martinis."

Joe's ambitions were nothing less than grandiose. Asked what he desired from his career, Kennedy replied, "everything." His wife and children would later credit the elder Kennedy as being "the architect of our lives."

In 1941, Joe changed his legal residence from New York to Florida, to escape state income and inheritance taxes. He established *Kennedy Enterprises* at 235 Park Avenue in the Manhattan financial district. By 1957, *Fortune* magazine listed Kennedy among the *top twenty* wealthiest individuals in the United States, estimating his net worth at between *200* and *400 million* dollars. By the time his oldest children were young adults, he owned houses in New York, Palm Beach, Cape Cod, and the French Riviera.

Robert Kennedy's mother, the former Rose Fitzgerald, came from a well-connected political family. Rose's father, John P. Fitzgerald, nicknamed *Fitzie* and *Honey Fitz,* had been elected mayor of Boston and had also served in the Massachusetts State Senate and the U.S. House of Representatives. Unlike her aggressive and domineering husband, Rose was stoic, even distant, and piously embraced the tenets of Catholicism (having attended two years of convent school after graduating high school). After her marriage on October 7, 1914, Rose quietly endured a lifetime of blatant philandering by her husband, yet managed to birth nine children. Rose seemingly ignored Joe's repeated infidelities, and contented herself with traveling, shopping sprees, and daily Mass.

Rose was not particularly affectionate with her children, and imposed a regimented upbringing. During summer vacations at the family's Cape Cod home, Rose employed a full-time physical fitness instructor. Beginning with 7:00 a.m. calisthenics on the front lawn, the Kennedy children attended tennis, golf, swimming, and sailing instructions. Rose kept an index card file on each of her children, enumerating their childhood diseases, allergies, immunizations, and shoe sizes.

Both parents were frequently absent from home, delegating much of their child rearing responsibilities to paid employees; yet, their influence left dual imprints. Two generations later, Rose and Joe's grandson, Christopher Kennedy Lawford, wrote of their legacy: "My grandfather believed that experience shaped character. My grandmother believed that religion shaped character."

Robert Kennedy was the third of four sons; ten years younger than Joe, Jr. and eight years junior to Jack. Bobby spent much of his early childhood surrounded by his sisters and their female playmates, and the older Kennedy males feared he might become a "sissy." Rose Kennedy believed that her three other sons were separated by too many years from Bobby, and none of them "were much use to him as boyhood pals."

As the seventh child and third son, RFK explained his unique position in the family hierarchy: "When you come from that far down, you have to struggle to survive."

Quiet and sometime insecure, he was often referred to as the "runt" of the family, and subjected to taunts from other children. As an adult, RFK reflected on his childhood: "What I remember most vividly about growing up was going to a lot of different schools, always having to make new friends, and that I was very awkward. I dropped things and fell down all the time. I had to go to the hospital a few times for stitches in my head and leg. And, I was pretty quiet most of the time. I didn't mind being alone."

Bobby developed an interest in American history, and his bedroom was decorated with pictures of various Presidents, while his bookshelves contained volumes on the Civil War. He also became an avid stamp collector, once receiving a handwritten letter from another philatelist— President Franklin Roosevelt.

Rose Kennedy served as the family disciplinarian, and often resorted to corporal punishment. Bobby's younger brother, Ted, remembered her harsh discipline: "Mother would have made a great featherweight—she had a mean right hand."

Bobby's father did not have to resort to physical punishment—a simple glare from his cold blue eyes would immediately bring his offspring into line. Joe emboldened his children with stern resolve and repeatedly instructed them: "You either win or lose—there's nothing else in life. If you don't place first, you may as well come in last."

On one occasion, Bobby and a group of his friends returned to the Kennedy residence after participating in a sailing contest. Joe, who was eating lunch, asked his son how the morning race had gone.

"We came in fifth," Bobby replied.

The elder Kennedy pounded the table top in anger, overturning his drink glass: "Lunch is over!"

Jack Kennedy's long time pal, Lem Billings, once told Joseph Kennedy that Bobby was "the most generous little boy." The elder Kennedy quickly replied: "I don't know where he got that."

At age ten, Bobby wrote a self-revealing essay: "I have pretty good character on the whole, but my temper is not too good. I am not jealous of anyone. I have a loud voice, and talk a lot, but sometimes my talk is not very interesting…"

Lem Billings later reflected on young Bobby's relative obscurity: "We barely noticed him in the early days, but that's because he didn't bother anybody."

Between the ages of seven and seventeen, RFK attended six different schools, as his wealthy father drifted between business ventures. His grades were undistinguished, and while at preparatory school, Bobby received scolding letters from his mother concerning his mediocre academic performance. The headmaster at Milton remembered RFK as a "very intelligent boy, quiet and shy, but not outstanding, and he left no special mark on Milton."

One of Bobby's middle school instructors once announced that two "great things" had occurred in the recent past: "Rommel was surrounded in Egypt," and RFK "had passed a math test."

Away from the classroom, Bobby tended to isolate himself and often appeared melancholy. His sister, Jean, believed that RFK's awkwardness favorably shaped his personality: "Nothing came easy for him. Perhaps that gave him sympathy, later in life, for those who were less fortunate. He, in some peculiar way, understood their soul."

"He didn't make friends, easily," a prep school classmate recalled.

Rose Kennedy offered a blunt assessment: "He is the most unsociable of my sons."

Like his mother, Bobby embraced religion, and served as a Catholic altar boy. His strong faith fostered a rigid mindset, and early on, RFK divided the world into two camps—*good* and *bad*.

Bobby also identified with the underdog; if a bully targeted a smaller child, RFK stepped in to help the latter fight back. On one occasion, after an awkward little girl lost her eyeglasses during a swim outing, Bobby repeatedly dove underwater, until he retrieved the missing glasses.

As a child of privilege, Robert Kennedy was never forced to work. When he did take on a newspaper route, Bobby was afforded the luxury of making his deliveries from the rear seat of his father's chauffeur-driven Rolls Royce.

At times, RFK could be reckless. When he was ready to learn how to swim, Bobby simply jumped off a sailboat into the choppy seas of Cape Cod. Flailing in the water, he was rescued by his oldest brother, Joe. A bemused Jack Kennedy summed up his younger brother's impulsive act: "It showed either a lot of guts or no brains at all, depending on how you looked at it."

During his teen years, Bobby's willpower partially eclipsed his awkwardness. A prep school classmate later recalled RFK's budding adolescence: "He was neither a natural athlete, nor a natural student, nor a natural success with girls, and had no natural gift for popularity. Nothing came easy for him. What he had was a set of handicaps and a frustrated determination to overcome them. The handicaps made him re-double the effort."

Another classmate describe Bobby's withdrawn nature, a trait that distinguished him from his older brothers: "I don't think he went out of his way to make friends...He was not a politician in the usual sense of the world—he wasn't looking for votes."

When Bobby was eighteen years old, his oldest brother, Joe, Jr., an American bomber pilot, was killed over the skies of Europe. In a top secret World War II project, code named *Aphrodite,* Allied bombers were filled with up to *ten tons* of TNT, to be employed as guided missiles against seemingly impenetrable German *V-1* rocket launch sites. To match his younger brother's combat bravery (Jack had become a decorated war hero after his *PT* boat was sunk in the Pacific, and he oversaw the rescue of the majority of his crewmates), Joe, Jr. volunteered to pilot one of the explosive laden bombers. In August of 1944, he took off from England, and was supposed to bail out of the plane near the target, allowing the remote controlled aircraft to crash into its target. The bomber, however, exploded in midair, instantly killing the young naval aviator.

Joe, Jr.'s death devastated his father and younger siblings. Bobby had established a close relationship with his older brother during the course of the war, and the two often exchanged letters. During Joe Jr.'s flight training at the Naval Air Station in Jacksonville, Florida, he invited Bobby for a visit. After his older brother smuggled him aboard his trainer aircraft, Bobby was able to briefly take the plane's controls from the copilot's seat.

In May of 1948, tragedy struck again, when Jack and Bobby's older sister, Kathleen, was killed in a plane crash. The two brothers questioned if there was truly a *Kennedy Curse,* and resolved to live each day to its fullest.

The tragic deaths of their older siblings emboldened both Jack and Bobby with fatalistic outlooks and reckless disregard for their own safety.

"Under the law of averages, either Jack or I will be killed in an auto accident," RFK announced to a college classmate, as he sped down the road in his beat up, balding-tired convertible.

Like his father and older brothers before him, Robert Kennedy attended college at Harvard, earning mostly C's and D's, and spent a portion of his junior year on academic probation. Bobby also enrolled in Naval Officer's Candidate School, and wrote his naval pilot brother, Joe, an amusing letter about his participation in the war effort: "We haven't had too much action here on Harvard Square, but we're on alert at every moment for an attack, and I'm sure that when it comes, we will conduct ourselves according to Navy standards."

After failing the flight school aptitude test, a disgusted RFK resigned his commission and enlisted as a naval Seaman. In 1945, Bobby's college education was interrupted by a one year military tour of duty, a portion of which was served on a newly commission destroyer, the *Joseph P. Kennedy, Jr.,* named in honor of his deceased brother. Seaman Kennedy spent most of his time chipping paint aboard the destroyer, which was stationed in a Cuban port during much of his tour.

At the end of World War II, Bobby's military record was largely mundane, and unlike his older brothers, he never ventured into a combat zone. After receiving his honorable discharge from the military on May 30, 1946, RFK reflected on his time in Navy: "There I was, on a ship named for my brother, sailing the placid waters and watching beautiful sunsets. Jack had been a hero. Joe died a hero. Okay, I didn't especially want to be a hero, but it was galling not have seen any action, at all."

While serving in the Navy, RFK made a move to secure his position in the family hierarchy. Writing to his father, Bobby asked for guidance: "I wish, Dad that you would write me a letter as you used to Joe and Jack about what you think about different political events and the war, as I'd like to be able to understand what's going on better than I do."

After discharge from the Navy, RFK returned to Harvard to complete his undergraduate education. Though undersized at five feet eight inches tall and 155 pounds, Bobby played end on the Crimson football team. Compensating for his lack of size, RFK was a savage blocker and tackler, and was often the first one to arrive at practice and the last one to leave. In the opening game of his senior year, Bobby caught a touchdown pass against Western Maryland. Shortly afterwards, he broke his leg in practice, causing him to miss the majority of the season. In the final game of his collegiate career, against archrival Yale, the coach allowed him to briefly enter the game, earning RFK a coveted varsity letter (an honor that neither of his older brothers had achieved).

The most *straight-laced* of the Kennedy male offspring, Bobby was the only son to win his father's *$1000.00* reward by not smoking or drinking alcohol until his twenty-first birthday.

In spite of his shyness, RFK vigorously defended his opinions on sociopolitical issues of the day. A fellow dorm room inhabitant described him as "kind of a nasty, brutal, humorless little fellow when he got going." Bobby also possessed a fiery temper; once shattering a beer bottle over the head of a college classmate.

Bobby also demonstrated willingness to court controversy. When Catholic Priest, Father Leonard Feeney, spoke at Harvard and declared that the college was a "pesthole" for Jews and Atheists, RFK was enraged. Much to his mother's chagrin, Bobby wrote a letter to the Cardinal, requesting that Feeney be excommunicated from the Church.

When his brother, Jack, ran for Congress in 1946, RFK volunteered to help with the campaign. JFK was less than enthusiastic: "It's damn nice of Bobby wanting to help, but I can't see that sober, silent face breathing new vigor into the ranks."

A campaign adviser offered his own assessment of Jack's younger brother: "When Bobby came into campaign headquarters, he was very polite, nice, and what I would call very shy. He wanted very much to help out in the campaign. What struck me was the first thing he said to me, 'Give me the toughest part of the District. I'll take it.'"

RFK was assigned to the East Cambridge area, believed to be the opponent's stronghold. In his successful election bid (winning *seventy-three* percent of the vote), JFK failed to carry those East Cambridge precincts, but earned impressive vote totals, proving that Bobby was willing to confront difficult challenge. RFK developed a fierce loyalty toward JFK, telling campaign advisor, David Powers: "My brother has more courage than anyone I have ever met."

Robert Kennedy graduated Harvard University in 1948 with an A.B. in Government. With lackluster grades, he was not a candidate for Harvard Law School, and enrolled at the University of Virginia's School of Law in September of that same year.

As a law student, RFK was active in the *Student Legal Forum*, and utilized family political connections to invite distinguished speakers to Charlottesville. Among the notable lecturers was his older brother, John F. Kennedy, the newly elected Congressman from Massachusetts.

Bobby also invited United Nations peace negotiator and Nobel Prize winner, Ralph Bunche, to address the legal forum. After learning that the audience in Virginia would be segregated, as was the prevailing custom of the time, Bunche refused to speak. RFK passionately appealed to the school's Governing Board, who subsequently mandated integrated seating during Bunche's lecture.

While attending law school, Bobby became engaged to Ethel Skakel, a wealthy, Catholic debutante from Connecticut. The couple had been introduced by Bobby's sister, Jean.

Ethel was the sixth of seven children born to George and Anna Brannack Skakel. George was a self-made millionaire, beginning his career as a railroad clerk, before founding the *Great Lakes Carbon Corporation*. Like Rose Kennedy, Anna was a devout Catholic, attending daily mass—an intense faith that was passed along to her daughter.

Two years younger than Bobby, the five feet four inch tall Ethel was a vivacious tomboy and a fierce competitor. During a "touch" football game, Ethel blindsided Bobby's younger brother, Teddy, spraining the stocky young man's ankle and dislocating his elbow. Athletic and energetic, Ethel regularly defeated her fiancée on the tennis courts, which made her all the more appealing to RFK.

Bobby and Ethel were married on June 17, 1950 at the Skakel family home in Greenwich, Connecticut; Jack served as his younger brother's best man. Ethel readily settled into married life, becoming her husband's chief supporter and biggest fan.

"She believed that Bobby could do no wrong," a mutual friend later remembered.

RFK graduated law school in June of 1951. He finished *fifty-sixth* in a class of *124*, with a cumulative grade point average of *2.54*.

Eight years apart in age, Bobby and Jack had never been particularly close. In October of 1951, Joseph Kennedy insisted that RFK accompany his older brother on a seven-week tour of Asia (the pair visited Japan, Vietnam, India, Iran, Pakistan, Thailand, Singapore, Korea and Israel). During the 25,000 mile trek, the brothers grew much closer, and forged an enduring bond.

Joseph Kennedy wrote of Bobby's *need* to make such an excursion: "He is just starting out, and has the difficulty of trying to follow two brilliant boys. This, in itself, is quite a hardship, and he is making a good try against it."

Suffering from an acute worsening of his adrenal insufficiency *(Addison's disease)*, Jack became violently ill during the Asian sojourn, and was admitted to a military hospital in Okinawa. Throughout his life, JFK was plagued by bouts of weakness, weight loss, vomiting, hypotension, and a diminished immune response, and had spent much of his childhood in the sick bed. Bobby related an oft told family joke: "If a mosquito bit Jack Kennedy, the mosquito would die."

As Bobby sat by his brother's bedside in Okinawa, Jack's temperature soared to 106 degrees, and a priest was summoned to administer the last rites.

"Everyone expected him to die," RFK later recalled.

When desoxycorticosterone acetate (DOCA) was developed, JFK was finally able to gain some control of his adrenal insufficiency. The steroid pellets were implanted in back of his thigh, supplying the needed hormone to his weakened system (the invention of oral corticosteroids, a decade later, replaced the sometimes poorly absorbed DOCA injections, and markedly improved JFK's overall health).

Jack eventually recovered from his near death experience in Okinawa, but returned home much thinner and weaker. He also realized that his younger brother would stick by him during difficult times, and came to view RFK in a much different light.

At age twenty-one, each of Joseph Kennedy's children received a *one million dollar* trust fund, giving them the luxury to choose between working or pursuing other interests. Nonetheless, after his tour of Asia, RFK devoted considerable energy to studying for, and passing, the New York state bar examination.

Near the end of 1951, RFK took a job as a lawyer in the *Internal*

Security Section of the Criminal Division of the United States Department of Justice, which specialized in the investigation of suspected Soviet intelligence agents. The first of Bobby and Ethel's eleven children was born that same year, and was christened, Kathleen, in honor of RFK's deceased sister.

In 1952, John F. Kennedy announced his candidacy for the United States Senate. Unseating the Republican incumbent, Senator Henry Cabot Lodge, would be a challenge for the upstart Kennedy, and would require ample financing and meticulous organization.

Joseph Kennedy had actively promoted Jack's political career, and was convinced his son would defeat Lodge. The elder Kennedy had once been a rising star in politics and was appointed by President Roosevelt to serve as the first Irish Catholic American Ambassador to Great Britain during the 1930s. As Nazi Germany began to overtake much of Europe, Ambassador Kennedy feared that Hitler could not be stopped. After Great Britain entered the war in September of 1939 (following Germany's *blitzkrieg* invasion of Poland), Ambassador Kennedy was devastated: "It's the end of the world—the end of everything!"

While the Luftwaffe attempted to bomb England into rubble, an anxious Kennedy declared that "democracy is dead." He also opposed American military or financial intervention in the European war. Kennedy's popularity plummeted, and British citizens mocked him as "Jittery Joe." Desperate to keep America out of the war, Kennedy unsuccessfully tried to arrange a personal meeting with Adolf Hitler (leading to speculation that he would bribe the Fascist leader to seek peace).

Ambassador Kennedy courted controversy in a widely publicized speech: "I should like to ask you if you know of any dispute or controversy existing in the world, which is worth the life of your son, or anyone else's son?"

Eventually, Ambassador Kennedy's outspoken defeatism unnerved President Roosevelt, who recalled him to the United States. His own political career now ruined, the elder Kennedy shifted his focus to his sons. After Joe, Jr. was killed (fulfilling his father's worst fears about the war), Jack was designated as heir apparent for his father's political ambitions.

JFK reluctantly entered politics to placate his father. Shortly after being discharged from the Navy, while resting and recuperating at the family home in Cape Cod, Jack discussed his future with Navy buddy, Red Fay, pointing to his father, who was pacing on the lawn: "God! There goes the old man. There he goes, figuring out the next step. I'm it now, you know. It's my turn. I've got to perform."

"I can feel Pappy's eyes on the back of my head...When the war is over and you are out there in sunny California...I'll be back here with Dad, trying to parlay a lost *PT* boat and a bad back into political advantage," JFK complained to Fay.

Prior to her brother's maiden campaign for Congress in 1946, Eunice Kennedy questioned her father: "Daddy, do you really think Jack can be a Congressman?"

"You must remember—it's not what you are that counts, but what people think you are," Joe quickly answered.

The savvy, elder Kennedy realized that his nearly unlimited bankroll would be a huge advantage in the campaign: "With what I'm spending, I could elect my chauffer."

Early in his career, Congressman Kennedy trumpeted the views of his overbearing father: "I guess Dad has decided that he's going to be the ventriloquist, so I guess that leaves me the role of dummy."

When asked about his job as a Congressman, JFK was often nonchalant: "Well, I guess if you don't want to work for a living, this is as good a job as any."

As his confidence grew, Jack gradually charted a course independent of his father. Ultimately, JFK supported the *Truman Doctrine* and *Marshall Plan* to rebuild war ravaged Europe, in defiance of Joe, Sr.'s vehement isolationist stance.

In spite of his initial misgivings, Jack soon found that politics suited his personality and ripening ambitions. By 1952, he had grown tired of being a small fish in the ocean of the House of Representatives, and was ready to move to the Senate, after briefly contemplating the Massachusetts Governorship. JFK quickly abandoned interest in the latter, believing that the Governor "sat in an office, handing out sewer contracts." In the end, Jack was more interested in foreign policy than domestic affairs.

Joseph Kennedy was prepared to finance his son's Senate campaign, but realized that Jack needed a loyal and determined campaign manage. Joe soon cast his eye on his third son.

"Bobby's my boy. When Bobby hates you, you stay hated," Joe proudly proclaimed, likening father to son.

RFK, however, was reluctant to undertake such an awesome responsibility, uncertain of his abilities: "I'll just screw it up."

JFK also had misgivings about his younger brother directing the Senate campaign. Jack was wary of his brother's abrasive, often self-righteous personality, and feared that he might become a "pain in the ass."

As usual, Joe Kennedy got what he wanted. After only three months on the job, RFK resigned his position with the Justice Department to manage JFK's Senate race. As his father had predicted, RFK devoted maximum effort to his new job, often working sixteen hour days, and quickly established a reputation as a stern, no-nonsense taskmaster. He was the first one to arrive at campaign headquarters on Kilby Street, and, late at night, the last one to leave.

"I don't care if anyone here likes me, as long as they like Jack," Bobby explained to a campaign worker.

JFK's long time friend, Lem Billings, was blunt in his assessment: "Bobby could be a royal pain. You either loved him or hated him—there was no in between."

Though he was stern and caustic, RFK eventually earned the respect of many Kennedy supporters, who admired his sense of purpose, and willingness to perform any of the necessary campaign chores. More than once, overcoming his fear of heights, Bobby climbed ladders to nail Kennedy campaign posters on walls and light poles.

RFK successfully targeted women voters, and arranged for his mother and sisters to host numerous "teas," where the handsome, young candidate wooed the often overlooked female segment of the electorate. The Kennedy sisters proudly wore skirts monogrammed with *Vote for John F. Kennedy.* The Kennedy camp also delivered over *one million* campaign brochures to nearly every home in Massachusetts.

Defying established political tradition, RFK did not rely on the Massachusetts *political machine* to dictate the tone of his brother's Senate campaign. The Kennedy team established its own distinct electoral organization, which was nicknamed the *Irish Mafia.*

Bobby preferred to remain behind the scenes during the campaign. Public speaking was a chore for the shy campaign manager, as evidenced by a rare public appearance: "My brother Jack couldn't be here. My mother couldn't be here. My sister Eunice couldn't be here. My sister Patricia couldn't be here. My sister Jean couldn't be here. But if my brother Jack could be here, he'd tell you that Lodge has a very bad voting record. Thank you."

Once Bobby took charge of campaign, his father remained in the background, emerging only rarely to bolster JFK's determination. JFK spent most of the race in intense pain, having reinjured his temperamental back while sliding down a fire pole at a campaign stop. Conscious of promoting an image of youthful vitality, Jack refused to use his crutches during public appearances. By the end of each day, the candidate often collapsed in agony. Joe intervened to lift his son's spirits, with hope for future political advancement: "I will work out plans to elect you President. It will not be any more difficult for you to be elected President than it will be to win the Lodge fight."

At the conclusion of the hard fought campaign, RFK was frazzled, exhausted, and gaunt, having lost some ten pounds from his already thin frame. At the same time, Bobby had developed a powerful political machine—an organization that would be enlarged to a national scale in future elections.

On Election Day, 1952, Republican presidential candidate, Dwight D. Eisenhower, soundly defeated his Democratic opponent, Adlai Stevenson. In spite of Eisenhower's *208,000* vote landslide victory in Massachusetts, JFK defeated the incumbent Republican, Henry Cabot Lodge by a narrow margin (*70,000* out of *2,353,231* votes cast—*three* percentage points).

Key JFK political operative, Kenneth O'Donnell, attributed the victory to RFK: "If Bobby hadn't come up to take over that campaign, and if he hadn't been Jack Kennedy's right hand man from that point on, without a question, Jack Kennedy would have lost."

At the conclusion of the hard fought senatorial race, Lem Billings described RFK's newfound position in the family hierarchy: "I don't think Jack had been aware that Bobby had this tremendous organizing ability. But, during the campaign, Bobby had proved himself, again and again, forging a partnership that would last until the two of them died."

The newly elected Senator paid his younger brother the ultimate compliment: "…He's the only one who doesn't stick knives in my back—the only one I can count on when it comes down to it."

Robert Kennedy's debut as a campaign manager had been a rousing success. Joe Kennedy, however, would not allow his younger son to savor the moment.

"You haven't been elected to anything," he told Bobby, "Are you going to sit on your tail for the rest of your life? You'd better go out and get a job."

In December of 1952, RFK was appointed by Wisconsin Senator Joseph McCarthy as Assistant Counsel to the *Senate Permanent Subcommittee on Investigations*. McCarthy, a hard drinking Republican and long time friend of the Kennedy family, willingly provided RFK with a high profile position on Capitol Hill.

McCarthy's subcommittee was designed to investigate communist infiltration into the United States Government. During the height of the *Cold War,* the communist menace seemed very real, and the original charter of the investigation was both noble and patriotic. McCarthy, however, engendered fear and distrust by utilizing smear tactics to make unsubstantiated, treasonous allegations against many loyal Americans. Fueled by raging alcoholism, McCarthy grew more reckless with his accusations, and drew scorn from his peers and respected members of the news media. Disillusioned and frustrated by McCarthy's behaviors, RFK resigned his position on June 29, 1953.

As McCarthy's attacks grew more outrageous, his Senate colleagues voted to censure him. JFK was recovering from back surgery in Florida, when the censure resolution was passed (he was the only Senate Democrat to skip the historic vote). Jack's non-vote and RFK's brief membership on the McCarthy subcommittee staff would be used again them by future political opponents. After his official censure, Joseph McCarthy completely self-destructed, and drank himself to death before the decade was out.

Years later, RFK reflected on his ill-timed role as counsel to the McCarthy Committee: "I thought there was a serious internal security threat to the United States; I felt, at that time, Joe McCarthy seemed to be the only one who was doing anything about it. I was wrong."

JFK's back surgery in 1954 not only hurt him politically (the skipped censure vote on McCarthy), but was nearly fatal. Several surgeons refused to operate on Kennedy, because of the risks associated with his adrenal insufficiency. At the *New York Hospital for Special Surgery,* Jack found a willing surgeon, and was adamant about his decision: "I'd rather be dead than spend the rest of my life on these God damn crutches."

In the post-operative period, JFK developed a potentially deadly *Staphylococcus* infection and lapsed into a coma. A priest was summoned to perform last rites, before the patient finally recovered.

Jack's recovery was long and painful, suffering with a raw, open wound that exuded pieces of necrotic bone. JFK spent much of his convalescence at his father's Palm Beach, Florida home, where an ever-loyal Bobby stood guard outside his bedroom, as Jack went through agonizing withdrawal from narcotic pain medications.

For a fleeting period after the McCarthy debacle, Bobby thought of moving out West, establishing residence, and running for the Senate (perhaps in Nevada). As usual, Joseph Kennedy took charge and arranged for his son to be appointed to the Presidential Commission spearheading government reform (headed by former President Herbert Hoover). RFK found the commission work tedious, and eventually sought another job. In 1954, he returned to Capitol Hill as the Democratic Minority's Chief Counsel. When the Democrats took control of the Senate in January of 1955, RFK became Majority Counsel.

RFK had also grown mightily in the eyes of his father. In 1955, the elder Kennedy revised his will, naming Bobby as the executor, believing that his third son was the one to "keep the Kennedys together in the future."

In 1954, RFK was named President of the *Joseph P. Kennedy Foundation,* which provided aid to homeless and mentally retarded children. He gained further recognition that same year, when he was chosen as one of ten "Outstanding Young Men" by the National Junior Chamber of Commerce.

To broaden his son's knowledge of foreign policy, Joseph Kennedy arranged for Bobby to travel to Europe and Asia with Supreme Court Justice, William O. Douglas. RFK grew ill while in the Soviet Union, but stubbornly refused to allow Douglas to summon a "Communist doctor."

RFK's family suffered further tragedy in October of 1955, when Ethel's parents were killed in a private plane crash. Still a month shy of his thirtieth birthday, Bobby had already endured the tragic deaths of two siblings and both of his in-laws.

In the summer of 1956, John F. Kennedy unsuccessfully sought the Democratic vice-presidential nomination. RFK was assigned the last minute task of soliciting delegate support for his brother (after presidential nominee, Adlai Stevenson, decided to allow the convention delegates to select his running mate). Joseph Kennedy was none too happy about Jack's pursuit of the vice-presidency. Bobby drew the unenviable job of telephoning his father, who was staying at his home on the French Riviera. After absorbing verbal blows from the elder Kennedy, RFK hung up the phone and informed Jack: "Whew is he mad!"

Joseph Kennedy's anger over his son's blatant defiance was slow to abate. When Massachusetts Congressman, Tip O'Neill, complained that RFK never thanked him for relinquishing his delegate slot (such that

Bobby could participate in the convention), the elder Kennedy bluntly retorted: "Never expect any appreciation from my boys. These kids have had so much done for them by other people, that they just assume it's coming to them."

Though his vice-presidential bid fell short (the convention delegates ultimately selected Tennessee Senator, Estes Kefauver), JFK gained national exposure during his presidential nomination speech for Adlai Stevenson. Charismatic, energetic and polished, Kennedy's speech thrust him the national political limelight, transforming him into a prime contender for the 1960 Democratic presidential nomination. JFK was fully aware of his potential: "With only about four hours of work and a handful of supporters, I came within 33.5 votes of winning the vice-presidential nomination. If I work hard for four years, I ought to be able to pick up all the marbles."

Unwilling to appear over eager, JFK offered a nonchalant answer when questioned about his presidential aspirations: "I guess it is the only thing I can do."

When his book, *Profiles in Courage* (a collection of stories about statesmen, who had made principled, but unpopular decisions) won the *Pulitzer Prize*, JFK's reputation as a youthful intellectual was firmly established.

A 1957 *Gallup Poll* showed Estes Kefauver with *forty-one* percent of the vote (compared to *thirty-three* percent for JFK) in the 1960 race for the Democratic presidential nomination. After Kennedy was awarded the *Pulitzer Prize*, a repeat poll showed JFK leading Kefauver by a margin of *forty-five* to *thirty-three* percent.

Dedicating his efforts to the promotion of Jack's political career, RFK became his brother's unofficial protector. Shortly after the 1956 Democratic National Convention, JFK left the country for a Mediterranean cruise, leaving his pregnant wife behind. In late August, Jackie Kennedy began hemorrhaging, and was rushed to the hospital. An emergency C-section was performed, but the baby girl was stillborn. Meanwhile, Jack was on a private yacht, thousands of miles away, enjoying the company of other women. When he received the tragic news, JFK initially refused to end his vacation and return home to his wife.

Two days later, Senator George Smathers, who had accompanied Jack on the pleasure cruise, convinced the seemingly insensitive and uncaring husband to return home: "You'd better haul your ass back to your wife, if you ever want to run for President."

During Jack's absence, Bobby remained at his sister-in-law's hospital bed, and was the one who broke the news to her about the baby's death. RFK also arranged for the infant to be buried in the family cemetery in Boston.

Jackie would remain forever grateful for Bobby's kindness and support: "You knew that if you were in trouble, he'd always be there."

JFK's marriage barely survived this episode of cavalier disregard for Jackie. Rumors surfaced that Joseph Kennedy paid his daughter-in-law *one million* dollars to forego divorce. In the end, the couple remained together, and Jackie continued to overlook her husband's continuous infidelities, just as her mother-in-law had done for so many years. Had the couple divorced during that conservative political era, JFK's presidential hopes would have most likely been destroyed.

"It was closest they ever came a full-blown divorce," George Smathers later remembered, after Jack's Mediterranean misadventure.

In anticipation of his brother's quest for the presidency in 1960, Robert Kennedy shadowed the Stevenson campaign during the 1956 election. Finding the Democratic candidate indecisive and weak, RFK was not surprised when Eisenhower won re-election in a landslide. Stevenson was now zero for two in presidential elections, reinforcing the need for a fresh face in the Democratic Party.

A Stevenson campaign advisor summarized RFK's take home message from the 1956 presidential campaign: "Bob learned what not to do."

"Nobody asked me to do anything, nobody wanted me to do anything, nobody consulted me, so I had time to watch everything—I filled complete notebooks with notes on how a presidential campaign *should* be run," Bobby remembered.

Aware that the Stevenson campaign lacked focus, RFK privately criticized the presidential candidate: "He's got no balls. He sits around with his staff for hours, talking about nothing. He can't even give a speech—he has to read it aloud from a script. There's no organization in the camp— nobody knows what anybody else is doing…"

On Election Day 1956, Robert Kennedy quietly cast his ballot for Eisenhower.

After the 1956 election, Robert Kennedy turned his attention to a new assignment, after being named Chief Counsel for the Senate *Labor Rackets Committee,* chaired by Arkansas Senator, John L. McClellan. Under RFK's direction, the bipartisan committee (consisting of five Democrats and three

Republicans, including John F. Kennedy) initiated an investigation of labor union corruption and potential links between labor and organized crime. From February of 1957 through March of 1960, the Rackets Committee held numerous hearings, interviewing scores of witnesses. RFK's staff eventually grew to over *100* investigators.

Nationwide, union membership represented *27.1* percent of the civilian work force, posing a delicate and serious dilemma for RFK. Nonetheless, the Chief Counsel, with his characteristic *all or nothing* thinking, quickly identified the *good unions* (like the United Auto Workers) and the *bad unions* (namely the Teamsters).

The Teamsters Union quickly became the focus of the Racket Committee's investigation. Teamsters' President, Dave Beck, was called to testify before the committee, where it was revealed that he had embezzled some *320,000 dollars* from the union pension fund, including *185,000* dollars to purchase his private residence. Beck was forced to resign his leadership position, and was later imprisoned for larceny and income tax evasion.

Beck's successor, Jimmy Hoffa, soon found himself under the microscope of the Rackets committee, but proved to be a much tougher customer. The committee members and their Chief Counsel, Robert Kennedy, rightfully suspected the new Teamsters President was using union pension funds to finance organized crime activities and was contracting with Mafia figures to intimidate (and possibly murder) dissident union members. At the same time, committee investigators found it difficult to pin anything on the elusive Hoffa.

In 1957, the Teamsters were the largest organized labor union in America, with a membership of *1.3 million* workers, and its pension fund was valued at a *quarter of a billion* dollars. At the center of it all, was forty-four year old James Riddle Hoffa.

At five feet five inches tall and 185 pounds, the squat, powerfully built Hoffa began his career as a *blue collar* worker, unloading trucks, before working his way up the labor ladder. Never afraid to match fists or wits with his enemies, Hoffa was not the least bit impressed by the Rackets Committee Chief Counsel: "This Kennedy kid is nothing more than a spoiled brat."

When he received his summons to appear before the Rackets Committee, an enraged Hoffa fired a verbal warning shot: "You can tell Bobby Kennedy that he's not going to make his brother President over Hoffa's dead body."

Prior to his Congressional testimony, a mutual acquaintance arranged for RFK and Hoffa to meet for dinner. Each man refused to be intimidated by the other, and Hoffa surmised that Kennedy *thought* he was tough, because he had played football at Harvard. RFK, in turn, was critical of the Teamsters President: "When a grown man sat for an evening and talked continuously about his toughness, I could only conclude he was a bully hiding behind a façade."

Evasively answering questions during his committee appearances, Hoffa did his best to unnerve Robert Kennedy by calling him "Bob," and winking at him.

"I used to love to bug the little bastard," Hoffa bragged.

As RFK continued his relentless questioning of Hoffa, the union leader's annoyance gave way to rage. He felt that Kennedy was unfairly targeting him and "got his jollies from playing God." For the next eleven years, Robert Kennedy and Jimmy Hoffa would engage in repeated battles, before the labor leader was finally convicted and imprisoned for jury tampering.

RFK characterized Hoffa as the embodiment of *absolute evil,* and later wrote about his mission to uncover wrong doing: "The investigative work we have done…revealed that there is in America, today, an incredible web of underworld enterprise. This underworld is not the figment of a detective story writer's imagination. It is a real and present danger to the economy or our nation; powerful, cunning, well-organized and financed. So successfully masked have been these operations, that they're seldom exposed to the public eye."

While serving as Chief Counsel to the Rackets Committee, Robert Kennedy developed a keen interest in law enforcement. On weekends, he sometimes traveled to New York and spent time with agents from the *Federal Bureau of Narcotics (FBN).* The FBN, a forerunner to the present day *Drug Enforcement Agency (DEA),* was renowned for its freewheeling law enforcement policies. Unlike the FBI, which was a *strictly by the book agency,* the FBN did not require a subpoena or search warrant if they suspected a residence was harboring drug dealers. The FBN's liberal search, seizure, and arrest methods appealed to RFK's need for action, and his clear cut delineation between the *good guys* and the *bad guys.* More than once, Kennedy joined FBN agents on their daring raids against drug dealers.

RFK relished direct confrontation with the criminal element. As the Rackets Committee investigated potential links between the labor movement and organized crime, several Mafia leaders were called to testify.

The Chief Counsel was a relentless investigator, as evidenced by a cartoon caption on his office wall: "If at first you don't succeed, file a subpoena."

The Mafia leaders called to testify before the committee, frequently invoked their Fifth Amendment rights against self-incrimination. When the *bad guys* refused to answer his questions, RFK sometimes demonstrated reckless disregard for decorum.

In an arrogant, accusatory voice, RFK asked Chicago mob leader, Salvatore "Sam" Giancana, if he actually disposed of his opponents by killing them and stuffing them in car trunks. A surprised Giancana responded with a laugh, infuriating Kennedy.

"Would you tell us anything about any of your operations, or will you just giggle every time I ask you a question?" RFK inquired, with righteous indignation and remarkable naiveté.

Giancana's tone hardened: "I decline to answer, because I honestly believe my answer might tend to incriminate me."

"I thought only little girls giggled, Mr. Giancana," RFK retorted.

Bobby was disgusted by organized crime leaders: "They are sleek, often bilious and fat, or lean and cold and hard. They have the smooth faces and cold eyes of gangsters. They wore the same rich clothes, the diamond ring, the jeweled watch, the strong, sickly-sweet smelling perfume."

While RFK's friends and associates viewed him as just and heroic, others believed that his interrogation style was an affront to civil liberties. A prominent college professor criticized RFK's "juvenile tactics," and suggested that the Chief Counsel should entitle his memoirs as *Profiles in Bullying,* a satirical reference to JFK's Pulitzer Prize winning book. The adjective *ruthless* became a frequent modifier associated with the name Robert Kennedy.

Joseph Kennedy was not happy with Bobby's relentless interrogative style or Jack's membership on the Rackets Committee. The elder Kennedy was concerned that publicity generated by the harassment of organized labor would cost JFK votes in the 1960 presidential election.

The recognition afforded to the Kennedy brothers during the Rackets Committee investigation, however, was mostly positive. Sitting side by side in the Senate chambers, images of Senator Kennedy and his crusading younger brother were shown on nationwide television. *Look* magazine featured an article entitled "Rise of the Kennedy Brothers," while the *Saturday Evening Post* published a piece called "The Amazing Kennedy's."

Around that same time, RFK received a measure of praise from the most unlikely of sources. After the Soviet Union launched the world's first satellite, Senate Majority Leader, Lyndon Johnson, suggested that someone *like* Robert Kennedy would be a good choice to head a committee to explore America's efforts to catch up with Russian space dominance. After hearing about LBJ's recommendation, Bobby wrote in his journal: "Am very pleased with myself."

Kennedy family confidant, Lem Billings, noted a profound change in RFK: "For the first time in his life, he was happy. He'd been a very frustrated young man, awfully mad most of the time, having to hold everything in and work on Jack's career, instead of his own. I think he found himself during the Hoffa investigation."

With growing confidence, Bobby's privately shared his family's political aspirations: "One day, my brother Jack will be President, and I'll be a Senator from Massachusetts, and Teddy will be elected Senator from Connecticut. Those are the long term plans."

While RFK's prediction did not shape up exactly as outlined, in a mere *six* years, all *three* Kennedy brothers would hold high-profile positions in Washington D.C. (President, Attorney General, and U.S. Senator).

In 1958, John F. Kennedy handily won re-election to the Senate, earning *73.2* percent of the vote. Given JFK's token opposition, RFK spent little time with the campaign, and was able to remain in Washington D.C. with the Rackets Committee.

Robert Kennedy, once awkward and inexperienced, had evolved into a seasoned, aggressive crusader and respected political operative. Lacking JFK's innate charisma, RFK was viewed by many as arrogant and brooding. His harshest critics labeled him ruthless and condescending. Bobby's closest friends, however, realized that his abrasive exterior masked his true sensitivity, shyness, and uncertainty about the future.

Bobby continued a pattern of infidelity exemplified by his father and older brother, but was never as blatant with his extramarital affairs. RFK ultimately fathered eleven children, and his marriage appeared rock solid. Ethel Kennedy, while undoubtedly aware of her husband's indiscretions, adored him and tolerated no criticism of Bobby's motives, words, or actions.

RFK and his ever growing family lived at *Hickory Hill*, a sprawling estate in McLean, Virginia, near the Pentagon. The Georgian manor at 1147 Chain Bridge Road sat on six acres, with stables, a chicken coop, two swimming pools, a tennis court, and a Marine-style obstacle course. The house had once served as the headquarters of Union Army General George McClellan and as home to Supreme Court Justice, Robert H. Jackson. *Hickory Hill* had been originally purchased by JFK, but after the stillbirth of their child in 1956, Jackie felt haunted by the empty bedrooms of the large house. In 1957 Jack sold the property to Bobby (who had already fathered a half dozen children), for 125,000 dollars.

Hickory Hill's raucous grounds were filled with screaming children and a veritable menagerie of pets, including cats, dogs, pigs, horses, goats, rabbits, ducks, chickens, snakes, and turtles. At one point, a sea lion occupied the swimming pool and an anteater resided in a make-shift zoo in the basement. A warning sign was erected in the front yard: "Trespassers will be eaten."

Bobby was most comfortable with animals and children, where he was free to reveal the playful and sensitive side of his personality. On the weekends, RFK, the ruthless champion of right versus wrong and arch enemy of gangsters, would often be found in the yard, wrestling with his children and their dogs.

As much as he loved his children, Bobby also preached self-reliance, along with physical and mental toughness. RFK often reminded his brood: "Kennedys never cry."

If he encountered one of his children reading a comic book on sunny day, RFK quickly admonished them: "Put that junk down, right now, and get outside and do something!"

RFK preferred the comfort of a poolside barbecue to the pomp and circumstance of Washington D.C. galas. Ethel Kennedy echoed her husband's preferences for social discourse: "We did not feel easy in the company of highbrows."

In September of 1959, RFK resigned as counsel to the Rackets Committee and authored *The Enemy Within,* chronicling his investigation of labor union corruption and organized crime. The popular book briefly ascended to number two on the bestseller's list. In a gesture that was anything but ruthless, Bobby donated the royalties from his story to a charity benefitting retarded children (a tribute to his mentally challenged sister, Rosemary).

By late 1959, RFK knew that the most formidable task of his young life lay on the horizon. He was poised to pursue the ultimate prize; the election of John F. Kennedy to the presidency.

Chapter 4

Son, you've got to learn to handle a gun like a man

At the end of 1959, Lyndon Johnson carefully surveyed the political landscape. With Dwight Eisenhower in his second and final term, the 1960 presidential race promised to be a wide-open affair. LBJ was certain that his qualifications matched or exceeded those of any of the other likely Democratic candidates, which included John F. Kennedy, Hubert Humphrey, Stuart Symington, and Adlai Stevenson (who was decidedly handicapped by twin presidential election defeats). His legacy as Senate Majority Leader etched in stone, Johnson had little else to prove on Capitol Hill, and the lure of the Oval Office was nearly irresistible.

LBJ had long since earned the respect of fellow legislators, even those who resented his strong-arm tactics. Senator Barry Goldwater, who would play a prominent oppositional role in Johnson's later political life, readily acknowledged the Texan's power and influence: "I'll say this about him. He was a very good Majority Leader. He worked the Senate. If he had a job to do, we didn't go home at five or six o'clock. We went home when we got the job done, and it might be two to three days later, having been there all night, several nights."

In the fall of 1959, LBJ remained coy about his plans for the coming year. Unlike modern day politics, presidential campaigning did not begin two to three years in advance of the actual election. Ever the master politician, Johnson was careful not to tip his hand.

Instead, Johnson downplayed his interest in the Oval Office: "I don't really have the disposition, the training, or the temperament for the presidency. I don't want to get a bug in my mouth I can't swallow."

LBJ also ruminated about his health, in the wake of his previous heart attack. Fully aware that Johnson men tended to die from heart disease at a young age, he contemplated his own mortality.

"There are times, now, when my heart feels like lead," LBJ proclaimed, with a tinge of melodrama and self-pity.

Those who knew Johnson best doubted the sincerity of his philosophical meanderings. A longtime aide was fully aware of LBJ's ultimate goal: "He wants to be President, so bad, his tongue is hanging out."

LBJ skillfully hedged his bets, strong arming Texas State lawmakers to enact legislation allowing him to simultaneously run for the presidency and re-election to the Senate. Barring an unlikely upset, Johnson would retain his Senate seat, even if his presidential ambitions were thwarted.

Lyndon Johnson and Robert Kennedy were on an inevitable collision course. While fully aware of RFK's growing stature as Majority Counsel for the Senate Rackets Committee, LBJ still considered Bobby a political lightweight. When he encountered RFK on Capitol Hill, Johnson frequently addressed the younger Kennedy as *sonny boy*.

Over the years, Lyndon Johnson and the Kennedy family had warily eyed each other; occasionally flirting. In the fall of 1955, Joseph Kennedy made LBJ an unprecedented offer. Using a trustworthy intermediary, Joe promised LBJ *considerable* campaign funding if the Texan pursued the 1956 Democratic presidential nomination, and selected JFK as his running mate. Though intrigued by the offer, LBJ was a realist, and doubted than any Democrat could unseat the popular incumbent, Dwight Eisenhower. Moreover, Johnson was unwilling to be JFK's stalking horse, realizing that if the Democratic ticket went down to defeat, his charismatic running mate would emerge largely unscathed, and would be well positioned to win the 1960 presidential nomination (ironically, LBJ won *eighty* delegate votes at the 1956 convention as Texas' *Favorite Son* presidential candidate).

Robert Kennedy was appalled and angered when LBJ turned down his father's "generous offer" and viewed the Texan's decision as "discourteous." Johnson merely chuckled at Bobby's political naiveté.

LBJ had long been puzzled by the public's fascination with John F. Kennedy. Johnson rated his Massachusetts colleague as high on image and low on accomplishment. When JFK absented himself from Joe McCarthy's censure vote, LBJ questioned Kennedy's courage and maturity. If Kennedy was unwilling to challenge an old family friend, like McCarthy, Johnson doubted that he was man enough to make even more difficult choices as President.

Johnson also derided Kennedy's well-crafted reputation as an intellectual. When unsubstantiated rumors arose that JFK's Pulitzer Prize winning book, *Profiles in Courage*, had been ghost written by his legislative aide, Ted Sorensen, LBJ eagerly perpetuated the gossip.

In spite of his many misgivings about Kennedy, LBJ had helped promote JFK's senatorial career, appointing him to choice committee positions. Johnson had also backed Kennedy's unsuccessful bid for the 1956 vice-presidential nomination.

"Texas proudly casts its vote for the fighting sailor, who wears the scars of battle," LBJ had proclaimed to the '56 convention delegates, citing JFK's World War II heroism.

In reality, Johnson had little to lose by supporting Kennedy for the vice-presidency, as he had already decided to sit out the 1956 presidential election. Though Kennedy was unsuccessful in winning the nomination, LBJ had earned JFK's respect and gratitude.

Four years later, the 1960 election remained foremost in Lyndon Johnson's mind. With Eisenhower's retirement, LBJ sensed that it was time make his move, *with* or *against* John F. Kennedy.

John F. Kennedy had already made up his mind to run for President prior to the 1960 election. The Massachusetts Senator was aware that two of his most formidable potential opponents would be Lyndon Johnson and Missouri Senator, Stuart Symington. On March 15, 1958, JFK addressed the annual *Gridiron Dinner* in Washington D.C., and joked about his political future: "I dreamed about 1960 the other night, and told Stuart Symington and Lyndon Johnson about it yesterday. I told them how the

Lord came into my bedroom, anointing my head, and said, 'John Kennedy, I hereby anoint you President of the United States.' Stu Symington said, 'that's strange, Jack, because I had a similar dream last night, in which the Lord anointed me President of the United States and outer space.' Then Lyndon Johnson said, 'that's very interesting, gentlemen, because I, too, had a similar dream last night, and I don't remember anointing either one of you!'"

In a private, sober conversation, Kennedy analyzed his Southern-born opponent's strengths and weaknesses: "The Democratic Party owes Johnson the nomination. He's earned it. He wants the same things for the country that I do. But, it's too close to Appomattox for Johnson to be nominated and elected. So, therefore, I feel free to run."

At the same time, JFK refused to be labeled by either wing of his party, hoping to position himself as a *centrist*. He specifically refused to characterize himself as a liberal: "I'm a realist."

In the fall of 1959, JFK sent Bobby to Texas to gauge LBJ's presidential ambitions. Kennedy planned to formally announce his candidacy at the beginning of the coming year, but was already carefully eyeing the competition. RFK's mission was simple, consisting of three basic questions. Did LBJ plan to run for President in 1960? If not, would he attempt to block JFK's nomination? Lastly, would Johnson actively support another presidential candidate?

Not surprisingly, Johnson refused to tip his hand, informing RFK that he did not *plan* to run for President, and had no *intentions* of backing another candidate. RFK doubted LBJ's sincerity, and quickly realized that the Texan was not going to give him any straight answers.

The meeting at the LBJ Ranch remained uneventful, until the very end. As was his custom with male guests, LBJ insisted that RFK join him on a deer hunting expedition.

RFK was not familiar with weapons and had no interest in hunting, but realized that this masculine rite of passage was a political necessity. In the extravagant style of a gentleman rancher, LBJ drove RFK and his fellow hunters to the kill zone in his convertible. The hunters did not have to stalk their prey; they merely climbed atop a tower adjacent to an open area.

LBJ's hunting perch sat forty feet above the ground, with a carpeted and air conditioned dining room. A shooting deck overlooked a field baited with oats to attract deer from the protected wooded areas.

As he centered a deer in the telescopic cross hairs of the borrowed rifle, RFK endured silent torment: "This isn't hunting. It's slaughter."

Reluctantly squeezing the trigger, Bobby's half-hearted shot missed the target. Unprepared for the rifle's powerful recoil, Kennedy was knocked to the floor of his perch; his brow bloodied by the jerking weapon.

Helping RFK to his feet, LBJ sternly admonished his guest: "Son, you've got to learn to handle a gun like a man."

Embarrassed and angry, Robert Kennedy held his tongue, but was fully aware that round one of the Kennedy/Johnson feud had been decided in the Texan's favor.

Chapter 5

LBJ now means let's back Jack

In October of 1959, John F. Kennedy hosted his first formal presidential campaign strategy session. RFK peppered the candidate with questions: "Jack, what has been done about the campaign? What planning has been done? Jack, how do you expect to run a successful campaign if you don't get started?"

"A day lost now, can't be picked up at the other end. It's ridiculous that more work hasn't been done, already," Bobby complained.

Turning to another adviser, JFK mimicked his younger brother's staccato, high-pitched voice: "How would you like looking forward to that voice blasting in your ear for the next six months?"

Kidding aside, Robert Kennedy was clearly in charge, and eager to get the campaign underway.

On Saturday, January 2, 1960, JFK formally announced his presidential candidacy. Addressing nearly *300* supporters and news reporters in the

Senate Caucus Room, Kennedy promised to offer energetic leadership as the country headed into a new decade. He also made it abundantly clear that he was interested only in the top spot, and would not settle for the vice-presidency as a consolation prize.

Under Robert Kennedy's skillful leadership, the Kennedy camp developed a *Counterattack Sourcebook.* The campaign manual served as a resource for responding to allegations concerning JFK's religion, relative inexperience, health problems, and poor attendance during his Senate career (as well as his failure to cast a censure vote against Joe McCarthy).

RFK was on the cutting edge of developing an innovative campaign strategy. Before 1960, presidential primaries were a minor event, and the nomination was customarily decided by party leaders in the proverbial smoke filled rooms at the national convention. The candidate with the best connections to state and regional political bosses usually prevailed.

Bucking tradition, JFK entered the spring primaries to win as many delegates as possible, while his campaign operatives cut deals with political bosses in the non-primary states. By the time the convention opened in July, Kennedy hoped to have enough committed delegates to secure a first ballot nomination.

Meanwhile, Lyndon Johnson plotted electoral strategy from his lavishly decorated seven-room suite inside the Capitol building (nicknamed the *Taj Mahal*). LBJ relished showing off his inner sanctum, with its plush furniture, crystal chandeliers, and green and gold color scheme. On the wall of the innermost office, guests were greeted by a lighted, full-length portrait of the Senate Majority Leader. The redecoration of Johnson's office had cost the taxpayers more than *100,000* dollars, and was emblematic of the Texan's oversized ego.

Johnson dismissed the presidential preference primaries as little more than "beauty contests," believing that the nomination would be decided, as usual, at the convention. LBJ was certain his influence with party bosses would outweigh JFK's: "When it gets down to the nut cutting, Kennedy won't have the old bulls with him."

Historian and LBJ biographer, Randall B. Woods, summed up the Majority Leader's early election year strategy: "His only chance, Johnson perceived, was to let the other Democratic hopefuls kill each other off, and then have the party turn to him at the convention."

While trudging through the primary states, John F. Kennedy kept close tabs on Lyndon Johnson's political machinations. JFK did not share Bobby's smoldering contempt for LBJ, and managed to maintain cordial relations with the Senate Majority Leader.   JFK respected Johnson's influence and leadership skills, and found his earthy sense of humor and bombastic style rather amusing.

"He's a son of a bitch, but he's got talent," Kennedy privately confided.

At the same time, JFK questioned Johnson's presidential electability: "He is a riverboat gambler. He is omnipotent in the Senate, but lacks power in the rest of the country."

LBJ was acutely aware of his limitations. Since the end of the Civil War, no Southerner had been elected President. While Johnson's racial attitudes were far more progressive than most of his regional peers, he was nonetheless a resident of the Deep South. In the eyes of many voters, a Southerner and a Segregationist were one in the same.

At heart, LBJ regarded the forty-two year old Kennedy as a "playboy and lightweight," and seriously questioned JFK's maturity and judgment: "I know ten times more about running a country than Jack Kennedy."

"That boy needs a little more gray in his hair," Johnson complained.

Johnson had little regard for JFK's apparent superficiality: "Kennedy was pathetic as a Congressman and as a Senator. He didn't know how to address the chair. Kennedy had the 'squealers' who followed him...The girls who giggle and people who are just happy to be with you."

LBJ mistakenly assumed that he had plenty of time to make his final move, doubting Kennedy would emerge from the primaries with an insurmountable lead in the delegate vote.

On March 3, 1960, JFK won *eighty-five* percent of the votes in the New Hampshire Presidential Primary (against a smattering of write in votes for Stuart Symington and Adlai Stevenson). In Indiana and Nebraska, Kennedy ran unopposed, compiling a perfect record in primary contests.

While LBJ adopted a *wait and see* strategy, Kennedy campaigned vigorously in the Wisconsin and West Virginia primaries against his chief opponent, Hubert Humphrey (many political pundits viewed the Minnesota Senator as merely as stalking horse for Lyndon Johnson). With RFK's tireless leadership and his father's unlimited bank roll, JFK crisscrossed Wisconsin, shaking hands and wooing voters. Bobby was determined that the Kennedy camp would not be outworked, and one occasion , walked *nine* miles in the bitter cold, after his train was caught in a snowdrift.

JFK's charm and good looks appealed to a new generation of voters. Kennedy campaign advertisements were slick and professional, and the voters who saw him on television longed to meet him in person.

"We'll sell him like soap flakes," Joseph Kennedy boasted, fully aware of his son's Hollywood appeal.

JFK defeated Humphrey in Wisconsin; earning *fifty-six* percent of the vote (winning the most popular votes in Wisconsin Presidential Primary history). Kennedy also won *two-thirds* of the state's delegates and carried *six* of ten congressional districts. Humphrey, however, ran strong in the heavily Protestant districts, suggesting that JFK had not yet fully overcome anti-Catholic prejudice.

The Democratic primary contest then moved to West Virginia. Humphrey hoped to capitalize on Kennedy's Catholicism in this conservative state, where *ninety-seven* percent of the population was Protestant. The Humphrey campaign attempted to exploit the issue of faith by adopting a provocative campaign theme: *Give me that old time religion.* The voters, however, seemed to identify with the youthful JFK and mostly ignored long standing religious prejudices

When the candidate's wife was privately questioned about the religious issue, Jackie Kennedy was refreshingly honest: "I think it's so unjust of people to be against Jack because he's a Catholic. He's such a poor Catholic. Now, if it was Bobby, I could understand it."

Humphrey's attempts to portray JFK as a man of privilege and totally out of touch with the common man never seemed to take root, even in this notoriously poverty ridden state. On a blustery cold day, as JFK stood outside a coal mine shaking hands with workers at shift change, he was approached by a grizzled miner.

"Is it true you're the son of one or our wealthiest men?" the man asked.

JFK answered in the affirmative.

"Is it true that you've never wanted for anything and had everything you wanted?" the miner continued.

The candidate nodded.

"Is it true you've never done a day's work with your hands, all your life?" he asked.

Jack nervously answered yes.

"Well, let me tell you this. You haven't missed a God damn thing!" the man explained, as he shook Kennedy's hand.

Kennedy political operatives called on Franklin Roosevelt, Jr. to campaign on behalf of their candidate. West Virginia had been hit particular hard by the *Great Depression,* and the name Roosevelt was still sacred to many mountaineer voters. FDR, Jr. immediately cast aspersions on Humphrey's masculinity and bravery, calling into question his lack of military service during World War II. Humphrey was angered by the subtle allegations of cowardice, and held RFK responsible for calling his patriotism into question, railing at "that young, emotional, juvenile, Bobby."

"Anyone who gets in the way of the teacher's pet—I should change that to Papa's pet—is to be destroyed," Humphrey complained, deriding Joseph Kennedy's money and influence.

In West Virginia, Humphrey could not compete with Kennedy's seemingly unlimited financial resources. Humphrey spent a total of *25,000* dollars during the primary contest, while the Kennedy campaign spent *34,000* dollars on television advertising, alone.

JFK used his disarming wit to deflect the campaign finance issue: "I got a wire from my father that said: 'Dear Jack, don't buy one more vote than necessary. I'll be damned if I'll pay for a landslide.'"

After Kennedy won the West Virginia primary by an overwhelming majority (*60.8* to *39.2* percent), a demoralized Humphrey dropped out of the race. Following his victory in West Virginia, JFK won by a landslide in Maryland, capturing *seventy* percent of the vote. In Oregon, Kennedy defeated Favorite Son candidate, Senator Wayne Morse, by a margin of *fifty-one* to *thirty-two* percent.

Kennedy was undefeated in primary contests and had knocked LBJ's most powerful stalking horse (Humphrey) out of contention. Lyndon Johnson was the only obstacle between JFK and his party's presidential nomination.

While JFK campaigned and ignored his senatorial duties, Lyndon Johnson continued to oversee the legislative process. A resentful LBJ assumed the role of workhorse, while Kennedy emerged as the show horse and media darling.

As Johnson formulated his convention strategy, he was shocked to learn the depth of Kennedy's support in Democratic Party. LBJ approached Massachusetts Congressman, Thomas P. "Tip" O'Neill: "Now, I realize you're pledged to that boy. But, you and I both know he can't win. He's just a flash in the pan, and he's got no record of substance to run on. Will you be with me on the second ballot?"

O'Neill quickly informed Johnson that there would be *no* second ballot, as Kennedy would win during the first delegate roll call.

"I can't believe what I'm hearing," LBJ stammered.

LBJ simply could not understand how JFK had come so far, so fast: "He never said a word of importance in the Senate, and he never did a thing…He managed to create the image of himself as a shining intellectual, a youthful leader, who would change the face of the country. Now, I will admit that he had a good sense of humor, and that he looked awfully good in the God damned television screen. And, through it all, was a pretty decent fellow, but his growing hold on the American people was a mystery to me."

Johnson had committed a rare political blunder, assuming that old school political axioms were infallible. By the time he fully recognized his mistake, it was too late. Historian and LBJ biographer, Doris Kearns Goodwin, elaborated on Johnson's miscalculation: "Confusing the national campaign with bargaining in the Senate, he wrongly assumed that each Democratic Senator controlled the delegates from his state. While John Kennedy and his men crisscrossed the country, winning primaries, attending state conventions, and rounding up delegates, Johnson remained in his office in Washington, expecting somehow to make the right deals with right people."

Facing the prospect of being totally shut out of the nominating process, Lyndon Johnson finally announced his presidential candidacy on July 5, 1960, just days before the convention opened.

The Kennedy camp set up their convention headquarters on the eighth floor (Suite 8315) of Los Angeles' Biltmore Hotel, where RFK assembled his well-oiled political machine. Utilizing over *3000* note cards containing biographical information on each delegate, Bobby kept careful count of the votes needed for a first ballot nomination. Campaign workers were issued walkie talkies to facilitate instant communication from various spots in the convention hall. As he has shown during the primary season, RFK was a firm taskmaster, and refused to let his staff be outworked by the competition.

When a small group of Kennedy supporters took the afternoon off to visit California's most famous amusement park, RFK was furious: "It has come to my attention that some of you think Disneyland is more important than nominating the next President of the United States. Those, that do, can just resign."

On another occasion, an unpaid volunteer, who had been up until nearly three a.m. soliciting delegate support for JFK, was late to an early morning staff meeting. Bobby castigated the tardy worker: "Look, if it's too much for you to get here at seven, when we get here, just let me know, and you'll be excused."

A campaign advisor noted the sharp contrast between the candidate and his campaign manager: "John Kennedy was a charmer, but Bobby was no-nonsense—he couldn't fake it if he wanted to. I guess the bottom line is that with Bobby, you eventually learn to love him. But, you had to learn."

RFK cautioned his staff to carefully tally delegates: "I don't want generalities or guesses. There's no point in fooling ourselves. I want the cold facts. I want to hear only the votes we are guaranteed to get on the first ballot."

During the course of the convention, RFK cemented his image as a "heartless, cold, axe man." Many loyal Democrats, who liked and respected JFK, grew to despise his younger brother.

Once the convention was underway, Lyndon Johnson realized his odds of overcoming the Kennedy juggernaut were remote. Nonetheless, LBJ mounted a vigorous challenge from his campaign headquarters (also located in the Biltmore Hotel).

At first, LBJ's attacks against JFK were light hearted, focusing on his opponent's youth: "Did you hear the news? Jack's pediatricians have just given him a clean bill of health."

The contest soon grew bitter, when LBJ resurrected long standing concerns about Kennedy's Catholicism, and then focused on an even more sensitive subject—JFK's health. Johnson operatives pointed out that the youthful appearing Kennedy actually suffered from Addison's disease—a credible accusation, since JFK did take corticosteroids to combat his potentially life threatening adrenal insufficiency. For years, however, the Kennedy family had publicly maintained that Jack's periodic health crises were attributable to *malaria*. On more than one occasion, Jack had termed his bouts of sickness as "something like walking leukemia." In reality, Joe Kennedy had hoarded corticosteroids in safety deposit boxes across the United States, in the event of an unexpected emergency. During the 1960 presidential primary season, JFK had experienced near panic, when the bag containing his medications was misplaced (fearing that his political enemies might learn of its contents).

Alarmed by the potential fallout from full disclosure of his brother's medical history, Robert Kennedy offered a disingenuous disclaimer: "He does not have an ailment *classically* described as Addison's disease."

At the same time, LBJ embellished Kennedy's physical ailments, with characteristic hyperbole: "He's a scrawny little fella, with rickets."

"Have you seen his ankles? They're about so round," LBJ exaggerated, making a small circle in the air with his index finger.

Johnson also attacked Joseph Kennedy, citing the former Ambassador's pre-World War II Nazi appeasement: "I never thought Hitler was right."

Hour by hour, LBJ's attacks grew more scurrilous. Journalist and historian, Theodore White, who was covering the convention, received a phone call from an unidentified Johnson supporter: "I think you should know that John and Bobby Kennedy are fags."

Aware that politics often turned ugly, RFK was nonetheless amazed by the savageness of LBJ's attacks: "I knew he hated Jack, But, I didn't think he hated him that much."

The Kennedy campaign was forced to launch a counterattack, and called into question Lyndon Johnson's cardiac problems. When an LBJ adviser cried foul, Bobby exploded: "You've got some nerve! Lyndon Johnson has compared my father to the Nazis, and said my brother is dying from Addison's disease. You Johnson people are running a stinking damned campaign, and you'll get yours, when the time comes. We'll fucking kill you!"

In a last ditch effort to demonstrate his maturity and leadership, Johnson proposed a one-on-one debate in front of the Massachusetts and Texas convention delegations. Against the advice of a number of his closest advisers, who were fearful of Johnson's personal attacks, Kennedy accepted his opponent's challenge.

During his opening remarks, JFK wittily disarmed both LBJ and the assembled delegates: "You're a great Majority Leader, and I hope you'll be the same for me."

Adding to his woes, LBJ had overestimated his strength in Western states, where Kennedy operatives managed to secure impressive inroads. With *761* delegates needed to win the nomination (out of a total of *1520* votes), Johnson mistakenly assumed that he had considerable support in the South and West, counting on the support of *526.5* delegates.

"There I was, looking for a burglar coming in the front door, and little did I know that the fox was coming through the fence in back. When I woke up, the chickens were gone," LBJ lamented, realizing that JFK had already secured pledges from what were believed to be Johnson-committed delegates.

On July 13, 1960, Minnesota Governor, Orville Freeman, nominated John F. Kennedy for President. Lyndon Johnson's nominating speech was delivered by fellow Texan and Speaker of the House, Sam Rayburn.

"This is not (a) time to experiment. We must offer a man who has demonstrated that he can lead," the legendary Rayburn proclaimed, contrasting Johnson's proven leadership to Kennedy's youth and inexperience.

In the end, LBJ was unable to overcome JFK's momentum. When the Wyoming delegation announced that their *fifteen* delegates were pledged to John F. Kennedy, the first ballot nomination was his (the final delegate tally was *806* for Kennedy, *409* for Johnson, *86* for Symington, *79.5* for Stevenson, and a combined *140.5* for a handful of lesser candidates).

Ever the consummate politician, Lyndon Johnson immediately set aside his disappointment and sent Kennedy a congratulatory telegram: "LBJ now means 'Let's Back Jack.'"

As far as LBJ was concerned, unflattering accusations made during the heat of the campaign were a necessary part of politics, and subject to forgiveness. To a lesser degree, JFK shared Johnson's philosophy, and was willing to let bygones be bygones.

Robert Kennedy, however, was unwilling to forgive or forget LBJ's scurrilous attacks against the Kennedy family. Joe Kennedy's prophetic warning about his younger son was right on the money: "Once Bobby hates you, you stay hated."

Chapter 6

I want to be Vice-President

At first glance, a JFK/LBJ presidential ticket seemed preposterous. The prospect of Kennedy offering his chief rival the vice-presidency appeared remote. The likelihood of Johnson accepting JFK's offer seemed even more far-fetched.

Over the years, LBJ's domineering manner had earned him powerful enemies, many of whom were prepared to do just about anything to keep him from becoming JFK's running mate. The liberal wing of the Democratic Party unfairly assumed that Johnson, as a Southerner, was also a Segregationist. Labor leaders identified LBJ's voting record as hostile to their cause. Most importantly, Robert Kennedy detested Johnson, and it was assumed that JFK shared his brother's disdain for the powerful Texan.

Most political pundits doubted LBJ would give up his post as Senate Majority Leader for the vice-presidency—a position that was high on symbolism, but low on substance. John Nance Garner, who served as Vice-President under Franklin Roosevelt and was one of LBJ's early political idols, likened the number two position to a "pitcher of warm piss."

The day before the Democratic National Convention opened, LBJ had appeared on the *NBC News* weekly program, *Meet the Press,* and was asked if he was interested in the vice-presidency.

"No," LBJ responded, "Most Vice-Presidents don't do much."

Political analysts had already formulated a list of JFK's potential running mates, including Senators Hubert Humphrey, Stuart Symington, and Henry "Scoop" Jackson, along with Minnesota Governor, Orville Freeman. Lyndon Johnson's name appeared on none of those lists.

JFK, however, was a practical politician and keenly aware of his own strengths and weaknesses. Kennedy counted on the unwavering support of Democratic liberals and labor leaders, and was confident of his appeal to voters in the Northeast and Midwest. His greatest challenge would be attracting votes in the conservative and Southern and Border States. In the end, Johnson's strengths complemented JFK's shortcomings.

The convention vote on the vice-presidential nominee was scheduled for the day after JFK's nomination, leaving the Kennedy camp less than twenty-four hours to choose a running mate. Doubting the availability of Lyndon Johnson, JFK focused on less controversial choices, like Humphrey and Symington, before receiving surprising signals from LBJ operatives.

Philip Graham, publisher of the *Washington Post* and close friend to both JFK and LBJ, urged Kennedy to consider Johnson for the number two position. Congressman Tip O'Neill also approached Kennedy, suggesting that LBJ was actually interested in becoming JFK's running mate.

"Of course I want Lyndon Johnson. The only thing is, I would never want to offer it to him and have him turn me down—I would be terribly embarrassed," Kennedy explained, genuinely surprise by O'Neill's revelation.

LBJ expressed interest in joining the ticket, to the utter amazement of many of his advisers. Johnson's mentor and fellow Texan, Sam Rayburn, offered the strongest opposition. Rayburn, who detested the Republican nominee, Richard Nixon, soon changed his mind, and advised LBJ to accept JFK's potential offer.

In many ways, Johnson was in a *no lose* position. If the Kennedy/Johnson ticket went down to defeat, barring a major upset in the senatorial race, LBJ would be reelected to his powerful legislative seat.

LBJ could also see the handwriting on the wall concerning his future as

Majority Leader. If elected President, JFK would become the *most powerful* Democrat in Washington, and unlike Eisenhower, would not *need* Johnson to serve as a powerful liaison between the Oval Office and Capitol Hill. If Nixon was elected, the new Republican President would never be as respectful and deferential to LBJ as Eisenhower had been.

If elected Vice-President, Johnson would be well positioned to succeed JFK after eight years. Of perhaps greater importance, the Vice-President was just a heartbeat away from the presidency, even though such a morbid possibility seemed remote with a man of Kennedy's young age. In the end, LBJ quoted a familiar political axiom: "Power is where power goes."

Mid-morning, on July 14, 1960, Kennedy privately conferred with Lyndon Johnson in the Texan's hotel room. After the meeting, a stunned JFK quickly located his brother.

"You just won't believe it. He wants it!" Jack told Bobby (JFK's surprise was somewhat disingenuous, as he had already received feelers from Johnson intermediaries).

"Oh, my God!" RFK replied.

"Now, what do we do?" JFK asked.

In addition to RFK's firm opposition, most other Kennedy supporters were appalled at the idea of LBJ joining the presidential ticket. Kenneth O'Donnell, the campaign's liaison to organized labor and RFK's long-time friend, was aghast, directing his anger at JFK: "This is the worst mistake you have ever made. You came out here to this convention like a knight on a white charger—the clean-cut Ivy League college guy, who's promising to get rid of the old hack politicians. Now, in your first move after the nomination, you go against all the people who supported you. Are we going to spend the campaign apologizing for Lyndon Johnson, and trying to explain why he voted against everything you ever stood for?"

O'Donnell warned JFK that Civil Rights supporters (who distrusted any Southerner) and labor leaders (who opposed Johnson's legislative voting record), would feel "double crossed." When leaders of the party's liberal wing learned about Kennedy's offer to LBJ, they were also enraged. JFK's suite soon filled with disenchanted supporters, who gave the presidential candidate an angry earful.

JFK was suddenly gripped by indecision. Robert Kennedy later recalled the uncertainty of the moment: "It was the most indecisive time we ever had...We changed our minds eight times...How could we get him out of it?"

Feeling trapped, Jack dispatched Bobby to discuss the awkward situation with LBJ. Johnson refused to meet with RFK, and insisted that Sam Rayburn and John Connally serve as intermediaries. Unable to secure a face to face meeting with LBJ, RFK talked with Rayburn and Connally, pointing out that the labor wing of the party was "revolting" against the prospect of Johnson appearing on the Democratic ticket.

"Lyndon just can't accept the nomination. It was a mistake," Bobby explained, asking that Johnson decline the offer before it was made public.

"Aw, shit, Sonny!" an angry Rayburn replied, before storming out of the hotel suite.

John Connally, Lyndon Johnson's long time political protégé (and future Secretary of the Navy, Governor of Texas, and Secretary of the Treasury), informed RFK that it was "ludicrous" to suggest that labor leaders would "revolt" against the Democratic Party.

"Who's the candidate, you or your brother?" Connally challenged RFK.

Unable to secure Johnson's withdrawal, Bobby returned to his brother's hotel suite. At the same time, Philip Graham, who was huddling with LBJ, exchanged phone calls with JFK, hoping to clarify the mixed messages coming from the Kennedy camp.

"It's all set. Tell Lyndon I want him," Jack reassured Graham.

Desperately hoping to keep Johnson off the ticket, RFK returned to LBJ's suite. Speaking once again with John Connally, Bobby warned that organized labor leaders were now threatening to disrupt the convention if Johnson was nominated for the vice-presidency.

Disgusted and disgruntled, Connally cut to the chase: "Bobby, there is no point in your talking to me, or to Lyndon. Your brother came down here and offered him the vice-presidential nomination, and Johnson accepted. Now, if he's changed his mind, he's going to have to call and ask him to withdraw, because Johnson is not going to do it himself."

Having failed, once again, to meet face to face with Lyndon Johnson, a frustrated RFK returned to confer with his brother. Meanwhile, JFK had telephoned Johnson and read the press release announcing LBJ's spot on the ticket.

"Do you really want me?" Johnson asked, hoping for solid affirmation.

"Yes," JFK replied, in a less than enthusiastic tone

"Well, if you really want me, I'll do it," Johnson vowed.

Assuming that his selection was a done deal, LBJ was stunned when Robert Kennedy appeared at his door for a *third* time. Before accepting the inevitability of a Kennedy/Johnson ticket, RFK was determined to speak directly to LBJ: "I went down there to see if I could get him to withdraw."

Amidst growing confusion, Bobby was unaware that his brother had just confirmed Johnson's selection as his running mate. LBJ quietly listened to RFK's concerns about the negative reactions from organized labor and liberal party leaders. Bobby suggested that Johnson accept the Chairmanship of the Democratic National Committee, in lieu of the vice-presidency.

RFK, who had expected an angry eruption from the temperamental Texan, was surprised by Johnson's forlorn expression. Instead, Bobby feared that LBJ was "going to burst into tears."

"I want to be Vice-President," Johnson replied, in an anxious and mournful tone, "If he will have me, I'll join in making the fight for it."

Boxed into a corner, RFK realized LBJ was not going to voluntarily withdraw his name. Vulnerable, yet manipulative, Johnson had transformed RFK into the bad guy.

"Well, then, that's fine," Bobby reluctantly answered, "He wants you to be Vice-President, if you want it."

For the first time as a campaign manager, RFK had been unable to shape the outcome of a major policy decision. Dejected and demoralized, Bobby left Johnson to deal with the press. Standing on a chair in the hotel hallway, LBJ addressed reporters: "If my country thinks I can serve better as a Private, I want to serve. If they want me as a General, I want to serve. Jack asked me to serve—I accept."

JFK tried to console his younger brother, reminding him that LBJ would be much easier to "control" as Vice-President than as Senate Majority Leader; as a powerful lawmaker, Johnson could single handily block Kennedy's legislative agenda. While Jack appeared ready to move forward, Bobby was temporarily inconsolable.

JFK also attempted to cheer up his dismayed adviser, Kenneth O'Donnell: "I'm forty- three years old. I'm not going to die in office. So, the vice-presidency doesn't mean anything."

On Thursday evening, July 14, 1960, Lyndon Johnson was nominated as JFK's running mate by acclamation. While there were no public demonstrations or *revolts,* Robert Kennedy absorbed considerable heat from the party's labor leaders.

"Robert Kennedy was never so savagely attacked in his life," Kenneth O'Donnell later recalled.

At day's end, RFK was mentally and physically exhausted: "Yesterday was the best day of my life, and today is the worst day of my life."

Lyndon Johnson's presence on the ticket was a bitter pill for Robert Kennedy to swallow. Unlike his brother, RFK could not forgive the man who had ridiculed his father, exposed his brother's medical history, and spread rumors that the Kennedy brothers were homosexuals.

Joseph Kennedy, the sage mastermind of an emerging Kennedy dynasty, believed that Johnson would ultimately add strength to the Democratic ticket. Joe calmly reassured his sons about LBJ: "It will be the smartest thing you ever did."

Outwardly elated by his ability to outfox Robert Kennedy, Lyndon Johnson was also angry and resentful. He held RFK personally responsible for the humiliating events of earlier in the day—Bobby had made him *beg* for the vice-presidential nomination.

It had been one of longest, most stressful days of Johnson's colorful life, and he would never forget RFK's treachery.

Chapter 7

Little brother is watching you

In the summer of 1960, the Republican Party nominated incumbent Vice-President, Richard Nixon, as its presidential candidate. Nixon subsequently selected Henry Cabot Lodge as his running mate. Even though he had his Senate seat to John F. Kennedy in 1952, Lodge remained popular in the voter rich northeast.

While the Republicans assembled a formidable ticket, Robert Kennedy could not wait to begin the General Election campaign. After a brief post-convention vacation, RFK hit the ground running. The Kennedy brain trust devised an innovative election year strategy—for the first time ever, television cameras, computers, and image consultants would play major roles in a presidential campaign. The Kennedy camp also hired a full time pollster, Lou Harris, to track JFK's progress.

Bobby summed up his plans for the interval between Labor Day and Election Day: "Run and fight and scramble for ten weeks—all the way."

RFK led by example, working from dawn until late into the night. Not until days' end did Bobby relax, rewarding himself with a large bowl of ice cream, and a bottle of *Heineken* beer.

With single-minded devotion to the task at hand, RFK showed little interest in making new friends. Addressing a group of Democratic leaders in New York, Bobby was particularly blunt: "I don't give a damn if the state and county organizations survive after November, and I don't give a damn if you survive. I want to elect John F. Kennedy."

Tough and demanding, RFK exacted unwavering loyalty and tireless devotion. Kennedy campaign workers adopted an unofficial motto: "Little brother is watching you."

"I'm not running a popularity contest," Bobby explained to a reporter, "It doesn't matter if they like me, or not."

RFK's brashness generated enmity among many seasoned politicians. While President Eisenhower jokingly referred to JFK as "Little Boy Blue," he privately condemned Robert Kennedy as "that little shit." Florida Senator, George Smathers, JFK's long time friend and key Deep South party leader, remembered several unpleasant confrontations with RFK.

"He was an arrogant guy, Bobby was. He didn't have respect for anyone's views, but his own. He was just like the old man," Smathers recalled, likening RFK to his infamous father.

For the most part, Joseph Kennedy stayed in the background, serving as the campaign's paymaster. The elder Kennedy wanted JFK to bask in the limelight, and hoped that RFK would earn credit for orchestrating a campaign victory: "I don't want them to inherit my enemies. It's tough enough they inherit my friends!"

Republican strategists poked fun at the Kennedy campaign in rhyme: "Jack and Bob will run the show, while Ted's in charge of hiding Joe."

Though he was unhappy with Lyndon Johnson's presence on the ticket, Robert Kennedy was determined to make the best of an unlikely political marriage. At the start of the General Election campaign, RFK crudely outlined his expectations for LBJ: "We put that son of a bitch on the ticket to carry Texas."

Knowing he must "deliver the South," LBJ barnstormed the region. In Nashville, Johnson hosted a *unity meeting* of Southern Governors, and implored them to work together on behalf of the Democratic Party: "It's all the way with JFK."

Starting in Kennedy's home state, where he mounted a policeman's horse and demonstrated his equestrian skills, LBJ began a campaign swing toward the Heart of Dixie; the aptly named *Boston to Austin axis.* As expected, the energetic Johnson was a crowd pleaser, and eventually earned begrudging praise from his long time nemesis.

"We are getting outstanding favorable reaction to your speeches, wherever you go. There is no question, but what these speeches are making a major difference," RFK wrote Johnson.

LBJ repeatedly reminded black voters that he was not a prototypical Southern Segregationist: "I assure you from the bottom of my heart that I have done my dead level best to make progress in the field of Civil Rights."

LBJ reassured African Americans that if Kennedy was elected President, "you will make more progress in *four* years, than you have in the last *104* years."

In October, Johnson boarded a special train, christened the *LBJ Victory Express,* and traveled *3500* miles across the Deep South, delivering *sixty* speeches in *eight* different states. The journalists covering the event jokingly referred to the whistle stop tour as the *Cornpone Express.*

Ironically, Johnson encountered the strongest resistance in his conservative home state. On November 4th, LBJ was confronted with a particularly ugly situation in Dallas. Republican Congressman, Bruce Alger, accompanied by a coalition of conservative citizens, accosted Lyndon and Lady Bird outside the Adolphus Hotel. Alger led the way, brandishing an accusatory placard: "LBJ sold out to Yankee Socialists." In the resulting melee, Lady Bird was struck by a picket sign and her gloves were thrown into a gutter by a hostile protestor.

The rowdy Dallas conservatives included a group of Junior Leaguers; derisively known as the "mink coat mob." Several crowd members spat on the Johnson party as they made their way through the crowd, and encountered another hostile sign: "Beat Judas." LBJ's willingness to face down a near lynch mob earned him the begrudging respect of liberal Democrats, who could not help but admire the Texan's courage.

LBJ was steadfastly determined to prove his worth to the Kennedy brothers. In a private conversation with John Connally, LBJ reminded his political protégé that it would be devastating to lose the state of Texas, even if JFK won the nationwide election.

JFK and LBJ usually campaigned alone, only occasionally crossing paths during the General Election season. As Johnson confronted angry conservatives in the Deep South, Kennedy waged his own unseemly battles.

Many liberals, including former First Lady, Eleanor Roosevelt, were less than enthusiastic about JFK's presidential candidacy, and openly criticized Kennedy's failure to cast a censure vote against Senator Joseph McCarthy. Taking direct aim at JFK's Pulitzer Prize winning book, Roosevelt reminded fellow liberals that Kennedy would have done better by displaying "a little less profile, and a little more courage."After reassuring Roosevelt of his support for traditional liberal causes, Kennedy eventually earned the former First Lady's endorsement.

Privately, JFK complained about Roosevelt's bitterness: "She hated my father, and she can't stand it that his children turned out so much better than hers."

He also earned the begrudging support of former President Harry Truman, who had long detested Joseph Kennedy. In early July, just prior to the Democratic Convention, Truman had publicly questioned JFK's qualifications for the presidency: "Senator, are you certain that you are quite ready for the country, or that the country is ready for you in the role of President in January 1961? May I suggest you be patient?"

"It's not the Pope, it's the Pop," Truman declared, explaining his concerns about the candidate's father, rather than his Catholicism.

On August 20th, Kennedy visited with the former President at the Truman Presidential Library in Independence, Missouri. After a forty minute meeting, Truman announced to the press: "The convention nominated this man, and I am going to support him, and what are you going to do about it?"

In the end, Harry Truman's animosity toward Richard Nixon outweighed his disregard for Joe Kennedy, leading to his endorsement of JFK.

Sensitive to concerns about his Catholicism, Kennedy displayed a wry sense of humor, after learning that Truman had told a group of Republicans to "go to hell."

"Our side will try to refrain from raising the religious issue," Jack quipped.

Kennedy jokingly applied a religious metaphor to describe his campaign itinerary: "It's coast to coast with the Holy Ghost."

Ultimately, religion proved to be a serious campaign issue, as many Protestant clergymen feared that a Catholic President would be "under extreme pressure from the church" and "duty bound to submit to its direction."

"I refuse to believe that I was denied the right to be President on the day I was baptized," Kennedy countered.

In private, JFK was clearly frustrated: "I'm getting tired of these people who think I want to replace the gold at Fort Knox with a supply of holy water."

In September, JFK addressed a conference of Protestant ministers in Houston, persuasively arguing that his religion would not affect his ability to govern the country. Kennedy's convincing performance partially defused the *Catholic issue.*

Even the normally unflappable Robert Kennedy was brought to tears by the controversy, citing his late brother's valor in World War II: "Did they ask my brother Joe whether he was Catholic, before he was shot down?"

During a rare joint campaign appearance in San Antonio, Lyndon Johnson chimed in on the religious controversy. Confronting a protestor's sign that read, "We don't want the Kremlin or the Vatican," Johnson recited the names of men who were massacred at the Alamo.

"No one knows whether they were Catholic, or not. For, there was no religious test at the Alamo," LBJ proclaimed.

At other campaign stops across the Deep South, LBJ used his colloquial manner to defend JFK, who was a decorated World War II PT Boat hero: "That little ole Massachusetts boy took his little ole torpedo boat and rammed into the side of a Japanese cruiser, and there wasn't nobody asking what religion he was. And, when he was saving those American boys that was (sic) in his crew, they didn't ask what church he belonged to."

Throughout the campaign, Robert Kennedy capitalized on his brother's photogenic image. Employing a professional media consultant, the Kennedy camp maximized television exposure, allowing voters the opportunity both see and hear the candidate.

On September 26, 1960, the first of *four* debates between John F. Kennedy and Richard M. Nixon was televised from Chicago. Under the harsh and unforgiving television lights, JFK appeared tan and handsome, while Nixon looked pale and unshaven (having unwisely coated his face with *Lazy Shave,* rather that professional makeup).

"My God, they've embalmed him even before he died!" Chicago

Mayor, Richard Daley, exclaimed, when Nixon appeared on the television screen.

Nixon, who had been hospitalized for treatment of an infected knee at the end of August, appeared tense and uneasy in front of the cameras. Kennedy, who had consented to the use of a light coat of professional facial make up, seemed confident and composed. Just prior to the start of the contest, RFK tried to relax his brother, and set the tone for the evening.

"Kick him in the balls," Bobby whispered, with a mischievous smile.

Potential voters listening to the debate by radio gave Nixon a slight edge, but the television viewers were more impressed with Kennedy. For many voters (an estimated *85,000,000* Americans watched at least one of the televised debates), the stark contrast in appearance between the two candidates remained a lasting image, as Election Day rapidly approached.

In the closing days of the campaign, JFK received an unexpected boost in support from African American voters. On October 19th, Civil Rights leader, Martin Luther King, Jr., was arrested after staging a sit-in at *Rich's* department store in Atlanta. A year earlier, King had received a suspended sentence for driving in Georgia with an Alabama driver's license (three months after moving to Atlanta). Judge Oscar Mitchell, an avowed segregationist, used the previous offense as an excuse to deny King bail, and sentenced him to four months hard labor on the state chain gang.

Harris Wofford and Louis Martin, who were part of the Kennedy campaign's Civil Rights division, contacted the candidate's brother-in-law, Sargent Shriver, who, in turned, urged JFK to telephone King's wife, Coretta, and offer his support. On the spur of the moment, Kennedy agreed to place the call, expressing appropriate sympathy and concern.

When Bobby learned about his brother's phone call, he was incredulous, fearing that white Southern voters would extract revenge on Election Day. RFK took his anger out on Shriver: "You dumb shit, you've blown the election!"

When Martin and Wofford intervened, explaining the harsh nature of King's sentence, RFK's anger abated: "How could they do that? Who's the Judge? You can't deny bail on a misdemeanor."

In short order, RFK telephoned Judge Mitchell and complained about the abuse of King's constitutional rights. After Bobby's call, the Judge agreed to release King from his harsh sentence.

The Kennedy brothers were lauded in the black communities. Martin

Luther King, Jr.'s father told his Ebenezer Baptist Church congregation: "I had expected to vote against Senator Kennedy because of his religion. But, now he can be my President, Catholic or whatever he is. It took courage to call my daughter-in-law at a time like this. He has the moral courage to stand up for what he knows is right. I've got all my votes, and I've got a suitcase, and I'm going to take them up there and dump them in his lap."

By Election Day, the Kennedy campaign had spent nearly *thirteen million* dollars. JFK had traveled over *200,000* miles, while RFK had toiled tirelessly behind the scenes.

"Jack works as hard as any mortal man can, but Bobby goes a bit further," Joe Kennedy reflected, as the moment of truth approached.

JFK also paid tribute to his younger brother: "I don't know what Bobby does, but it always seems to turn out right."

On Tuesday, November 8, 1960, nearly *sixty-five* percent of the electorate voted in the presidential election. The Kennedy team set up headquarters at the family compound in Cape Cod. The sunroom in RFK's house served as election central and was equipped with a state of the art communications center, including telephones, televisions, and Teletype machines. RFK constantly worked the phones to monitor voter turnout and gather returns—by day's end, his long distance telephone bill was more than *10,000* dollars.

As Election Night inched forward, a campaign adviser asked Bobby why he appeared so glum. Surprisingly, RFK wasn't thinking about the outcome of the election: "I'm worried about Teddy. We've lost every state he worked in, out west. Jack will kid him, and that may hurt his feelings."

The election was not decided until 5:30 a.m. the next morning, when Kennedy was declared a winner in the state of Michigan. Jack had gone to bed at half past three, while Bobby remained awake and in charge, until the race was decided. At 7:00 a.m., the Secret Service surrounded President-Elect Kennedy's ocean front house, signaling the beginning of a new era in American politics.

John F. Kennedy won by a mere *112,881* out of *66,832,818* votes cast—a margin of only *0.17* percent. Kennedy's Electoral College victory was more comfortable (*303* to *219*), but a transfer of only *12,000* votes in *five* states would have given Richard Nixon the presidency.

The issue of Kennedy's Catholicism had nearly cost him the election. The Kennedy/Johnson ticket won only *forty-six* percent of the non-Catholic votes, marking the first time a President had been elected with less than a majority of the Protestant vote.

Lyndon Johnson spent Election Night in Texas, focusing more on statewide returns than on national vote totals. The Kennedy/Johnson margin of victory in Texas mirrored the nationwide results, where they won by only *46,233* out of more than *2,000,000* votes cast. Johnson won reelection to the Senate, but only managed to defeat his Republican opponent, John Tower, by *56.5* to *43.5* percent—further evidence of the state's growing Conservatism.

LBJ should have been elated. His selection as JFK's running mate had paid huge dividends. The Democratic ticket won not only Texas, but also carried *five* other states of the Old Confederacy—South Carolina, North Carolina, Georgia, Arkansas, and Louisiana. Had Mississippi not pledged its electoral votes to Segregationist candidate, Harry Byrd, Kennedy would have likely won the Magnolia State. All toll, *eighty-one* of the *128* electoral votes in the eleven Deep South states went to the Kennedy/Johnson ticket.

The issue of whether LBJ was a Segregationist was finally laid to rest, when the Democratic ticket won *seventy* percent of the black vote (double Stevenson's total from four years earlier).

On Election Night, while the outcome was still in doubt, LBJ phoned JFK with an amusing progress report: "I see *you* are losing Ohio. *I* am carrying Texas and *we* are doing pretty well in Pennsylvania."

Once the final votes had been counted, LBJ received a phone call from Robert Kennedy. Bobby could not resist ribbing the Vice-President Elect: "Well, Lady Bird carried Texas for the President."

Lyndon Johnson was fully aware of his key role in the election of John F. Kennedy to the presidency. However, the normally boisterous Texan was less than enthusiastic, and some observers believed that he had hoped for a narrow loss in the presidential race. Having delivered the Deep South and proven himself to the liberal wing of the Democratic Party, Johnson would have been a hero of sorts, even if Kennedy had lost the election. Moreover, LBJ would have established himself as the frontrunner for the 1964 presidential nomination. Instead, he was a sullen Vice-President Elect.

A loyal Johnson aide described the Texan's mood on the morning after the election: "He looked as if he'd lost his last friend on earth."

In marked contrast to LBJ's ambivalence, Robert Kennedy was ecstatic. He had engineered the ultimate political triumph. RFK's aggressive attitude and caustic demeanor did not win many new friends, but his organizational skills and innovation established a new standard for presidential campaigns. The use of television, computer analysis of voting patterns, and pre-election polling proved highly successful, and helped elect the youngest President in American history.

A prominent newspaper editor wrote that the Kennedy campaign had "a great deal of the electronic age," and that RFK's efforts were "exacting, painstaking, and careful."

For the next *three* years and *thirteen* days, Robert Kennedy's career would be on the rise, while Lyndon Johnson would be banished to political exile.

Chapter 8

*Bobby **is** going to be Attorney General*

John Adams, the first man to hold the office, described his role very clearly: "I am Vice-President. In this I am nothing, but I may be everything."

Hubert Humphrey, who also served as Vice-President, poked fun at the number two position: "There is the old story about the mother who had two sons. One went to sea, and the other became Vice-President, and neither was ever heard (from) again."

Now that he was Vice-President-Elect, Lyndon Johnson's influential political journey had reached a dead end. His future appeared bleak; no Vice-President since Martin Van Buren (in 1836), had been elected to the presidency.

Rejecting historical precedent, LBJ tried to improve his position between Election Day and JFK's inauguration. Johnson envisioned a dual role as Vice-President; one, where he served in the executive branch of government, but directed the efforts of the legislative branch. His grandiose plans, however, met a rude awakening in early 1961.

On January 3rd, Johnson joined Senator Mike Mansfield, his handpicked successor as Senate Majority Leader, and *sixty-two* other Senators at a Democratic caucus on Capitol Hill. Senator Mansfield proposed that the newly elected Vice-President be allowed to preside over future meetings of the group.

Mansfield's suggestion met fierce opposition from several Senators, who were wary of interference from the White House in legislative matters. Many of the lawmakers had grown tired of Johnson's autocratic leadership, and were grateful to have him out of Congress. In the end, the Democratic caucus voted, *forty-six* to *seventeen,* in favor of Mansfield's resolution, but LBJ felt *unwanted,* and refused to accept the proposed leadership position.

Blindsided by the attitude of his former colleagues, Johnson realized that his base of power had evaporated. Moreover, he felt betrayed and humiliated: "I know the difference between a caucus and a cactus. In a cactus, all the pricks are on the outside."

Johnson's second gambit was centered on the President-Elect. He asked JFK to sign an Executive Order giving the Vice-President "general supervision" over several government agencies (including NASA), and require all cabinet heads to copy Johnson on memorandums sent to the President. Unwilling to cede that much power to his Vice-President, Kennedy simply ignored LBJ's request.

By mid-January of 1961, Lyndon Johnson could see the handwriting on the wall. His once powerful wings had been clipped at every turn.

President-Elect Kennedy was uncertain how to best deal with his disgruntled running mate. Aside from his appreciation of Johnson's *down home* charm, JFK sympathized with LBJ, realizing the proud Texan had voluntarily relinquished his powerful post as Senate Majority Leader for the political impotence of the vice-presidency.

Eight days after the election, JFK visited the Vice-President Elect at the LBJ Ranch openly embracing the Texan's hospitality. Much to LBJ's delight, Kennedy shot his requisite deer. Johnson later presented Kennedy with the stuffed deer head as a gift, hoping the new President would mount it in the Oval Office. Instead, JFK had Johnson's gift hung in the White House's Fish Room.

"The three most overrated things in the world are the state of Texas, the FBI, and hunting trophies," Kennedy privately quipped.

JFK managed to keep Johnson at arm's length, refusing his request for office space in the West Wing of the White House. Kennedy did allow the Vice-President to keep his "Taj Mahal" in the Capitol, and also assigned him a six-room suite in the *Executive Office Building (EOB)*, across the street from the Oval Office (LBJ was the first Vice-President in history to have an actual executive branch office).

While JFK was careful not to be eclipsed by LBJ's powerful personality, he also knew that Johnson possessed considerable knowledge and experience, and asked the Vice-President to attend all cabinet meetings, weekly sessions with congressional leaders, and national security meetings.

Kennedy also shared the spoils of victory with his Vice-President. LBJ's long time political protégé, John Connally, was appointed Secretary of Navy. Johnson was also allowed to control patronage in the state of Texas, much to the chagrin of the Lone Star state's Democratic Senator, Ralph Youngblood.

JFK instructed his aides to treat LBJ with dignity and respect, regardless of their personal feelings about him. Kennedy bluntly outlined those expectations with his Appointments Secretary, Kenneth O'Donnell: "Lyndon Johnson was the Majority Leader of the United States Senate. He was elected to office several times by the people. He was the number one Democrat in the United States, elected by us to be our leader. I'm President of the United States. He doesn't like that. He think he's ten times more important than I am—he happens be that kind of fellow…Elected officers have a code, and no matter whether they like each other or hate each other…You have never been elected to anything by anybody, and you are dealing with a very insecure, sensitive man, with a huge ego. I want you to literally kiss his ass from one end of Washington to the other."

Understandably, Lyndon Johnson failed to embrace the enthusiasm of his fellow *New Frontiersmen*. An adviser recalled LBJ's obvious unhappiness: "It was clear to me, and a lot of other people that he didn't want to be Vice-President."

In November of 1960, just after the General Election, *Newsweek* magazine boldly declared: "Robert Kennedy will be the new man to see in Washington."

In reality, Bobby was temporarily without a job, after orchestrating his brother's successful campaign. RFK was uncertain about the direction of his career. He briefly contemplated returning to Massachusetts and running for Governor. As expected, Joe Kennedy intervened and made the choice for him; RFK would be the new Attorney General.

Eunice Kennedy joked about her father's decision: "Bobby, we'll make Attorney General, so he can throw all the people Dad doesn't like into jail. They'll have to build more jails."

RFK was reluctant to accept his father's dictate: "In the first place, I thought nepotism was a problem. Secondly, I had been chasing bad men for three years, and I didn't want to spend the rest of my life doing that."

When rumors of RFK's pending appointment were leaked, public opinion was largely negative, as reflected in a *New York Times* editorial: "It is simply not enough to name a bright young political manager, no matter how bright or how young or how personally loyal, to a major post in the government, that, by rights, ought to be kept completely out of the political arena."

As an astute politician, JFK sensed the risks associated with appointing his brother to a major cabinet post. Jack offered to have the Governor of Massachusetts appoint Bobby to fill JFK's vacant Senate seat. RFK immediately refused, vowing to serve in the Senate only if elected by the voters (ultimately, JFK's former Harvard roommate, Ben Smith was appointed to fill the seat, until Ted Kennedy reached the required age of thirty to serve in the Senate).

In late November, JFK asked his personal attorney and long-time Washington insider, Clark Clifford, to visit his father at the Kennedy estate in Palm Beach and discuss the inadvisability of RFK serving as Attorney General. Clifford made a careful presentation to the aging Ambassador: "Bobby is very valuable. He is young. He has time—start him somewhere else, perhaps number two at Defense. Give him the chance to grow. He will be outstanding."

Joe Kennedy was unfazed by the arguments of nepotism, youth, and legal inexperience: "Thank you very much Clark. I am so glad to have heard your views. I do want to leave you with one thought, however—one firm thought. Bobby *is* going to be Attorney General. All of us have worked our tails off for Jack, and now that we have succeeded, I am going to see to it that Bobby gets the same chance that we gave Jack."

In mid December, RFK breakfasted with his brother at Jack's Georgetown home. After instructing Bobby to comb his hair, the Kennedy brothers greeted reporters, and JFK announced RFK's appointment as Attorney General.

"Don't smile too much, or they'll think we are happy about the appointment," Jack whispered to Bobby.

As expected, a public outcry followed the announcement. The *Nation* protested that it was the "greatest example of nepotism this land has ever seen." The *Atlantic Monthly* considered the action a "slap in the face to all law abiding citizens."

JFK deflected the criticism with his wry sense of humor: "I don't know why people are so mad at me for making Bobby Attorney General. I just wanted to give him a little legal practice before he becomes a lawyer."

Surprisingly, RFK's arch nemesis, Lyndon Johnson, did not object to the appointment, and offered a backhanded endorsement: "The Senate ought to confirm him. It's a different matter if some ole boy hasn't got sense enough to pour piss out of a boot, but I don't think you can say that about Bobby Kennedy. He may be a snot-nose, but he's bright."

LBJ reassured his mentor, Senator Richard Russell, who was alarmed by RFK's lack of legal experience: "I don't think Jack Kennedy's gonna let a little fart like Bobby lead him by the nose."

Unfazed by the negative publicity, the Senate, with only one dissenting vote, confirmed Robert Kennedy as head of the Justice Department. On January 21, 1961, at age thirty-five, Robert Kennedy, was sworn in as the sixty-fourth Attorney General of the United States in the second floor family quarters at the White House. RFK celebrated the occasion by sliding down the banister of the Executive Mansion's grand, curved staircase.

While JFK sometimes poked fun at his serious minded younger brother, he was also profoundly appreciative of the sacrifices Bobby had made on his behalf. At Christmas, Jack and Jackie gave RFK a leather-bound edition of his book, *The Enemy Within*. Inside the front page, JFK humorously wrote: "To Bobby—*The Brother Within*, who made the easy difficult."

On January 21, 1961, the sun broke through the clouds and illuminated the seven-inch snowfall from the day before. At midday, the temperature was a bone-chilling twenty-two degrees, as steam clouds puffed from the mouths of the Inauguration Day speakers.

Just over *100* people occupied the inaugural platform, and *sixteen* of them were members of the Kennedy family. *Twenty thousand* spectators gathered at the base of the Capitol to witness not only a presidential change of guard, but the emergence of a new generation of leaders.

At 12:40 p.m., Speaker of the House, Sam Rayburn, administered the vice-presidential oath of office to Lyndon Johnson. During the course of the inaugural ceremony, LBJ's glum countenance betrayed his inner feelings. As JFK boldly articulated his plans for the *New Frontier,* Lyndon Johnson politely applauded, but displayed little enthusiasm.

In a metaphorical sense, the proud Texan had already been put out to pasture.

Chapter 9

The New Frontier

The thousand days of the *New Frontier* were the best of times for Robert Kennedy and the worst of times for Lyndon Johnson. The time period between January of 1961 and November 22, 1963, commonly remembered as *Camelot,* has been mythologized in scores of books and movies. Those *thirty-five* months were a time of momentous domestic and foreign strife—the Bay of Pigs, the Cuban Missile Crisis, the gradual escalation of American involvement in Viet Nam, the Space Race, the ongoing tensions of the Cold War, and the tumultuous Civil Rights movement.

JFK's cabinet officers were considered the *best and brightest,* and included an influx of younger men, many of whom came from academia and the private sector. Kennedy hoped to revive the idea that public service was a noble pursuit for all citizens, and not the exclusive domain of aging, career politicians.

The new President hailed his cabinet as a "ministry of talent," and was not afraid to cross party lines to select the most skilled advisers. Secretary of Treasury, Douglas Dillon, Secretary of State, Robert McNamara, and National Security Adviser, McGeorge Bundy, were all registered Republicans.

"I don't care if the man is a Republican or a Democrat or an Igorat, I just want the best person available for the job," JFK proudly explained.

In spite of his reputation as a powerful political wheeler-dealer, Lyndon Johnson was somewhat intimidated by the academic achievements of his fellow *New Frontiersmen.* Among the Kennedy staffers were Harvard and Yale graduates, Phi Beta Kappa's, a former college dean, and a Rhodes Scholar. LBJ thought his education at Southwest Texas State paled in comparison to the majority of JFK's appointees.

Journalist and historian, David Halberstam, explained LBJ's intellectual insecurity: "He did not suffer a bad education; he suffered from the belief he had a bad education. So, he didn't trust his instincts, which were a lot sounder, in many ways, than Kennedy's."

When LBJ bragged to his mentor, Sam Rayburn, about the number of scholars in JFK's cabinet, the Speaker of the House was less than impressed with their political pedigrees: "Well, Lyndon, you may be right, and they may be every bit as intelligent as you say, but I'd feel a whole lot better about them, if just one of them had run for sheriff, once."

Robert Kennedy was emblematic of the fresh-faced leadership in Washington, D.C. Energetic and ambitious, RFK hoped to transform the Department of Justice into a dynamic organization. Acutely aware of his limited legal experience, the new Attorney General surrounded himself with gifted deputies, including Byron White (a future Supreme Court Justice), Nicholas Katzenbach (who would succeed Kennedy as Attorney General), and Ramsey Clark (another future Attorney General).

Katzenbach believed that RFK was in a unique position, oblivious to politics as usual: "Bobby had no need to prove himself to anyone but his brother."

RFK expected both loyalty and frankness from his deputies: "Look you guys, I've got a problem. You are all better lawyers that I am, but I'm the Attorney General, so it has to be my decision. But, that doesn't mean it has to be uniformed, so let's hear what you think."

"He wanted the President to get the facts and the law from the person closest to the problem, and unlike some other cabinet officers, he did not have to be that person," Katzenbach later recalled.

The Attorney General carefully focused his energy on issues that interested him. Much to the chagrin of a number of his fellow *New Frontiersmen,* RFK regularly skipped Cabinet meetings, terming them a "waste of time."

In spite of his reputation for brusqueness, RFK was a motivator. On Washington's Birthday, a federally sanctioned holiday, Kennedy noticed that a large number of automobiles were parked in the Justice Department's garage. The Attorney General requested that an aide write down all the license plate numbers; he later sent each employee a personal note of appreciation for coming to work on a holiday.

Nicholas Katzenbach remembered his years in the Justice Department among the most rewarding of his career: "What Bobby was able to do was to communicate his own enthusiasm and energy to others, to make them feel that they were members of a team and what they were doing was important."

The ornate Justice Department building at the corner of Ninth Street and Pennsylvania Avenue was the product of a Depression Era, WPA building project. Above the entrance to the Attorney General's office suite, a simple message greeted visitors: "The Department wins its case whenever justice is done."

Robert Kennedy occupied a spacious wood paneled office with high ceilings and an ornate fireplace. A private elevator directly accessed RFK's individual office suite, which featured a conference room, private bathroom, and small bedroom.

RFK brought an air of informality to his stately surroundings, and could often be seen, tie loosened and sleeves rolled up, with his feet propped on his desk. With frayed shirt collars and scuffed shoes, RFK, in the words of journalist, Ben Bradlee, dressed like a "Brook's Brothers beatnik." Ever fashion conscious, President Kennedy made fun of RFK's button down collars: "Bobby doesn't know any better."

The Attorney General's office walls were lined with his children's crayon drawings. A life sized, stuffed tiger (a gift from novelist Ernest Hemingway) greeted visitors, with its menacing paws raised in the air. Many considered the striped feline a perfect metaphor for the restless man who occupied the office. During staff meetings, RFK and his aides often tossed a football or threw darts at a target on the wall. On one occasion,

Bobby grilled hamburgers for his staff member's children in his office fireplace.

A handful of experienced Justice Department officials were particularly appalled by RFK's habit of bringing his dog, Brumus, a hulking Newfoundland, to work. The *General Services Administration* contacted Kennedy's secretary, Angie Novello, and explained that it was against the law to bring dogs into federal buildings. When Novello explained the regulation to her boss, he simply shrugged his shoulders.

"Well, Ethel and the kids have gone to the Cape for the summer, and Brumus is home alone. It's just Brumus and me. I can't leave Brumus home alone, all day. He'll be lonely," Bobby explained.

In spite of his propensity to stain the carpets in his master's office, Brumus remained a frequent visitor at the Department of Justice. RFK also continued to throw darts at the wall, even though Hoover condemned the activity as "desecration of government property."

During his tenure as Attorney General, RFK remained a controversial figure. While loved by many, he was detested by others for his abrasiveness and arrogance. On Inauguration Day, a photographer for *United Press International*, who had known Bobby for many years, jokingly asked: "Well, Bobby, what are we supposed to call you now? Is it Bobby, or Attorney General, or General, or Sir?"

"Just call me son of a bitch, because that's what everybody else is going to be doing," Bobby replied.

RFK drew particular enmity from J. Edgar Hoover. Hoover had been appointed Director of the *Federal Bureau of Investigation* in 1924, a year before Robert Kennedy was born, and was accustomed to being treated with deference. Humorless, authoritarian, and fastidious, the FBI Director commanded respect, and sometimes fear, from Washington insiders. Even though the Attorney General was technically Hoover's superior in the organizational structure of the Justice Department, the FBI director was accustomed to answering directly to the President of the United States.

When RFK was appointed Attorney General, Hoover's power and influence were significantly weakened. The FBI director was forced to install a special telephone on his desk, such that RFK could summon him at will. Whenever he wanted to speak directly with President Kennedy, Hoover was required to use the Attorney General as an intermediary. Understandably, the tension between the two principle officers in the Department of Justice grew by the day.

Hoover viewed RFK as arrogant and juvenile. At the same time, the

Attorney General privately characterized the FBI Director as "rather a psycho."

As brother of the President of the United States, Robert Kennedy was careful to avoid conflicts of interest: "When I became Attorney General, I was forced to put politics aside, in order to do my job, and do it well. To be a successful Attorney General, politics can have nothing to do with your decisions."

True to his word, when New York State Judge, Vincent Keough, was accused of taking bribes in exchange for lenient sentences, RFK refused to back down. As the brother of Congressman, Eugene Keough, who had played a key role in swaying the New York Democratic delegation to support JFK at the 1960 Democratic convention, Judge Keough hoped political connections would protect him from prosecution. The Attorney General, however, instructed the Justice Department to aggressively pursue its case against Keough.

In a separate case, the mayor of Gary, Indiana, George Chacharis, was accused of accepting bribes and income tax evasion. Even though Chacharis had been responsible for delivering the Indiana delegation to JFK in 1960, RFK refused to interfere with prosecution of the case.

The President joked about his brother's unwillingness to compromise on principle: "You know what this administration needs more than anything is an Attorney General we can *fix.*"

In the end, Robert Kennedy's overriding mission was to serve his brother. Assistant Attorney General, Ramsey Clark, remembered RFK's sole motivation: "His brother's presidency was his consuming passion. It was not important to him whether he was considered a great Attorney General, except insofar as it meant a great Kennedy presidency. If something didn't serve his brother's presidency, he would dismiss it."

While Robert Kennedy's power and influence grew, Lyndon Johnson was politically impotent for the first time in his career. JFK's principal advisers mimicked RFK's disdain for the Vice-President and sometimes *forgot* to notify LBJ about White House meetings. President Kennedy, who was insulated from much of his advisor's anti-Johnson machinations, did his best to give the Vice-President specific, meaningful tasks.

"I've got to keep him happy, somehow," the President revealed in an off the record interview with a *New York Times* columnist.

To massage LBJ's enormous ego, JFK allowed the Vice-President to descend the grand staircase with him at the beginning of formal White House events. Kennedy also appointed LBJ to head the newly created *Committee of Equal Employment Opportunity (CEEO)*. The CEEO was chartered to lessen racial discrimination in federal government jobs and private businesses with government contracts.

As head of the CEEO, Johnson demonstrated his commitment to Civil Rights. Between 1962 and 1963, the percentage of federal jobs held by African Americans rose from *seventeen* to *two-two* percent—a significant improvement, in a time when racial prejudice still permeated society.

Not surprisingly, RFK was critical of LBJ's leadership of the cabinet level agency: "The CEEO could have been an effective organization if the VP gave it some direction."

During CEEO meetings, the Attorney General openly criticized LBJ in front of other committee members. RFK was particularly unhappy with the Vice-President's lack of leadership skills: "That man can't run this committee. Can you think of anything more deplorable than him trying to run the United States? That's why he can't ever be President of the United States."

LBJ was appointed chairman of the *National Aeronautics and Space Council*, befitting his long-standing interest in exploration of outer space. The Vice-President ultimately played a major role in JFK's ambitious goal of sending a man to the moon before the end of the decade. In a memo to the President, Johnson explained the global importance of the space program: "This country should be realistic and recognize that other nations, regardless of their appreciation of our idealistic values, will tend to align themselves with the country, which they believe will be the world leader—the winner in the long run. Dramatic accomplishments in space are being increasingly identified as a major indicator of world leadership."

LBJ's close ties to NASA enabled Texas to share in federal largess. Houston was selected as home to the *Manned Space Flight Center* (today, that facility bears Johnson's name).

Together, JFK and LBJ watched television coverage of the early manned space flights. When astronaut, Alan Shepard, became the first American launched into space, the President poked fun at his Vice-President: "You know, Lyndon, nobody knows that the VP is the Chairman of the Space Council. But, if that flight had been a flop, I guarantee you that everybody would have known that you were Chairman."

When John Glenn, was launched into orbit, LBJ's spontaneous

declaration, linking the space program to the Civil Rights movement, amused JFK.

"If only John Glenn were (sic) a Negro," Johnson announced in a mournful tone.

President Kennedy sought guidance on how to better utilize his unhappy Vice-President. JFK shared his concerns with Senator George Smathers: "I cannot stand Johnson's damn long face. He comes in, sits at cabinet meetings, with his face all screwed up, and never says anything. He looks so sad."

"Why not make him kind of Ambassador-at-large?" Smathers suggested.

"A damn good idea," JFK replied.

In short order, LBJ became the Kennedy Administration's designee for trips abroad. Johnson traveled thousands of miles, making *eleven* trips to *thirty-three* countries during his tenure as Vice-President. LBJ treated the foreign junkets like worldwide political rallies, often leaving his motorcade to mingle with the host country's citizens.

During a sojourn to Iran, Johnson berated the press corps for skipping a visit to a village: "What kind of bunch of God damn pansies have I brought *16,000* miles, only to have them sit around in air conditioned rooms, drinking whiskey, while I am meeting people? No wonder we are not getting anything in the newspapers back home!"

Among the Vice-President's destinations was South Vietnam. An uneasy LBJ initially balked at this assignment, fearing North Vietnamese guerillas might target an American dignitary.

"Mr. President, I don't want to embarrass you by getting my head blown off in Saigon," Johnson protested.

JFK laughingly reassured the Vice-President: "Don't worry, Lyndon. If anything happens to you, Sam Rayburn (Speaker of the House) and I will give you the biggest funeral Austin, Texas ever saw."

LBJ reluctantly agreed to visit Vietnam and beyond, but insisted on special services during his travels—an oversized bed, special shower head nozzles with needlepoint spray, cartons of cigarettes, and cases of his favorite *Cutty Sark* scotch. As always, Johnson took gifts emblazoned with the *LBJ* logo—*500* boxes of ball point pens and *seventy-two* cases of cigarette lighters.

JFK's sister, Jean Kennedy Smith, and her husband, Steve, accompanied the Vice-President on his sojourn to Southeast Asia (by sending family members on the trip, the President hoped to assuage LBJ's safety concerns). During a stopover in Hawaii, Jean playfully challenged Johnson.

"Tell us, Lyndon, which do you think is sexier Nancy (*NBC News* correspondent, Nancy Dickerson) or myself?" Pat inquired.

"Jean, you know I never mess around with Catholic girls," LBJ answered.

After arriving in South Vietnam, Johnson waded into crowds, handing out his ink pens and lighters, along with gallery passes to the United States Senate.

"Get your Momma and Daddy to bring you to the Senate, and see how the government works," Johnson shouted to a group of Vietnamese children.

During his tour of South Vietnam, LBJ developed a personal bond with the country's controversial President, Ngo Dinh Diem. Johnson believed that Diem (whose corruption and despotism were legendary) was an essential player in the battle against the spread of communism in Indochina. With characteristic hyperbole, Johnson described the diminutive South Vietnamese leader as the "Winston Churchill of Asia;" an opinion that was not shared by many in JFK's State Department.

When Diem and his brother were assassinated in a 1963 military coup (the overthrow was sanctioned by the American Ambassador to South Vietnam), LBJ believed that his ally had been betrayed by the United States.

While visiting Pakistan, Johnson's folksy persona was prominently displayed. Approaching a barefoot peasant leading a camel, the Vice-President extended a long distance invitation: "Y'all come visit us in the United States."

When the Pakistani later traveled to America, Johnson arranged for him to tour the country. Before returning to his native land, the Asian guest was given a pickup truck by the Ford Motor Company.

After the Berlin Wall was erected in August of 1961, tension between America and Soviet-backed East German Communists escalated; the threat of World War III suddenly seemed very real. To bolster the confidence of West Berliners and fortify anti-Communist solidarity, President Kennedy asked LBJ to travel to Berlin.

"There'll be a lot of shooting, and I'll be in the middle of it. Why me?" Johnson complained

To calm LBJ's fears, the President asked General Lucius Clay, the hero of the 1948 Berlin Airlift, to accompany the Vice-President to Germany.

In spite of his initial misgivings, LBJ enthusiastically travelled through the streets of West Berlin in an open car. Wading into the appreciative crowds, the Vice-President pumped hands and passed out his monogrammed ballpoint pens.

"This island does not stand alone," Johnson proclaimed to a crowd of 300,000 West Berliners.

Ultimately, LBJ's role in the *New Frontier* was mostly symbolic. President Kennedy refused to use Johnson in his natural domain, as a legislative liaison. JFK did not want LBJ overshadowing him on Capitol Hill, and failed to seek advice in areas where the Vice-President could have provided considerable insight—namely Civil Rights. Deputy Attorney General, Nicholas Katzenbach, later reflected on the Kennedy Administration's oversight: "...In retrospect, not to have used LBJ much more on Civil Rights legislation seems incredibly stupid. Bobby must be the principal suspect, because of his aversion to the Vice-President..."

As he endeavored to keep the Vice-President occupied, JFK grew frustrated by LBJ's continual moping. The President frequently attempted to engage Johnson in cabinet level discussions: "What do you think, Mister Vice-President?"

"Well, I don't know enough about that to express an opinion," Johnson often replied—a passive-aggressive protest, which only angered JFK.

LBJ's misery deepened when Sam Rayburn, died of cancer in November of 1961. Along with Richard Russell, Rayburn had been a surrogate father to Johnson, and LBJ desperately missed his mentor's reassurance and sage advice.

With demoralizing frustration and overt self-pity, LBJ watched his nemesis, Robert Kennedy, attract the headlines. *U.S. News and World Report* proclaimed RFK to be the "number two man in Washington" and the "Assistant President."

In January of 1963, RFK gave the opening address at an exhibition commemorating the centennial of the *Emancipation Proclamation*. As the Attorney General delivered his remarks, Civil Rights and labor activist, Joseph Rauh, passed a note to presidential adviser, Arthur M. Schlesinger, Jr.: "Poor Lyndon."

After the speech, Schlesinger asked for clarification, and Rauh explained: "Lyndon must know he is through. Bobby is going to be the next President."

Desperately seeking acceptance from the Kennedy brothers, Johnson made attempts to narrow the breach with the Attorney General. LBJ never understood why RFK was impervious to his homespun charm, and he often pushed the matter to embarrassing extremes.

At a White House reception, LBJ cornered RFK: "Bobby, you don't like me. Your brother likes me. Your sister-in-law likes me. Your daddy likes me. But, you don't like me. Why don't you like me?"

Bobby simply ignored Johnson's diatribe, adding to LBJ's humiliation. The Attorney General would not forgive LBJ for his slanderous remarks about the Kennedy family at the 1960 Democratic convention, and questioned the Vice-President's veracity: "He lies all the time...He lies even when he doesn't have to."

Historian, Randall Woods, explained Bobby Kennedy's intransience: "RFK refused to observe the dictum that in democratic politics, no one has permanent enemies, that a person who opposes you one day, may be your ally the next."

The feud between the Attorney General and the Vice-President was common knowledge in Washington D.C. Kennedy advisor, Arthur M. Schlesinger, Jr., explained the impasse in simple terms: "It was a pure case of mutual dislike."

On December 19, 1961, the Kennedy brothers suffered a jolting blow, when the guiding force in their lives was permanently disabled. While playing golf in Palm Beach, Florida, Joseph Kennedy, Sr. suffered a massive stroke. Lingering near death for several days, the elder Kennedy survived, after RFK convinced the treating physicians to not withdraw life support: "Let him fight."

When Joe Kennedy emerged from a coma, he was left with paralysis and severe aphasia. For the remaining eight years of his life (ironically, Joe would outlive three of his four sons), the elder Kennedy would be unable to utter more than two or three intelligible words.

With drool running from his mouth, and his partially paralyzed right hand drawn into a spasmodic claw, the once powerful patriarch was now an invalid. Rose, anticipating the worst, purchased a black dress, in the event of her husband's sudden death.

After his father's stroke, Robert Kennedy assumed an even greater role in his older brother's life—confidant, adviser, and protector. RFK's reputation as the *second most powerful man in government* was now undeniable.

With his brusque manner and single minded devotion to his brother, RFK accumulated more than his share of enemies. In November of 1961, during a White House reception, author Gore Vidal, who was visibly intoxicated, balanced himself by bracing against the First Lady (Vidal was near family, the stepson of Jackie Kennedy's stepfather). Offended by the writer's over-familiarity, Bobby removed Vidal's arm from his sister-in-law's shoulder, prompting a loud verbal altercation. At RFK's direction, Vidal was escorted from the White House.

RFK biographer, Evan Thomas, summed up the Attorney General's grasp on power: "He had vast influence when JFK was in the White House…His brother gave him virtually unlimited discretion—and he exceeded it."

As Attorney General, Robert Kennedy prosecuted organized crime leaders with unprecedented zeal. In contrast, J. Edgar Hoover was preoccupied with Communist infiltration, to the point that he barely recognized the existence of an organized crime element. Impatient with the pace of the FBI's efforts, RFK set up a special organized crime investigative group within the Department of Justice.

Feeding an obsession that began during his days as counsel to the Senate Rackets Committee, RFK targeted corruption in the Teamsters Union. Convinced the Teamsters President was corruptly using pension funds to finance an unholy alliance with Mafia leaders, the Attorney General established a *Get Hoffa* squad. RFK's tireless pursuit eventually paid dividends, when Jimmy Hoffa was ultimately convicted and imprisoned for jury tampering and pension fund fraud (receiving a *thirteen* year prison sentence).

In Robert Kennedy's *black or white* world, Hoffa and organized crime leaders were twin evils that threatened the country. RFK's legacy as Attorney General was defined by his pursuit of *bad guys.*

Driving past the Teamsters headquarters during the holiday season, Bobby pointed out the Yule tide decorations to his children: "See that? It's a bad Christmas tree. It was bought with money stolen from working people. It's a bad tree."

"Once he made up his mind, he was as dogged and fearless in pursuit of his objective as anyone I've ever known," Nicholas Katzenbach recalled, reflecting on the Attorney General's crusade against corruption.

Under the Justice Department's microscope, Jimmy Hoffa's hatred for RFK intensified. The Teamsters' President kept a .270 caliber rifle in his office, which he pointed to during fits of anger: "I've got to do something about that son of a bitch, Bobby Kennedy. He's got to go."

In the year before RFK became Attorney General, the Justice Department had obtained *forty-nine* indictments against members of organized crime. At the end of 1961, the number had grown to *121,* and continued to rise during the course of the Kennedy Administration (*350* in 1962 and *615* in 1963). More importantly, the number of convictions increased from *seventy-three* in 1961 to *288* in 1963.

As Attorney General, Robert Kennedy's enthusiasm for Civil Rights was slow to develop. Having been reared as a child of privilege, RFK had never known the pain of economic hardship or the ugliness of prejudice. In turn, he was reluctant to challenge the segregationist status quo: "Honestly, before I became Attorney General, I didn't give a shit for Civil Rights. It never touched my life."

The President and Attorney General had already made token concessions in protest against racism, resigning from segregated private clubs. JFK also refused to speak in front of segregated audiences.

At the same time, RFK was an astute Civil War historian, and believed that if the federal government forced desegregation, it would invoke bitter memories of Reconstruction across the Deep South. The Attorney General warned African American lawyer Thurgood Marshall (who would later become Solicitor General and a Supreme Court Justice): "The problem with you people, is that you want too much, too fast."

Cognizant of his brother's narrow victory in the 1960 presidential race, RFK was leery of alienating white voters: "Don't forget we are political geniuses by *119,000* votes."

Black leaders sensed the Kennedy Administration's ambivalence on matters of race. Martin Luther King voiced his impatience with JFK's lukewarm interest in Civil Rights: "I'm convinced that he has the political skill, but so far, I'm afraid the moral passion is missing."

During his presidential campaign, JFK vowed that desegregation of federal housing could be achieved by Executive Order, with "a stroke of the pen." Once elected President, fearful of alienating white Southern Democrats in Congress, JFK found it difficult to find "a useful and appropriate time" to issue the desegregation order. Not until November 20, 1962, did JFK finally sign *Executive Order 11063,* prohibiting discrimination by race, creed, or nationality in federal housing.

While RFK added some *200* lawyers to the Justice Department's Civil Rights Division, his commitment to end desegregation never quite matched his ardor for criminal prosecution. The Kennedy Administration earned justifiable criticism for its appointment of Mississippi's William Harold Cox to the judiciary. As a newly appointed federal judge, Cox referred to a group of African American plaintiffs as "a bunch of Niggers."

Presidential adviser, Ralph Dungan, later reflected on the Kennedy Administration's tepid support of desegregation: "I'm really sorry to say, on Civil Rights, we were not very good. We never asked ourselves the question—'What's right?'"

The Attorney General found himself in an unpleasant position during the formative years of the Civil Rights movement by making himself, rather than the President, the focus of "attention and resentment." Many black leaders believed that RFK was well-intentioned, but unduly cautious.

After the *Freedom Riders* were savagely beaten in Alabama, RFK recommended a "cooling off period," before blacks furthered challenged the racial *status quo.* Martin Luther King defiantly refused to heed the Attorney General's advice: "Wait means never!"

"We've been cooling off for one hundred years," Civil Rights leader, James Farmer, proclaimed, "If we get any cooler, we'd be in a deep freeze!"

RFK unsuccessfully tried to focus Civil Rights leaders on what he believed was a more meaningful and attainable goal: "The long range solution for Negros is voting rights. I think all other rights for which they are fighting will flow from that. Political power comes from votes and rights. Nobody could really oppose voting. You register those people to vote and Jim Eastland (the segregationist Senator from Mississippi) will change his mind."

Martin Luther King and other prominent Civil Rights leaders disagreed with the Attorney General's prioritization of voting rights. When King led full scale protests in Birmingham, Alabama, RFK grew frustrated: "The Negro leadership didn't know what they were demonstrating about... And, none of the white community knew what they were demonstrating about."

At the same time, many white Southerners accused the Attorney General of showing little respect for the region's established social customs. RFK underestimated the resolve of Southern segregationists and the violent tendencies of some racists. Supreme Court Justice, Hugo Black, an Alabamian who evolved from one time Ku Klux Klan member to ardent desegregationist, tried to educate Deputy Attorney General, Nicholas Katzenbach: "Neither you or Bobby understand the South."

As the *New Frontier's* chief law enforcement officer, Robert Kennedy took considerable heat from Civil Rights advocates. When RFK met with a group of African Americans at the Kennedy family apartment in New York City, Jerome Smith, a veteran Freedom Rider, openly attacked the Attorney General: "I feel like vomiting being here in this room with you."

When RFK defended the Kennedy Administration's progressive views on Civil Rights, famed singer, Lena Horne, grew belligerent: "Mr. Attorney General, you can take all those pious statements and stuff them up your ass!"

After absorbing verbal blows from Smith, Horne, and others, Bobby was clearly frustrated: "They didn't know anything. They don't know what the laws are. They don't know what we've been doing or what we are trying to do. You can't talk to them the way you can talk to Martin Luther King or Roy Wilkins (both of whom espoused non-violent resistance against the forces of Segregation)."

The stark brutality of racism, enforced by fire hoses, Billy clubs, and attack dogs, eventually forced the Kennedy brothers to adopt a proactive stance. Using the force of the Justice Department, backed by the might of the military, RFK led the successful fight to integrate two of the remaining bastions of educational segregation—the University of Mississippi and the University of Alabama.

While the integration of the University of Alabama was non-violent, the same could not be said for Ole Miss. During riots with angry Segregationists in Oxford, *twenty-eight* federal marshals were wounded and *two* innocent bystanders were killed. RFK vividly recalled the violent confrontation in Mississippi: "It was the worst night I've ever spent."

The Kennedy brothers found it increasingly difficult to push aside the Civil Rights issue, as the brutality of white racists dominated newspaper headlines and television news broadcasts. Justice Department aide, Burke Marshall, remembered the more RFK saw of violent racism, the "madder he became."

In June of 1963, the same day that Alabama Governor, George C. Wallace stood in the door of the registrar's office at the University of Alabama in symbolic defiance of integration, President Kennedy appeared on national television, announcing plans to submit a *Civil Rights Bill* to Congress. That night, Civil Rights leader, Medgar Evers was shot to death outside his Mississippi home by a white racist. RFK attended Evers' funeral and provided the slain man's brother, Charles, with his personal telephone numbers.

"Whenever I had the need to call him, I never found it too late or too early," Charles Evers later recalled.

RFK privately referred to the proposed Civil Rights legislation as "Bull Conner's Bill" (referring to Birmingham, Alabama's racist Police Commissioner). Connor's use of fire hoses and attack dogs against black demonstrators, had ultimately generated widespread sympathy for the plight of African Americas

While the Kennedy brothers earned newfound respect from Civil Rights leaders, their popularity nosedived among most whites in the Deep South.

"If Khrushchev was running against Kennedy here, Khrushchev would beat him. And, if Bob Kennedy was the candidate, Khrushchev would beat him worse," a Mississippi segregationist proudly proclaimed.

After introducing his Civil Rights Bill, President Kennedy's nationwide popularity fell from *sixty* to *forty-seven* percent. During a June 22, 1963 meeting with Civil Rights leaders, JFK warned his visitors: "I may lose the next election because of this."

As the Attorney General was experiencing an epiphany on Civil Rights, J. Edgar Hoover remained steadfast in his belief that the entire movement was Communist inspired. Hoover learned that Stanley Levison, a top advisor to Martin Luther King. had once been associated with the Communist Party (Levison apparently ended that association in 1955). In the eyes of the FBI Director, however, *once a Communist* meant *always a Communist.* Hoover pressured RFK to authorize wiretaps on King's private and business telephones. At first, the Attorney General resisted Hoover's machinations. Instead, both the President and RFK warned King to break off his ties with Levison and Jack O'Dell (a one-time Communist Party fund raiser).

"If they shoot you down, they'll shoot us down, too. So we're asking you to be careful," JFK warned King, during a private conversation in the White House Rose Garden.

King, who believed the Communist allegations against Levison and O'Dell were totally unfounded, only temporarily limited his contacts with the two white activists. In October of 1963, confronted with evidence from Hoover that King was maintaining contact with the alleged Communists, RFK reluctantly agreed to authorize FBI wiretaps of the famed Civil Rights leader. Conflicted over the necessity and morality of the surveillance, the Attorney General rationalized his decision: "There would have been no living with the Bureau, if I refused to sign."

As the Justice Department battled the forces of segregation, RFK was reluctant to utilize a gifted resource—Lyndon Johnson. Personal animosity clouded the Attorney General's judgment, and he simply ignored the Vice-President's proven commitment to Civil Rights, believing that LBJ's opposition to segregation was little more than political posturing.

In reality, LBJ's passion for Civil Rights was much greater than the Kennedy brothers. The Vice-President's opinions were on record: "Until justice is blind to color, until education is unaware of race, until opportunity is unaware of the color of men's skin, emancipation will be a proclamation, but not a fact."

After JFK introduced his Civil Rights Bill to Congress, the Vice-President encountered Mississippi's segregationist Senator, John Stennis, who informed LBJ that the South would never accept interference in States' Rights. An indignant LBJ confronted his former colleague: "Well, you know John, the other day, a sad thing happened. My cook, Zephyr Wright, who has been working for me many years—she's a college graduate—and her husband drove my official car from Washington down to Texas… They drove through your state, and when they got hungry, they stopped at grocery stores on the edge of town, in colored areas, and bought Vienna sausages and beans, and ate them with a plastic spoon. And, when they had to go to the bathroom, they would stop, pull off on a side road, and Zephyr Wright, the cook of the Vice-President of the United States, would squat in the road to pee. And you know, John, that's just bad. That's wrong. And, there ought to be something to change that. And, it seems to me that if the people in Mississippi don't change it voluntarily, that it's just going to be necessary to change it by law."

When finally consulted by Justice Department staffers for his input into the proposed Civil Rights legislation, Johnson shared his frustrations: "I don't know who drafted it—I've never seen it…I got it from the *New York Times.*"

LBJ was never allowed to use his considerable skills to lobby on behalf of the historic bill, even though he had clear ideas about how to promote the legislation. The Vice-President shared his proposed strategy with JFK's speechwriter, Ted Sorensen: "…The Negros feel, and they're suspicious that we're doing what we got to (do)…The Negros are tired of this patient stuff, and tired of this piecemeal stuff, and what they want more than anything else is not an executive order or legislation, they want a moral commitment that he's (JFK) behind them. I want to pull out the cannon. The President is the cannon. You let him be on all the television networks, just speaking for his conscience…I know the risks are great and it might cost us the South, but those sorts of states may be lost, anyway. The difference is if your President just enforces court decrees, the South will feel it's yielded to force. He ought to make almost a bigot out of nearly anybody that's against him; a high lofty appeal; treat these people as Americans."

RFK's activities on behalf of his brother reached well beyond the normal job description of the Attorney General. After the disastrous, CIA-orchestrated Bay of Pigs invasion in 1961, President Kennedy sought greater oversight of the intelligence agency. The Attorney General had received only a cursory briefing on the plot to overthrow Fidel Castro, and JFK regretted excluding his brother from the deliberations: "I should have had him involved from the very beginning."

JFK was convinced the CIA had bungled the covert operation against Cuba, and had provided him with misinformation prior to the mission. To ensure greater oversight of the military and intelligence community, the President appointed the Attorney General to the *Executive Committee of the National Security Council (Ex-Comm)*.

RFK grew angry with the finger pointing that occurred among administration members in the wake of the Bay of Pigs: "We've got to do something. All you bright fellows have gotten the President into this, and if you don't do something now, my brother will be regarded as a paper tiger by the Russians."

When Undersecretary of State, Chester Bowles, sent President Kennedy a memorandum explaining his opposition prior to the Bay of Pigs of invasion (the correspondence was delivered to JFK *after* the failed mission) RFK's trademark temper was unleashed.

"That's the most meaningless, worthless thing I've ever heard," the Attorney General announced, attacking Bowles memo, "You people are so anxious to protect your own asses, that you're afraid to do anything. All you want to do is dump the whole thing on the President. We'd be better off if you just quit, or left foreign policy to someone else."

RFK's tirade against Bowles occurred in front of JFK. The President's conspicuous silence gave tacit approval to the Attorney General's *ruthless* attack on the Undersecretary of State.

Describing the Bay of Pigs invasion as "the worst experience of my life," President Kennedy was determined to prove to both Cuba and the Soviet Union that the United States was not an international weakling. JFK took full responsibility for the failed invasion, and sarcastically told

Arthur Schlesinger, Jr. (who was expected to one day write a history of the *New Frontier*) that he could entitle his book, *Kennedy—The Only Years.*

After the President publicly accepted full responsibility for the Bay of Pigs fiasco, Kennedy's approval ratings increased to *eighty-three* percent. JFK was amazed: "Jesus, it's just like Ike. The worse you do, the better they like you!"

As the newly appointed watchdog over the CIA, RFK was determined to adopt a *get tough* policy with Cuba, and approved a series of covert operations to topple Fidel Castro. Included in those plans, were failed efforts to assassinate the Cuban dictator. In an ironic twist of fate, Mafia leaders had already been contracted to carry out assassination plots in August of 1960 by CIA Chief of Covert Actions, Richard Bissell (during the Eisenhower Administration). When he learned the very gangsters that the Justice Department was so aggressively prosecuting were also working for the federal government, RFK was appalled, and ended their involvement in the covert operations.

The details of CIA plots to overthrow Castro during the Kennedy Administration would not be revealed to the public until 1975, when a Senate investigation (the *Church Committee*) uncovered *eight* separate murder plots (between the years 1960-65). The Church Committee, however, was unable to determine if the Kennedy brothers approved any of the assassination attempts; Richard Bissell testified that neither the President nor the Attorney General was made aware of the plots to murder Fidel Castro. Other CIA operatives, however, later claimed that both JFK and RFK were party to the plans.

Vice-President Johnson, as usual, was kept out of the loop, and did not learn of the CIA plots until later in the decade, after he became President. LBJ was appalled at the reckless behavior of the Kennedy brothers: "They were funding a damned *Murder Inc.* in the Caribbean."

In addition to his official duties, Robert Kennedy was forced to cover for his brother's reckless indiscretions. JFK's sexual appetite was voracious and his choice of partners was often indiscriminate. All three surviving Kennedy brothers modeled the behaviors of their philandering father, forcing their spouses to rationalize the hurt and humiliation.

"Kennedy men are like that. They'll go after anything in a skirt. It doesn't mean a thing," Jackie Kennedy explained to her sister-in-law, Joan (Ted's wife).

Jackie adopted a philosophical stance on Jack's infidelity: "I don't think there are any men that are faithful. Men are such a combination of good and evil."

Speculating on her husband's post-presidential career, Jackie said, in half jest: "He'll probably take a job as headmaster of an exclusive, all-girls prep school."

Bobby was never as reckless or promiscuous as his older brother. Jack's conquests included White House secretaries, movie starlets, friends' wives, and prostitutes. The media operated under a different standard in the early 1960s, and the President's sexual escapades were never reported to the public. The First Couple's seemingly idyllic marriage remained fodder for flattering magazine articles and newspaper headlines.

The President's many infidelities, however, did not escape the attention of certain observers, including the fastidious and pious director of the FBI. J. Edgar Hoover maintained secret files on the private lives of numerous politicians and other public figures. Given his tenuous relationship with the Attorney General, Hoover's possession of incriminating documents about the Kennedy brothers provided the aging FBI director with an added measure of job security. When asked why he chose to re-appoint Hoover as Director of the FBI, JFK privately explained: "You don't fire God."

Vice-President Johnson offered a simpler explanation: "J. Edgar Hoover has Jack Kennedy by the balls."

On at least two occasions, after receiving confidential reports from Hoover, RFK warned his brother to end sexual liaisons with controversial partners (actress Marilyn Monroe and the known girlfriend of a Chicago Mafia leader).

JFK's compulsive philandering remained a well kept secret during his presidency. On one occasion a journalist approached Press Secretary, Pierre Salinger: "I am beginning to get information that Kennedy has mistress."

"Listen, this man is the President of the United States," Salinger answered, "He works fourteen or fifteen hours a day—he has to deal with international problems. If he does that all day long, and still has time to have a mistress, what the hell difference does it make?"

Salinger later recalled the reporter's response: "The guy laughed and walked out, and that was the end of it."

Concerned about JFK's physical health, RFK was appalled by the *medical treatment* his brother received from Doctor Max Jacobsen, a New York physician, who treated many other notables, including actress, Greta

Garbo, movie director, Cecile B. Demille, and baseball star, Mickey Mantle. Jacobsen, known as *Doctor Feelgood,* frequently injected President Kennedy with a mysterious elixir, which lessened his back pain, improved his mood, increased his energy, and fueled his already overactive libido. Jacobsen occasionally administered similar injections to the First Lady to treat her fatigue and depressed mood. When President Kennedy traveled to Vienna for a summit with Soviet Premier, Nikita Khrushchev, *Doctor Feelgood* accompanied him to Europe.

RFK eventually confiscated one of Jacobsen's vials, turning it over to the FBI for analysis. The laboratory tests revealed a mixture of vegetable oil, steroids and amphetamines.

When Bobby confronted his older brother about the contents of Jacbosen's magic potion, Jack was nonplussed: "I don't care if it's horse piss. It works."

Jacobsen's controversial and poorly documented treatments eventually caught up with him. In 1975, the medical board in New York stripped the physician of his license.

Robert Kennedy was his brother's designated "hatchet man." When Jack's close friend, Frank Sinatra, was designated *persona non grata,* because of his close association with Mafia leaders, the Attorney General orchestrated a formal break between the President and the famed crooner. After being learning that the President would not be staying at his house during a forthcoming trip to California, Sinatra exploded into rage, and blamed Bobby for JFK's betrayal.

The Kennedy brothers were not above using the immense powers of the presidency to intimidate their enemies. In April of 1962, Roger Blough, President of *U.S. Steel,* announced plans to increase the price of steel by six dollars per ton, in defiance of the Kennedy Administration's established wage-price guidelines. In response to Blough's betrayal, the Attorney General unleashed the full powers of the Justice Department against U.S. Steel. FBI agents raided the homes of company executives before dawn, confiscating private business records.

Less than a week later, withering under the scrutiny of the Justice Department, the steel producer agreed to rescind the price hikes. While the Kennedy Administration's aggressive tactics brought the steel industry executives to their knees, civil libertarians blamed RFK for employing "Gestapo police state tactics."

RFK defended his actions: "...I picked up all their records and told the FBI to interview them all...It was a tough way to operate. But, under the circumstances, we couldn't afford to lose."

In private, the Attorney General joked: "They were mean to my brother. They can't do that to my brother."

On one occasion, President Kennedy asked the Attorney General to demonstrate his physical prowess. To promote physical fitness, Justice Department staffers were selected to participate in the *Marine Fitness Test*—a *fifty-mile* hike. RFK's fellow travelers quit before the end of the grueling walk along the Chesapeake and Ohio Towpath (between Washington D.C. and Camp David). Only the Attorney General and his loyal canine companion, Brumus, completed the march; in *seventeen hours* and *fifty minutes*.

While they maintained the closest of relationships, the Kennedy brothers were rather unalike in temperament and tastes. Ted Sorensen, who knew both men quite well, contrasted their personalities, noting that each believed in the principle of "forgive, but not forget," but an "angrier RFK was less likely to forgive."

"Jack and Bobby were very different. Bobby was more volatile and intense. He (RFK) particularly admired physical courage, whereas JFK particularly admired moral and intellectual courage. Bobby was less likely to keep his emotions concealed than Jack. Jack was more likely to accept people as they were, while RFK was more likely to love a person or hate him. Both were quick to grasp a problem, although RFK was more prone to make snap judgments, a trait he later outgrew," Sorensen recalled.

JFK enjoyed gossip and bawdy jokes that Bobby found tasteless. RFK did not care for movies featuring sex and violence, and found girlie magazines, like *Playboy*, revolting.

"He never lost that Puritan strain of moral conservatism," RFK biographer, Jack Newfield, wrote.

Charismatic and urbane, JFK enjoyed social galas, while RFK, shy and taciturn, preferred the intimacy of small groups. JFK erected strict barriers between his political and social life. Bobby, on the other hand, often mixed and matched his work colleagues with friends and acquaintances outside of government, including artists, athletes, and journalists.

Jackie and Ethel Kennedy were never close, and were occasionally contemptuous of one another. Ethel was unimpressed by Jackie's apparent snobbery, often referring to her as *The Debutant*. With boundless energy and biting sarcasm, Ethel earned a reputation for being "more Kennedy than thou." When Jackie revealed that she had once dreamed of becoming a ballerina, Ethel eyed her sister-in-law's size nine feet: "With those feet of yours? You'd be better off going into soccer, kid."

The First Lady found Ethel too boisterous and tomboyish for her tastes. Jackie was also resentful of Ethel's fertility: "She drops kids like rabbits. It's disgusting."

Unlike Ethel, Jackie focused on image and style. After JFK was elected President, Jackie gave her social secretary specific instructions: "The one thing I do not want to be called is *First Lady*. It sounds like a saddle horse. Would you notify the telephone operators and everyone else that I'm to be known simply as Mrs. Kennedy, and not as First Lady."

Paul "Red" Fay, JFK's long time friend and Undersecretary of the Navy during the Kennedy Administration, noted that the President seemed more comfortable in social situations with his youngest brother, Ted. According to Fay, when JFK wanted to relax, Bobby proved "too intense" and "too focused on issues."

"He related to Teddy more than he did to Bobby," Fay opined.

At the same time, Fay expressed admiration for RFK's intrinsic strengths: "I'd put Bobby's judgment against all those guys."

Jack enjoyed poking fun at his younger brothers. During a conversation with Fay, JFK speculated about his post-presidential career: "Of course, when Bobby or Teddy becomes President, then I'd probably be most useful as Secretary of State. I'm just not sure that I would ever get adjusted to addressing Bobby or Teddy as 'Mr. President.' Let's not dwell too long on the prospect of taking orders from loveable Bob."

When the Attorney General argued his first case before the Supreme Court *(Gray v. Sanders),* JFK offered a light hearted assessment: "He did a very good job; according to everyone I talked to—Ethel, Jackie, (and) Teddy."

The President Joked that RFK's Supreme Court appearance proved that his brother could no longer be type cast by a single slogan: "Stop the world—I want to get Hoffa."

While Jack and Bobby were infrequent social companions, the President never questioned his younger brother's unfailing loyalty. In an interview with *Miami News,* Editor, William Beggs, JFK expressed admiration for the Attorney General: "I wish so very much I had two Bobbies."

The President also gave his younger brother an engraved cigarette case as a Christmas present, hinting at a *Kennedy Dynasty*: "After me, how about you?"

In a casual conversation with Press Secretary, Pierre Salinger, JFK speculated about his post-presidency: "I'm going to buy a newspaper in Boston—you'll be the editor, and we'll be reporting on Bobby's presidency."

Like his older brother, Robert Kennedy was driven to educate himself about new subjects. In late 1961, RFK asked *New Frontier* historian, Arthur Schlesinger, Jr., to set up monthly gatherings of notable academics to discuss social, economic, artistic, and political subjects. Hosted at RFK's home, the *Hickory Hill Seminars* became a popular feature during the Kennedy Administration.

Social gatherings at RFK's home were often accompanied by raucous horseplay. *New York Times* Washington correspondent, Tom Wicker, later recalled the mix of glamour and chaos: "It was very chic to be pushed into Bobby Kennedy's pool."

Throughout his career as Attorney General (and later as a United States Senator), RFK accumulated an eclectic mix of friends and acquaintances. Robert Kennedy, Jr. later recalled the criteria for admission into the inner circle: "My father surrounded himself with people who overcame, had proven themselves with physical courage—John Glenn, Jim Whittaker (the first American to climb Mount Everest), and Rafer Johnson. Our house was filled with Cubans, who had fought at the Bay of Pigs to distinguish themselves. You know, he liked those guys, because they were kind of tough guys, and he thought that although war was horrible and unspeakable, and should be avoided at all cost, that it was also the time when not the worst, but the best of human virtues emerged."

The Kennedy brothers often appeared isolated from life in the real world. Like Jack, RFK had never been forced to worry about money, and rarely carried cash on his person. Staffers were forced to pay for Bobby's restaurant and hotel bills, cab fares, and tips, before submitting monthly reimbursement claims to the Kennedy family accountants.

Reporter, Peter Maas, remembered attending church with RFK. When the offering plate was passed around, Maas contributed a dollar bill on behalf of the Attorney General.

"Don't you think I'd be more generous than that?" RFK whispered.

Some Kennedy Administration appointees found it all but impossible to work with the prickly Attorney General. When the President asked General Lucius Clay to serve as an ambassador to West Berlin during the tense months after the East Germans erected the Berlin Wall, the famed military officer accepted the offer with one stipulation—under no circumstances would he deal one-on-one with RFK.

"I understand," JFK laughingly responded.

In June of 1961, when Dominican Republic dictator, Rafael Leonidas Trujillo Molina was assassinated, President Kennedy and Secretary of State Rusk were in Europe for a summit meeting with Soviet leaders, leaving Undersecretary of State Chester Bowles as the ranking foreign policy officer in Washington. Many administration officials feared that the unrest in the Dominican Republic was the beginning of a Communist revolution. Robert Kennedy, now accustomed to functioning as a major foreign policy adviser, suggested that U.S. warships be moved closer to the Dominican coast.

When Bowles discounted the Attorney General's advice, RFK grew angry: "You're a gutless bastard."

Bowles telephoned the President in Europe and complained that he was being pressured into sending the Marines into the Dominican Republic. JFK urged Bowles to act with caution.

"Well, I'm glad to hear it," Bowles replied to the President, "And, in that case, would you clarify who's in charge here?"

"You are," the President replied.

"Good. Would you mind explaining that to your brother?" Bowles pleaded.

As his brother's devoted protector, RFK was seemingly unconcerned about how his words and actions might alienate others. Alabama Governor, John Patterson, remembered his interactions with the Attorney General in the early 1960s: "He called me up one night at the Governor's Mansion in Montgomery, about 2:00 a.m., and told me we didn't have enough police on Dexter Avenue (adjacent to the capitol building and the church were Martin Luther King coordinated Civil Rights protests). I said, 'God almighty, Robert, that's not any of my business or yours, either!'"

"If you were having a drink of whiskey with Robert Kennedy, he was just a hell of fine fellow," Patterson recalled, "But, every decision that he made about anything was based upon what was best for them politically. He didn't consider the fact you had a career and had a political agenda, yourself."

Historian, James Hilty, described RFK's unprecedented role in the

Kennedy Administration: "Robert Kennedy did and said things the President could not, tested the water in places the President could not step, and served as his eyes and ears in councils where the President could not go."

A few *New Frontiersmen* believed that RFK exceeded the limits of his office. Ralph Dungan, Special Assistant to the President, was among those alarmed by the Bobby's unchecked authority: "Frankly, I thought that lots of things he did as Attorney General were wonderful. But, in other areas, especially the foreign affairs field—although JFK relied a lot on him—I thought Bobby's judgment was not very good."

President Kennedy was aware of the criticisms directed against the Attorney General. Only on rare occasions, however, did JFK undercut his brother's authority.

After the Bay of Pigs fiasco in April of 1961, President Kennedy was no longer willing to unquestionably accept the advice of military leaders and intelligence officers. The President and Attorney General also lost a measure of their naiveté and overconfidence. RFK lamented about the administration's image during the early months of the *New Frontier*: "Those were the days when we thought we were succeeding because of all the stories on how hard everybody was working."

Justice Department aide, John Seigenthaler, reflected on lessons learned after the Bay of Pigs: "I really felt it was a disaster that was based on false intelligence and I don't think the President ever trusted the CIA after that. I don't think Bobby did, either."

During the *Cuban Missile Crisis* in October of 1962, when the world was on the brink of nuclear war, RFK played an active role in formulating administration policy. Unlike many of JFK's hawkish advisers, including Secretary of Treasury Dillon, CIA Director McCone, National Security Adviser Bundy, and the Joint Chiefs of Staff, RFK opposed a pre-emptive strike against Soviet missile sites in Cuba: "For 175 years, this has not been the kind of country which launches Pearl Harbor attacks on Sunday morning. The first American President to do anything like this would not be forgiven by history, by his own people, or by the world."

As a back channel negotiator, the Attorney General met with Soviet Ambassador, Anatoly Dobrynin, and explained that American military leaders were pressuring the President to invade Cuba. RFK warned Dobrynin that he was was uncertain how much longer JFK could hold the military at bay. As a result of those clandestine meetings, a secret deal was cut; the Soviet Union agreed to remove their offensive missiles from Cuba, in exchange for a promise that the United States would not invade Cuba, and also remove its now obsolete *Jupiter* missiles from Turkey.

By the narrowest of margins, the two super powers had avoided war and potential nuclear holocaust. Over the course of two tense weeks, JFK had listened to *all* of his advisers, and did not limit his options to military action, alone.

"During the Cuban Missile Crisis, President Kennedy had ice water in his veins," Secretary of State, Dean Rusk, remembered.

Once the threat of nuclear war had been averted, JFK eerily invoked the image of Abraham Lincoln during a conversation with Bobby: "This is the night I should go to the theater."

"If you go, I want to go with you," RFK chuckled

Not surprisingly, RFK minimized the Vice-President's usefulness during the confrontation with the Soviet Union: "Lyndon Johnson never made any suggestions or recommendations to what we should do at the time of the Cuban Missile Crisis. He was displeased with what *we* were doing, although he never made it clear what *he* would do."

RFK's harsh assessment was not entirely accurate. While LBJ was not a frequent speaker during the Ex-Com meetings, he was neither objectionable nor argumentative. In fact, Johnson was one of the early advocates for removing the Jupiter missiles from Turkey, setting up a *quid pro quo* with the Soviet Union. Nonetheless, RFK came away from the Cuban Missile Crisis believing that Johnson was ineffectual in times of crisis.

Robert Kennedy was party to America's expanding military involvement in Southeast Asia. Ascribing to the prevalent *Domino Theory* of spreading Communism in the Third World, the Kennedy Administration drew the earliest battle lines in Vietnam.

As Attorney General, RFK was regarded as a hawkish opponent of Communism. Between 1961 and 1963, the number of U.S. military advisors in Vietnam increased from *692* to *16,700,* setting the stage for what would become a full scale war later in the decade.

RFK also journeyed outside the country on behalf of the Kennedy Administration. In February of 1962, the Attorney General traveled to Germany, not quite six months after the Berlin Wall was erected.

During a speech to a cheering crowd of West Germans, RFK referred to an overhead cluster of red-flagged balloons released by East Berliners: "They will let their balloons come over, but not their people."

Throughout JFK's thousand-day presidency, Robert Kennedy did nothing to mask his dislike of Lyndon Johnson. In spite of President Kennedy's instructions to treat the Vice-President with dignity and honor, many *New Frontiersmen* mimicked the Attorney General's scornful attitude, and *Uncle Corn Pone* became the frequent butt of jokes. In October of 1963, RFK's Justice Department aides gave him a LBJ *voodoo doll,* emblematic of the Attorney General's incessant needling of the hapless Vice-President.

In spite of his political emasculation, Lyndon Johnson remained intensely loyal to JFK. He never voiced any disagreement with the President in front of cabinet officers or other staff members. Johnson kept a lid on his ego, generally refusing to offer an opinion unless JFK specifically asked. All the while, LBJ endured rude treatment at the hands of Bobby Kennedy and his minions. More than once, the Attorney General barged into private meetings between the President and Vice-President, changing the subject, without acknowledging LBJ's presence.

New York Times White House correspondent, Hugh Sidey, observed LBJ's humiliation first hand, and described the behavior of RFK and other Kennedy advisers as "awful" and "inexcusable." Secretary of State, Dean Rusk, who was not among Robert Kennedy's admirers (the Attorney General had made it known that he considered Rusk as an ineffectual Cabinet member), marveled at the Vice-President's intense loyalty: "Johnson showed great self-discipline and strength. I think it was a major effort of self-control to fit that role—with all that volcanic force that was part of his very being."

Journalist and Kennedy family friend, Charles Bartlett, remembered Johnson's stoic response to the repeated humiliations: "There was never a word that ever drifted back to Jack Kennedy of any criticism from Lyndon Johnson. I don't think Kennedy knew how tough certain members of his staff were being on the Vice-President, but there certainly was not one word—and I'm very sure of this—of disloyalty that the Vice-President ever uttered."

Even among friends, Johnson deflected criticism of President Kennedy. In 1962, during a private dinner at the LBJ Ranch, a Texas millionaire railed against JFK. The Vice-President quickly interrupted the man: "Either you quit your talk about the President or you leave this table."

"I'm sorry, Lyndon. I didn't mean to offend you," the stunned tycoon replied.

"Well, God damn it, you did, and you better stop it now!" LBJ demanded.

LBJ made sure that everyone knew that he was "hunkering down" to JFK: "I have tried to be the kind of Vice-President I would have wanted to have, if I had been President."

During the Kennedy presidency, the Vice-President's office in the Executive Office Building was only a short walk from the Oval Office, but historian, William Manchester, succinctly characterized it as an "unbridgeable chasm."

As Lyndon Johnson stood in the shadows and watched Robert Kennedy consolidate his power, he became disinterested in government service and often lapsed into maudlin bouts of self-pity. Kennedy adviser and future Democratic Senator, Daniel Patrick Moynihan, aptly described LBJ's powerlessness: "This is a bull castrated very late in life."

During the closing months of 1963, LBJ heard rumors that he might be dropped from the 1964 presidential ticket. In reality, the Attorney General would have liked nothing better than to dump Johnson, and carefully investigated allegations that the Vice-President was tied to the corrupt business dealings and financial improprieties of the former Secretary to the Senate, Bobby Baker. RFK, however, could never directly link LBJ to any of the illegal activities, which ultimately resulted in Baker's imprisonment.

Ever paranoid, LBJ suspected that RFK was trying to orchestrate his downfall: "President Kennedy worked so hard at making a place for me, always saying nice things, giving me dignity and standing…In the back room, they were quoting Bobby as saying I was going to be off the ticket."

JFK was never known to have made any public or private statements about replacing Lyndon Johnson on the 1964 presidential ticket. In fact, many Kennedy aides maintained that Johnson's presence was necessary to attract disaffected Southern voters. LBJ, however, could not ignore the rumors that RFK was orchestrating a coup against him. As was his tendency during times of despair, Johnson actually spoke of retiring from politics and pursuing a university presidency or purchasing a newspaper. While few of LBJ's closest aides believed that he would voluntarily abandon the vice-presidency, they were forced to endure his unhappy monologues.

Johnson's relative anonymity became a running joke throughout America. The popular television program, *Candid Camera*, interviewed people on the street: "Who is Lyndon Johnson?"

"I don't know him," was a common answer.

One interviewee suggested looking up Johnson's name in the telephone book.

In 1962, the youngest Kennedy brother, Edward, was elected United States Senator from Massachusetts, triggering public speculation of a *Kennedy Dynasty*. Many political pundits predicted that Robert Kennedy would be the presidential nominee in 1968, after JFK's second term, and Lyndon Johnson's name was no longer mentioned as a potential successor.

While Lady Bird Johnson summed up her husband's vice-presidency as "Lyndon's quiet years, out of the arena," LBJ's assessment was far more graphic: "It was filled with trips around the world, chauffeurs, men saluting, people clapping, chairmanships of councils, but, in the end, it is nothing. I detested every minute of it."

Johnson also realized that his mere presence served as a grim reminder of the Commander-in-Chief's own mortality: "Every time I came into John Kennedy's presence, I felt like a God damn raven hovering over his shoulder."

On November 11, 1963, President Kennedy, RFK, Ted Sorensen, Kenneth O'Donnell, Larry O'Brien, and John Bailey (Chairman of the Democratic National Committee) held their first formal re-election strategy session. The three hour meeting began with a measure of alarm—the latest *Gallup Poll* numbers showed that JFK's popularity rating had dropped from *seventy-six* to *fifty-nine* percent since the beginning of the year, in large part due to the proposed Civil Rights Bill, which was very unpopular in the Deep South.

The group focused on the two most likely Republican presidential nominees in 1964—Arizona Senator, Barry Goldwater, and Michigan Governor, George Romney (the father of 2008 Republican presidential candidate, Mitt Romney). The Michigan Governor, a devout Mormon, concerned RFK the most: "We have to watch Romney. People buy into that God and country stuff."

"Romney could be tough," JFK added, "You have to be a little suspicious of somebody as good as Romney—no vices whatsoever, no smoking and no drinking. Imagine someone we know going off twenty four or forty eight hours to fast and meditate, awaiting a message from the Lord, whether to run or not to run…"

The President hoped the ultra-conservative Goldwater would win the Republican nomination: "Give me, Barry—I won't even have to leave the Oval Office."

Collectively, the group adopted a theme for the 1964 re-election campaign—*Peace and Prosperity*. JFK ended the strategy session on an upbeat note: "This has been very helpful. We'll get together when I get back from Texas."

On Thursday, November 21, 1963 President Kennedy departed Washington, D.C. for a two day campaign swing through Texas. At half past noon the next day, an assassin's bullets abruptly altered the course of history.

The lives of Robert Kennedy and Lyndon Johnson would never again be the same.

Chapter 10

I will do my best

At 12:30 p.m., CST on Friday November 22, 1963, Lee Harvey Oswald, a misanthropic, self-proclaimed Marxist, fired three shots at President Kennedy's motorcade in downtown Dallas, Texas. From his sniper's perch on the sixth floor of the Texas School Book Depository, Oswald's marksmanship was deadly accurate.

Media studies showed that by 6:00 p.m. that same day, a remarkable *99.8* percent of the American public was aware that President Kennedy had been assassinated. Worldwide, millions were glued to their television sets when Air Force One landed in the twilight at Andrews Air Force Base.

Fearing that images of JFK's casket being unloaded from Air Force One might be too upsetting to television viewers; President Johnson's advisers recommended banning the press. LBJ disagreed: "It would look like we're panicking."

Lyndon Johnson stood at the open door of the presidential aircraft and watched as the gray hearse departed with his predecessor's body, waiting for a walkway to be rolled into place. Four minutes later, the new President debarked and greeted a solemn group of Washington dignitaries, including the Chief Justice of the Supreme Court, Earl Warren, Secretary of Defense, Robert McNamara, and Senate Majority Leader, Mike Mansfield.

"It's terrible, terrible," LBJ repeated to the men who greeted him.

At 6:14 p.m., President Johnson approached a bank of microphones eerily illuminated by television lights: "This is a sad time for all people. We have suffered a loss that cannot be weighed. For me, it is a deep personal tragedy. I know that the world shares the sorrow that Mrs. Kennedy and her family bear. I will do my best. That is all I can do. I ask for your help—and God's."

The new First Lady provided a written statement to the press: "I just feel it's all been a dreadful nightmare, and somehow we must find the strength to go on."

LBJ's short, but sincere address was well received by the public. *Life* magazine saluted the new President: "His eloquence at that moment, so simple as to be stately, defined both a nation's grief and its purpose."

Shadowed by Secret Service agents, Johnson was ushered to a waiting helicopter and flown to the White House. Joining LBJ on the short flight were the First Lady, Secretary of Defense, Robert McNamara, National Security Adviser, McGeorge Bundy, Under Secretary of State, George Ball, and three of LBJ's closest aides. The remainder of the cabinet was in route to Washington, after their summit trip to Japan was interrupted by the news of President Kennedy's assassination.

Raising his voice above the chop of the rotors, LBJ praised Jackie Kennedy: "I have never seen anyone so brave."

LBJ then shifted the conversation to the unexpected, painful transition: "Kennedy did something I couldn't have done. He gathered around him the ablest people I've ever seen—not his friends, not even the best in public service, but the best anywhere. I want you to stay. I need you. I want you to stand with me."

During the short flight, George Ball believed the new President was in state of shock, as if he had been drugged. Robert McNamara, on the other hand, thought LBJ was "surprisingly stable—much more so than I would have been in this situation."

After the Marine chopper landed on the South Grounds of the White House, Lady Bird was whisked away to the Johnson's' private residence, accompanied by a Secret Service detail. The new President walked from the landing area toward the West Wing of the White House. In the darkness, Johnson peered inside the open door to the Oval Office, where he could clearly see John F. Kennedy's desk, and the new carpeting that had been installed earlier in the day. An aide suggested that it was LBJ's right to immediately occupy the office (JFK appointees, McNamara, Bundy, and Ball concurred).

"That would be presumptuous of me," Johnson replied, before walking across the street to his suite of offices on the second floor of the Executive Office Building (EOB).

After arriving at his office, Johnson met with J. William Fulbright, the influential Chairman of the *Senate Foreign Relations Committee.* At 7:05 p.m., LBJ began a series of phone calls to past presidents—Herbert Hoover, Harry Truman, and Dwight Eisenhower (because of his poor health, Hoover was unable to speak directly with Johnson). The new President then telephoned FBI Director, J. Edgar Hoover, receiving an update about the investigation into JFK's assassination.

At 7:40 p.m., LBJ met for twenty minutes with a bipartisan group of Congressman and Senators. The shocked and grieving lawmakers pledged to support Johnson during the difficult transition period.

Following his meeting with congressional leaders, Johnson telephoned Supreme Court Justice, Arthur Goldberg, who had been inadvertently overlooked by LBJ during his arrival at Andrews Air Force Base. To shore up support among Kennedy loyalists, LBJ also called Democratic National Chairman, Dick Maguire, and long-time JFK speech writer, Ted Sorensen.

Before departing his office, Johnson dispatched a staff member to the West Wing to retrieve two sheets of presidential stationery. With a steady hand, the new President wrote brief letters to JFK's young children:

Dear John: It will be many years before you understand fully what a great man your father was. His loss is a deep personal tragedy for all of us, but I wanted you particularly to know that I share your grief. You can always be proud of him."

Dear Caroline: Your father's death has been a great tragedy for the nation, as well as for you, and I wanted you to know how much my thoughts are with you at this time. He was a wise and devoted man. You can always be proud of what he did for his country."

His office duties complete, the new President was escorted under heavy Secret Service guard to his home, *The Elms,* at 4040 Fifty Second Street, NW. Outwardly, Lyndon Johnson appeared calm and steady, but he was still smarting over Robert Kennedy's snub aboard Air Force One.

"For millions of Americans, I was illegitimate, a naked man with no presidential cover, a pretender to the throne, an illegal usurper," LBJ angrily complained.

At *The Elms,* drinking an orange soda, Johnson raised his glass to a portrait of the late Sam Rayburn: "Oh, Mister Sam, I wish you were here now. I need you."

Johnson's cardiologist, Dr. Willis Hurst, was waiting when the new President arrived home. After conducting a physical examination, Hurst determined that his now famous patient was medically stable.

Working the phones again, Johnson contacted the Director of the Secret Service, James Rowley, commending the bravery of Special Agent, Rufus Youngblood, who had used his body as a human shield to protect Johnson when the gunfire erupted in Dallas: "Jim, I don't know how your shop operates, but Youngblood deserves something—a decoration, a promotion, or whatever you do. He was great. If I'd been in his spot, I don't think I'd have had the nerve to knock the Vice-President to the floor."

It took several hours for LBJ to fall asleep at the end of that tragic day. For the first time since the turn of the century, when Theodore Roosevelt succeeded William McKinley, a Vice-President had become President after the assassination of his predecessor.

Reclining atop his bed in pajamas, LBJ chatted with his aides, Jack Valenti, Cliff Carter, and Bill Moyers. In a pressured, but precise monologue, Johnson outlined his ambitious agenda: "I'm going to get Kennedy's tax cut bill out of the Senate Finance Committee, and we're going to get this economy humming again. Then, I'm going to pass Kennedy's Civil Rights Bill, which has been hung up too long in Congress. And, I'm going pass it, without changing a single comma or word. After that, we'll pass legislation that allows everyone, anywhere in this country, to vote, with all barriers down. And, that's not all. We're going to get a new law that says every boy and girl in this country, no matter how poor, or the color of their skin, or the region they come from, is going to be able to get all the education they can by loan scholarship, or grant—right from the federal government."

Less than twelve hours after assuming the presidency, LBJ concluded future policy dissertation: "By God, I intend to pass Harry Truman's medical insurance bill. He didn't do it, but we'll make it into law."

At 3:09 a.m., LBJ finally drifted off to sleep, allowing his exhausted aides slipped out of the President's bedroom.

Robert Kennedy sat in the back seat of the hearse with Jackie Kennedy during the forty five minute drive to Bethesda Naval Hospital. Still dressed in her pink, blood stained dress; the former First Lady shared the horrific details of the assassination. Though pained by his sister-in-law's story, Bobby allowed her to vent.

At Bethesda, the Attorney General, former First Lady, and a handful of Kennedy aides were escorted to the seventeenth floor VIP suite, while JFK's body was transported to the morgue for autopsy.

Jackie steadfastly refused to shed her ruined clothes, telling friends and family who arrived at the hospital: "I want them to see what *they've* done."

Meanwhile, RFK masked his grief with activity, making a flurry of telephone calls. As the eldest surviving brother, Bobby was now the *de facto* head of the Kennedy family.

RFK took time to write his eldest son, Joseph Patrick Kennedy, II a letter explaining the change in family dynamics: "You are the oldest of all the male grandchildren. You have a special and particular responsibility now, which I know you will fulfill. Remember all the things that Jack started—be kind to others that are less fortunate than we—and love our country."

Bobby's brother-in-law, Sargent Shriver, was assigned the task of coordinating JFK's state funeral. Jackie requested that the funeral arrangements closely match the protocol used after the assassination of Abraham Lincoln.

Bobby dispatched his brother, Ted, and sister, Eunice, to Cape Cod to break the awful news to their father. The Attorney General also telephoned Marie Tippit, widow of Dallas Police Officer, J.D. Tippit, who had been shot to death by Lee Harvey Oswald, forty five minutes after President Kennedy was assassinated. RFK then phoned John Connally's wife, Nellie, to inquire about the condition of the seriously wounded Texas Governor.

Conferring with Kenneth O'Donnell, Bobby clarified his early afternoon exchange with Lyndon Johnson, concerning the oath of office ceremony aboard Air Force One. Bobby assured O'Donnell that he never *encouraged* LBJ to be sworn in before leaving Dallas. After learning the plane's departure had been delayed by the oath of office ceremony, RFK was livid. The Attorney General was particularly angered by LBJ's insistence that Jackie stand by his side during brief ceremony. In RFK's eyes, Johnson had immediately manipulated and abused the powers of the presidency.

Upon arriving at Bethesda, Ethel Kennedy offered solace to her sister-in-law: "At least you have the comfort of knowing that Jack has found eternal happiness."

"I would have hoped for more," Jackie answered, "You're lucky to have Bobby—he's here for you."

"He's here for you, too, Jackie," Ethel promised.

The autopsy and cosmetic preparation of JFK's body took most of the night. The undertakers prepared for the possibility of an open casket, and worked diligently to repair the massive damage inflicted on Kennedy's head by the assassin's bullet.

At 4:34 a.m. the hearse arrived at the White House. A military honor guard carried the flag draped coffin into the East Room, where it was placed atop a replica of the black draped catafalque used to display Abraham Lincoln's casket in 1865.

Bobby and Jackie silently opened the coffin and stared down at Jack's lifeless face. Robert McNamara, Arthur Schlesinger, and Nancy Tuckerman (Jackie Kennedy's Social Secretary) were asked to view the body and offer opinions about whether the casket should be left open for viewing. The observers reached a consensus—JFK's face appeared too "waxen." The grieving widow and brother quickly decided to keep the coffin closed.

Nearing dawn, RFK made his way upstairs to the Lincoln bedroom. Kennedy family friend, Charles Spalding, gave the Attorney General a sleeping pill.

"God, it's so awful. Everything was really beginning to run so well," RFK moaned.

After he exited the room, Spalding heard Bobby break into sobs: "Why now, God? Why now?"

Chapter 11

Can't you wait?

The series of events that occurred during the fourth weekend of November in 1963 became a tragic blur to most Americans—JFK's assassination, the President's flag draped casket lying in state in the White House and Capitol Rotunda, the murder of the accused presidential assassin, Lee Harvey Oswald, and Kennedy's massive state funeral. Television networks suspended commercial interruptions, providing continuous coverage that lasted for *seventy hours* and *twenty-seven minutes* (ending at1:16 a.m. on Tuesday, November 26th). *CBS, NBC,* and *ABC* delivered grainy black and white images of the unfolding tragedy to millions of viewers, worldwide.

After sleeping only four hours, LBJ awakened to begin his first full day as President of the United States. Johnson began his morning much like the evening before, pledging to implement progressive policies, and end the *New Frontier's* legislative stalemate.

"Do you realize that when I came to Washington tonight (actually last night) as President, there were on my desk the same things as when I came to Congress in 1937?" LBJ told his aide, Horace Busby.

Before the day ended, Johnson explained his progressive tendencies to another adviser: "I am a Roosevelt *New Dealer.* As a matter of a fact, Kennedy was a little too conservative to suit my taste."

Still angered and hurt by RFK's snub aboard Air Force One the previous night, LBJ complained to his aide, Jack Valenti: "Nobody said a word to me. And here I am the God damn President of the United States!"

At 8:40 a.m., Johnson was escorted by the Secret Service from his residence to the White House. A steady downpour drenched the nation's capitol, symbolic of the somber mood of its citizens. The new President immediately issued a proclamation, declaring November 23, 1963, as an official day of mourning for John F. Kennedy. The mourning period would last for *thirty* days, during which time the flag would remain at half mast, and no government-sponsored social functions would be held.

Robert Kennedy managed only an hour or two of fitful sleep in the Lincoln bedroom. After awakening, he visited with Jackie and her two children. The comments of his niece and nephew magnified the cruel events of the day before. Six-year-old Caroline Kennedy declared that her "Daddy is too big for his coffin." Her younger brother, John, about to turn three, explained that a "bad man" shot his father.

"Every time I look at Caroline and John, I want to cry," RFK told Kennedy adviser, David Powers.

At ten o'clock on Saturday morning, *seventy-five* Kennedy family members and close friends gathered in the East Room of the White House for a private mass. A portable altar was erected within sight of JFK's flag draped coffin, and the mourners substituted folding chairs for pews.

Disregarding the advice on his advisers on the evening of the assassination, Lyndon Johnson had resisted the temptation to occupy the Oval Office, believing such an act would be disrespectful. By the next morning, LBJ had changed his mind.

At 9:00 a.m., Robert Kennedy unexpectedly entered the West Wing to help clear his late brother's desk of papers and personal items. Bobby encountered JFK's long time personal secretary, Evelyn Lincoln, weeping inside her office. Lincoln explained that President Johnson was already inside the Oval Office.

"He told me, 'I have a meeting at 9:30, and would like you to clear your things out of your office, by then, so my own girls can come in,'" Lincoln cried.

The President and Attorney General briefly huddled in the anteroom across from the President's private bathroom, adjacent to the Oval Office; their first face-to-face discussion since JFK's murder.

"I need you more than the President needed you," LBJ implored, using the same phrase employed in earlier conversations with Kennedy staffers.

Bobby was in no mood to discuss his role in the new administration, and was hurt and angered by LBJ's hasty occupation of his late brother's office.

"Can't you wait?" Kennedy implored, before quickly departing.

Evelyn Lincoln managed to clean out her office that morning. But, much like Bobby, she viewed LBJ as an insensitive interloper.

In fairness to the new President, National Security Adviser, McGeorge Bundy had previously spoken with RFK, who asked to be given a few days to clear the Oval Office of his brother's personal possessions. Bundy had written Johnson a note to that effect, but LBJ did not receive until after his confrontation with Bobby.

To delay further conflict with RFK, LBJ decided not to occupy the Oval Office until after his predecessor's funeral. Johnson, however, was clearly bitter: "I think Bobby seriously considered whether he would let me be President."

Historian and writer, David Halberstam, later summarized the ever-widening chasm between LBJ and RFK: "Both men were jockeying for the right to be John Kennedy's legatee. Robert Kennedy had the right to it by blood and by emotion; Lyndon Johnson had no emotional base, but he had it by constitutional right."

As he had done the evening before, LBJ plunged into a busy schedule. At 9:15 a.m., the new President was briefed by CIA Director, John McCone, who reassured him there was no evidence of an international conspiracy behind President Kennedy's assassination. Fifteen minutes later, Secretary of State, Dean Rusk, who had been in route to Japan when JFK was murdered, met with his new Commander-in-Chief for the first time.

At ten o'clock, Johnson received a telephone update from J. Edgar Hoover about new developments in the case against Lee Harvey Oswald. A few minutes later, LBJ phoned George Meany, the powerful head of the AFL-CIO, hoping to shore up support from organized labor.

The new President and First Lady entered the East Room at 11:00 a.m. to pay their respects to his slain predecessor, standing in silence in front of the flag draped coffin. Kennedy's body would lie in state in the White

House for another *twenty-four* hours, before it was moved to the Capitol Rotunda for public viewing.

Afterwards, Lyndon and Lady Bird visited with Jackie Kennedy in the White House family residence. The widowed, former First Lady promised to vacate the living quarters as soon as possible.

"Honey, you stay as long as you want. I have a nice, comfortable home, and I'm in no hurry," Johnson replied (Jackie Kennedy took LBJ at his word, and did not move out of the White House until *two* weeks after her husband's assassination).

At 12:20 p.m., the President and First Lady attended a special service at St. John's Episcopal Church, located within walking distance of the White House. The rector prayed for his distinguished visitor: "Oh God, bless thy servant Lyndon, and all others in authority, so they may do thy will."

After the Saturday morning mass, Bobby Kennedy (along with his sisters, Pat and Jean) traveled to Arlington National Cemetery, accompanied by Secretary of Defense, Robert McNamara. McNamara had spent the early part of the day scouting for potential burial sites in the historic cemetery. While many news outlets speculated that JFK would be buried in the family gravesite in Boston, McNamara and other Kennedy aides favored Arlington. Standing in the steady rain, on a gentle slope just below the Custis-Lee Mansion, with its commanding view of the Lincoln Memorial, RFK decided to make this spot his brother's final resting place.

At half past two on Saturday afternoon, LBJ conducted his first official cabinet meeting. As Johnson entered the room, the cabinet secretaries all stood.

"Gentlemen, the President of the United States," Secretary of State Rusk announced.

LBJ began with a silent prayer, and once again reminded each cabinet officer that he "needed them more" than his predecessor. The meeting was soon interrupted by the late arrival of the Attorney General.

With no plans to attend the cabinet meeting, RFK happened to be in the West Wing, making sure that his brother's desk chair had been removed from the Oval Office, when National Security Adviser, McGeorge Bundy, corralled him. Bundy insisted that Kennedy attend the cabinet meeting; RFK reluctantly agreed, with the stipulation that no photographers be present.

When RFK arrived five minutes after the meeting began, LBJ quietly seethed. Afterwards, Johnson complained that RFK had deliberately *upstaged* the new President; an allegation Kennedy later denied. Believing Bobby Kennedy had planned his tardy entrance, LBJ angrily attributed a fictitious quote to the Attorney General: "We won't go in until he (the President) has already sat down."

During the cabinet meeting, Secretary of State, Dean Rusk, and Ambassador to the United Nations, Adlai Stevenson, offered prepared statements supporting the new President. After the meeting, Robert Kennedy questioned Rusk's and Stevenson's sincerity, since both men had *read* their statements, instead of giving extemporaneous, heartfelt displays of support. RFK was certain that LBJ would never inspire the same love and devotion as President Kennedy.

Secretary of Agriculture, Orville Freeman, recalled RFK's arrival at Johnson's maiden cabinet meeting: "His general demeanor as he came into the room and sat down—well, it was quite clear that he could hardly countenance Lyndon Johnson sitting in his brother's chair."

With escalating anger and paranoia, LBJ complained that the Attorney General had not uttered a single word of support for the new President.

That same day, LBJ met with former President, Dwight Eisenhower. Making notes on a yellow tablet, Eisenhower offered detailed advice concerning the executive branch transition. The former President encouraged LBJ to make a joint address to Congress, as soon as possible, to reassure a shocked and anxious country.

Eisenhower also advised Johnson to accept the resignations of all Kennedy cabinet members and advisers, and replace them with his own loyal appointees. LBJ ultimately disregarded this recommendation, urging all members of the Kennedy Administration to remain by his side.

President Johnson hoped to deliver his congressional address on Tuesday, one day after JFK's funeral, and attempted to clear the prospective date with the Kennedy family. National Security Adviser, McGeorge Bundy, was dispatched to meet with Robert Kennedy.

Bundy explained the situation to Kennedy, who requested that the address be postponed until at least Wednesday, allowing more time to pass after his brother's funeral. When Bundy emphasized LBJ's desire to deliver the speech on Tuesday, Bobby erupted in anger.

"Well, the Hell with it! Why do you ask me about it? Don't ask me about what you want done—you'll tell me what it's going to be anyway. Go ahead and do it," Kennedy spat out.

Unhappy with RFK's initial response, LBJ dangled the apple of political fortune in front of Kennedy brother-in-law, Sargent Shriver: "Well, Sarge, it's a terrible thing. I'm completely overwhelmed, but I do want to say that I've always had a very high regard for you. It hasn't been possible for me to do anything about it until *now*, but I intend to."

When Shriver asked if he could immediately to assist the President, LBJ foolishly asked him to approach RFK concerning the timing of the Congressional address.

"Why does he tell you to ask me? Now, he's hacking at you. He knows I want him to wait until Wednesday," Bobby snapped at Shriver, certain that LBJ was manipulating the Kennedy family.

After his dressing down from RFK, Shriver relayed the message to LBJ: "Bob prefers you wait a day, unless there are overriding reasons for having the address earlier."

Clearly disgruntled, LBJ scheduled the address for Wednesday, but was convinced that RFK valued the Kennedy legacy more than the continuity of the presidency. At the same time, RFK was nearing his breaking point, finding it difficult to accept that a petty interloper had seized his brother's mantle.

On Sunday morning, RFK and Jackie visited JFK's coffin in the East Room, before the body was transported to the Capitol Rotunda. Bobby placed an engraved silver rosary, his *PT-109* tie clasp (commemorating Jack's World War II torpedo boat), and a lock of his own hair inside the casket.

Lyndon Johnson attended church that morning, and then accompanied his predecessor's body to the Capitol. Meanwhile, accused presidential assassin, Lee Harvey Oswald, was shot to death in the basement of Dallas Police Headquarters by Jack Ruby, a vengeful, mentally unstable strip club owner—the third and final murder in the bizarre, weekend long tragedy. A stunned nation witnessed Oswald's murder on live television, and anxiously wondered what would happen next.

"It has been too much, too ugly, too fast," a television news commentator reported, after Ruby gunned down Oswald.

A similar refrain was echoed by a foreign ambassador, who was speaking on the telephone with Texas Congressman, Albert Thomas, when Ruby extracted his revenge: "My God, you Texans are just crazy! They've shot that boy!"

In the early afternoon, the President and First Lady rode in a limousine from the White House to Capitol Hill, accompanied by Jackie Kennedy, her two children, and RFK. To the muffled cadence of military, JFK's body was transported eighteen blocks by a horse-drawn caisson. A solemn and respectful crowd lined Pennsylvania Avenue as the flag draped coffin slowly passed, followed by a majestic stallion, with boots reversed in the rider-less stirrups. LBJ and RFK shared few words during the mournful ride.

Jackie Kennedy, however, tried to comfort the new President: "Oh, Lyndon, what an awful way for you to come in!"

Over the course of the next twenty-four hours, some *250,000* mourners passed by the coffin in the marbled Capitol Rotunda. Many citizens traveled from distant states, waiting for hours in a line stretching dozens of blocks, hoping to bid a personal farewell to President Kennedy.

Monday, November 25, 1963, was a sun-drenched, briskly cool day. Nearing mid-day, President Kennedy's body was transported from the Capitol Building, past the White House, to Saint Matthew's Cathedral. Much to the chagrin of the Secret Service, President Johnson joined the Kennedy family and other dignitaries, as they walked behind the caisson for the final eight blocks between the White House and the church. At first, LBJ had agreed to remain in his limousine during the funeral march, but, on the spur of the moment, reconsidered: "Lady Bird told me I should do it, so I changed my mind."

Security was tight during the funeral procession, with fears that the assassination impulse might be contagious. In addition to the Secret Service detail, *sixty-four* CIA agents, *forty* FBI agents, *two-hundred fifty* State Department bodyguards, and *twelve* French bodyguards (detailed to protect Charles de Gaulle) accompanied the mourners during their walk to the cathedral.

A distinguished group of American political leaders, along with *220* representatives from over *100* foreign countries, attended the solemn ceremony. After the funeral mass, JFK's body was taken to Arlington National Cemetery, where he was interred with full military honors. At the end of the ceremony, Jackie Kennedy lit a torch, representing an *eternal flame,* permanently marking the gravesite of the thirty-fifth President of the United States.

On the evening of the funeral, LBJ hosted a reception for foreign leaders at the Department of State. Many world leaders caught their first glance the new President, who appeared self-assured, and fully in command.

On the night of JFK's funeral, the Kennedy family mournfully celebrated John F. Kennedy, Jr.'s third birthday (Caroline's sixth birthday would follow two days later). Late in the evening, Bobby and Jackie returned to JFK's freshly filled grave. The eternal flame cast its flickering shadow, as the brother and widow knelt to pray. Afterwards, the grief stricken pair walked slowly down the gentle slope, hand-in-hand, wondering if either could face the future without Jack.

Chapter 12

All I have, I would have given gladly not to be standing here today

Lyndon Johnson was in the unenviable position of succeeding a tragic hero. Twenty eight years after the Kennedy assassination, respected Washington Insider, Clark Clifford, analyzed JFK's martyrdom: "...While he was alive, no one imagined that he would, after his death, become a mythical figure in American culture and history."

In the 1960 presidential election, JFK had won *49.7* percent of the popular vote. Shortly after his assassination, a full *sixty-five* percent of American voters claimed they had voted for Kennedy.

In short order, New York City's Idlewild Field was renamed the *John F. Kennedy International Airport.* Throughout the country, bridges, highways, town squares, and wildlife sanctuaries were renamed in honor of the fallen

President. Canada designated an unnamed peak as *Mount Kennedy* (two years later, RFK would scale the mountain).

Jackie Kennedy collaborated with historian Theodore White and *Life* magazine to commemorate her late husband's thousand day presidency as *Camelot*. JFK's favorite record was the cast album from the popular play, with lyrics written by the late President's friend and Harvard classmate, Alan Jay Lerner: "Don't let it be forgot; that once there was a spot; for one brief shining moment; that was known as *Camelot*."

"There will never be another *Camelot*," Jackie explained to White, "There will be great Presidents again—and the Johnsons are wonderful to me, but there'll never be another *Camelot*."

While the former First Lady fostered the notion of a glorious presidency, many *New Frontiersmen* were less than enamored by the moniker. Arthur Schlesinger, Jr. clarified the nature of the myth: "*Camelot* was, of course, unknown in Kennedy's lifetime. JFK, himself, would have regarded that with derision."

"*Camelot* is a creation of journalists. I'm sure that Jackie, in her romantic, fuzzy way, thought that it was neat," Ralph Dungan opined.

JFK Press Secretary, Pierre Salinger, was blunter: "*Camelot* is a fraud— the word never came out during the Kennedy Administration."

In the early months after the assassination, Lyndon Johnson consolidated his presidential powers, but remained courteous, compassionate, and considerate to the Kennedy family. Against the advice of the Secret Service, Johnson had demonstrated his loyalty by openly walking behind his predecessor's casket during JFK's funeral march.

The day after the funeral, LBJ received a hand written note from Jackie Kennedy: "Thank you for walking yesterday—behind Jack. You did not have to do that—I am sure many people forbid you to take such a risk—but you did it anyway."

Johnson and the former First Lady exchanged hand written missives and telephone calls during the weeks and months following the tragic events in Dallas. LBJ doubted that he could narrow the acrimonious breech with Robert Kennedy, but was determined to treat the slain President's family with as much dignity as possible: "I took his program and his family, after he was fallen, and I did everything that I would want a man to do for my program, or my family, if the same thing happened to me."

At the request of Jackie Kennedy, President Johnson renamed NASA's *Cape Canaveral* in honor of his martyred predecessor (this decision proved unpopular, as *Canaveral* was one of the oldest named geographical points in all of North America; in the mid 1970s, the rocket launch site was returned to its original name).

The gracious, former First Lady acknowledged Johnson's generosity on behalf of the Kennedy family: "Of course, I've always liked Lyndon Johnson. He has been very generous with me. Bobby gets me to put on my widow's weeds and go down to his office and ask for tremendous things, like renaming Cape Canaveral after Jack, and he has come through on everything."

On seventh of December, two weeks after JFK's assassination, the widow and her two children moved to a rented house in Georgetown. Caroline Kennedy, however, continued to attend a special school on the White House grounds until the end of December.

On December 17th, Jackie returned to the White House to attend her daughter's school Christmas program. She had planned to visit President Johnson in the Oval Office, but he was in New York delivering a speech. After that day, and for the the remainder of the Johnson Administration, Jackie did not return to the White House.

The telephone conversations between Jackie and LBJ were tender and sometimes flirtatious. Johnson addressed the widow with a bold sense of familiarity: "Give Caroline and John John a hug for me—tell them I'd like to be their Daddy."

After conversing with Jackie, Johnson was often exuberant. LBJ called Press Secretary, Pierre Salinger, shortly after a telephone chat with the former First Lady.

"This is screwy, but can you hold onto your chair? Would it be just terrible to ask Miz Kennedy to be Ambassador to Mexico?" Johnson asked Salinger.

The startled press secretary was non-committal, but this did not dampen the President's enthusiasm.

"God, Almighty! It'd electrify the Western hemisphere. She'd just walk out on that balcony and look down on them, and they'd just pee all over themselves, every day!" Johnson exclaimed (fearing that the former First Lady would turn him down, LBJ ultimately did not extend the offer).

Lady Bird Johnson offered to rename the historic Rose Garden, adjacent to the Oval Office, the *Jacqueline Kennedy Garden*. Jackie politely declined, believing that her name should not be permanently attached to the White House (a small flower garden near the East Wing, however, was later named in her honor).

In time, the relationship between Lyndon Johnson and Jackie Kennedy grew somewhat strained. Each time LBJ asked her to return to the White House to attend social functions, Jackie declined. In her grief, the widowed First Lady tried to erase all visible reminders of the Executive Mansion, to the point of telling her driver to avoid streets that were in close proximity to 1600 Pennsylvania Avenue. Jackie was also pressured by her brother-in-law to minimize contact with Johnson—RFK was concerned that LBJ would manipulate her to bolster his political image.

When Franklin Roosevelt, Jr. (son of the legendary President and a close friend of the Kennedy family), asked President Johnson to stop putting "pressure" on Jackie to return to the White House, LBJ erupted: "I've bent over backwards for that woman. I've done cartwheels and deep knee squats, and all I get is criticism!"

In the fall of 1964, Jacqueline Kennedy and her two children moved from Washington D.C. to New York City. For 200,000 dollars Jackie purchased a five bedroom/five bath apartment at 1040 Fifth Avenue. The new residence featured a private elevator and a commanding view of Central Park. The former First Lady believed it would be easier to achieve relative anonymity in the *Big Apple,* where she could properly raise her two children outside of Washington D.C.'s fishbowl.

After relocating to New York, Jackie occasionally spoke with LBJ, and their overall relationship remained friendly. Johnson believed that the former First Lady treated him with more respect than any other member of the Kennedy clan. Jackie, in turn, was appreciative of Johnson's concern for her well being, and managed to overlook his often overbearing demeanor.

At 12:30 p.m. on Wednesday, November 27, 1963 (Thanksgiving Eve), two days after JFK's funeral, President Johnson delivered a nationally televised address to a joint session of Congress. To promote continuity and good will, LBJ asked Kennedy's speechwriter and closest aide, Ted Sorensen, to help prepare his address. Johnson began the speech in a dignified and solemn manner: "All I have, I would have given gladly not to be standing here today. The greatest leader of our time has been struck down by the foulest deed of our time…"

Johnson mostly followed Sorensen's draft, but deleted this particular sentence: "I, who cannot fill his shoes, must occupy his desk."

Johnson boldly outlined the most pressing issue on his forthcoming legislative agenda: "No memorial or eulogy could more eloquently honor

President Kennedy's memory than the earliest possible passage of the Civil Rights Bill for which he fought so long..."

Johnson's maiden address was well received by lawmakers, the press, and the general public. Few Americans, outside of Texas, were familiar with LBJ, and the new President's reassuring words comforted a grieving nation.

Always image conscious, Johnson privately bragged that he had been interrupted by applause *thirty-four* times during the *twenty-four* minute speech.

Robert Kennedy sat on the front row with other cabinet members during Johnson's address. Though he politely applauded with the rest of the gallery, the Attorney General's mood was somber, and his countenance was grim.

Later that same day, Johnson asked RFK to join him in the Oval Office, hoping to temper their growing feud. The meeting lasted only twelve minutes, as Kennedy was in no mood for LBJ's platitudes.

"Your people are talking about me," Johnson said, "You can't let your people talk about me, and I won't talk about you."

Trying to defuse RFK's anger over the swearing in ceremony about Air Force One, LBJ declared that the oath had not delayed the plane's departure. Kennedy knew this was not true, as there had been nearly a half-hour wait for the judge to arrive to swear in the new President. Johnson explained that he had not wanted to occupy the Oval Office the day after President Kennedy's assassination, but had been pressured to do so by staff members and cabinet officers, which, at best, was a half truth. Kennedy left the meeting knowing that LBJ had once again lied to him.

Robert Kennedy was uncertain about his future. He did not want to serve as LBJ's Attorney General, but made no immediate decision to leave the Johnson Administration. To lessen the likelihood of conflict, Kennedy avoided face-to-face contact with LBJ for the remainder of 1963: "I'm not mentally equipped for it, or physically."

Consumed by grief, RFK was unable to perform his job duties for several weeks after his brother's murder. He often did not go to his office, delegating duties to various assistants. Bobby frequently wore articles of clothing belonging to his late brother, including Jack's tweed overcoat, leather naval jacket (emblazoned with the presidential seal), and cardigan sweater. Plagued by insomnia, he refused to take a sedative, and would often leave home in the middle of the night, driving around in his convertible, seemingly oblivious to the freezing temperatures.

RFK felt a measure of guilt, wondering if his zealous prosecution of the Mafia and supervision of CIA efforts to depose Fidel Castro might have backfired, and led to his brother's death. On the afternoon of JFK's assassination, Bobby told his adviser, Ed Guthman: "I thought they would get one of us, but Jack, after all he'd been through, (it) never worried me...I thought it would be me."

A handful of malcontents expressed regret that RFK had been on the receiving end of the bullets fired in Dallas. The National Director of the *Congress of Racial Equality (CORE),* James Farmer, was at a convention on the day of JFK's assassination, and was shocked when he overheard a conversation between two white businessmen: "They got the wrong damn Kennedy; they should have killed that Bobby son of a bitch!"

When he learned that President Kennedy had been assassinated, a vengeful Jimmy Hoffa refused to lower the Teamsters' headquarters flag to half-mast. Hoffa joyously confided to a colleague: "Bobby Kennedy's just another lawyer, now."

Thanksgiving vacation followed a week after JFK's assassination, and Bobby was too grief stricken to return to the family compound in Cape Cod. Instead, he took his family to Secretary of Treasury, Doug Dillon's home in Hobe Sound Florida. Presidential Press Secretary, Pierre Salinger vividly recalled RFK playing in a "vicious" game of "touch" football, where he was "getting his feelings out by knocking people down."

While vacationing in Antigua in the spring of 1964, Jackie Kennedy gave her brother-in-law a copy of Edith Hamilton's, *The Greek Way.* Jackie remembered Bobby underlining passages in the book. Trying to come to terms with his grief, RFK highlighted the words of Aeschylus: "All arrogance will reap a harvest rich in tears. God calls men to a heavy reckoning for overweening pride."

Bobby was also captivated by Michael Harrington's, *The Other America,* which vividly detailed the devastating consequences of poverty. The plight of the impoverished soon became one of RFK's prime areas of focus. U.S. Attorney Robert Morgenthau noted that after his brother's murder, the Attorney General no longer seemed interested in pursuing *bad guys*: "I saw him often after that, but he never mentioned organized crime to me again."

In the weeks following JFK's assassination, RFK exhibited a dark sense of humor. On one occasion, Bobby asked a friend: "Been to any good funerals, lately? I don't like to let too many days go by without a funeral."

Accompanied by adviser, Dave Hackett, Bobby attended the funeral of a mutual friend, and his morbidity shocked fellow mourners: "Hackett and I have so much experience at this thing, that we're offering a regular service for funerals. We select readings and songs of utmost simplicity, and then we pick out a cheap casket to save the widow money. You know, they always cheat you on a casket. We pick passages from the Bible, and do all that's necessary to ensure an interesting and inexpensive funeral. This is a new service we can provide all our friends."

The Attorney General also began to question the tenets of his faith, finding that long his standing piety was insufficient balm for intense grief. He concluded that the Catholic Church had grown too conservative and was out of touch with the needs of contemporary citizens. For the remainder of his life, RFK would cite the words of Greek philosophers more often than biblical references.

William Manchester, whose book, *Death of a President*, chronicled the events surrounding JFK's assassination, visited with RFK in the early months after his brother's death: "I was shocked by his appearance. I have never seen a man with less resilience. Much of the time, he seemed to be in a trance, staring off into space—his face a study in grief."

Bobby found it difficult to utter the word *assassination* or the name *Dallas*. Instead, he would simply reference the *events of November 22nd*. Senator Edward (Ted) Kennedy vividly recalled the magnitude of his brother's grief: "Hope seemed to have died within him, and there followed months of unremitting melancholia. He went through the motions of everyday life, but he carried the burden of his grief with him always."

Dealing with her own unspeakable sorrow, Jackie Kennedy tried to boost Bobby's moral, writing in a letter: "Now that Jack's gone, Caroline and John need you more than ever. Above all, the country needs you. It is time to honor Jack's memory—not to continue to mourn it. We would both, myself included, be negligent in our responsibilities to that memory, if we collapse. Jack would want us both to carry on what he stood for, and died for."

Included with Jackie's letter was a sheaf of yellow legal pad note sheets entitled: "Notes made by President Kennedy at his last Cabinet meeting—10-29-1963." RFK immediately framed the notes and displayed them on the wall of his study.

Ted Kennedy credited the most unlikely of individuals for helping alleviate Bobby's crushing depression. In January of 1964, Lyndon Johnson asked RFK to travel to the Far East to negotiate a cease fire between Indonesia and Malaysia. Ted was certain that LBJ sincerely "hoped the assignment would lift his (Bobby's) spirits," and ultimately "broke my brother's cycle of depression." In his memoirs, Ted Kennedy complimented LBJ for a "valuable act of compassion."

As he slowly emerged from his despair, RFK remained reluctant to discuss his future. In private conversations, Bobby explained that he *could not* leave the Attorney Generalship until Congress passed JFK's Civil Rights Bill.

Against the advice of seasoned political advisors, who felt that the new Commander-in-Chief should handpick his own staff, LBJ retained the entirety of JFK's cabinet and most of the late President's closest aides. Johnson enjoyed mixed success inspiring loyalty from the Kennedy men; many of them became devoted to the new President, while others were unable to accept the demise of the *New Frontier.*

A handful of Kennedy loyalists regularly supplied RFK with inside information from the Johnson White House. When he learned that RFK was kept apprised of the innermost details of his administration, LBJ grew even more suspicions about the Attorney General's ultimate political goals.

Kennedy loyalist, Arthur Schlesinger, Jr., later confided the injustices afflicted against LBJ: "To be charitable, the government would have been paralyzed if everyone had behaved like me and Ken O'Donnell."

While mournfully ambivalent, RFK was not entirely disinterested in the future. A month or so after JFK's assassination, Bobby instructed a small group of Kennedy loyalists to maintain their faith: "We worked hard to get where we are, and we can't let it all go to waste. My brother barely had a chance to get started. And, there is so much now to be done—for the Negros and the unemployed and the school kids and everyone else who is not getting a decent break in our society. This is what counts. The new fellow doesn't get this. He knows all about politics, and nothing about human beings."

The Attorney General reminded his loyal followers that the *New Frontier* would not officially end, until Lyndon Johnson was elected President in his own right: "The important thing for us to do now is to stick together. Our power will last for just eleven months. It will disappear the day of the election. What we have to do is use that power in these months to the best permanent advantage…There are a hundred men scattered throughout government, who are devoted to the purposes for which we came Washington. We must all stay in close touch, and not let them pick us off, one by one."

RFK privately criticized LBJ's management style: "He yells at his staff. He treats them just terribly; very mean. He's a very mean, mean figure."

RFK realized that many former *New Frontiersmen* were ill equipped to deal with Johnson's powerful personality: "He eats people up, even people who are considered strong figures. There's nothing left of them."

Kennedy was convinced that his own relationship with LBJ would never be cordial: "He wants people to kiss his behind all the time…I can't do that, and, so, therefore, I think it's probably difficult to get along."

Bobby was enraged when he learned that LBJ told Pierre Salinger that JFK's foreign policy might have led to his own assassination: "When I was young in Texas, I used to know a cross-eyed boy. His eyes were crossed, and so was his character. Sometimes, I think that, when you remember the assassination of Trujillo (the President of the Dominican Republic) and the assassination of Diem (South Vietnamese President), what happened to Kennedy may have been divine retribution."

RFK rarely passed up opportunities to impugn the character of the new President. Columnist, Rowland Evans, remembered private discussions with the Attorney General, shortly after JFK's death: "He'd just deluge me with stories about what a son of a bitch Lyndon was—how he was using Army personnel to spruce up his ranch, and things like that. The feeling was (one) of frustration and bitterness; they had built up this marvelous edifice, and just as they were completing it, they had to give it up."

RFK denigrated LBJ's leadership skills, which paled in comparison to his late brother's. In sharp contrast to President Kennedy, who openly debated policy decisions, RFK accused LBJ of acting as "his own judge and jury."

While his relationship with Robert Kennedy remained tense and volatile, President Johnson repeatedly accommodated the wishes of the Kennedy family. On December 23, 1963, Press Secretary, Pierre Salinger asked LBJ if several Kennedy family members and loyalists could travel with the President aboard Air Force One to the funeral of Pennsylvania Congressman, William Greene.

"Whatever you want, you get," Johnson told Salinger, "Just let them go with me. Wherever I go, Kenny O'Donnell and Ethel Kennedy go, and anybody else named Kennedy—or anybody that's ever smelled the Kennedy's. This is one team—period."

LBJ also forged a close relationship with Ted Kennedy, who had been elected to the Senate in 1962. Affable, with a self-deprecating sense of humor, Ted was much more like Jack than the brooding, grim faced Bobby. The younger Kennedy also understood LBJ's difficult position, succeeding a martyred hero.

In June of 1964, just seven months after JFK's assassination, Ted was seriously injured in a private plane crash in Massachusetts. The pilot and an aide were killed, while Kennedy suffered three fractured vertebrae, two broken ribs, a bruised kidney, a collapsed lung, and multiple lacerations.

In the wake of Ted's near fatal plane crash, RFK could not help but wonder if there was truly a *Kennedy curse:* "Somebody up there doesn't like us."

At the same time, Bobby displayed a brave front: "The Kennedys intend to stay in public life. Good luck is something you make and bad luck is something you endure."

RFK's Justice Department aide, Ramsey Clark, sensed the Attorney General's uncertainty about the future: "He was being pushed forward by a momentum outside him, carrying on less because he really wanted to than because people had told him he had to."

After Ted's tragic plane crash, President Johnson monitored the situation closely and maintained frequent contact with the Kennedy family. LBJ dispatched Army physicians to Massachusetts to provide consultation and treatment to the injured lawmaker.

When Ted was well enough to communicate by telephone, Johnson called him frequently. LBJ stressed the importance of cooperation between his administration and the Kennedy family, invoking JFK's memory: "The last thing that he would want us to do is to wind up disagreeing with each other. And, we're not going to do that. Nobody is going to come between us. And, anytime something happens that you or the Attorney General or your mother or your father or your sisters feel ought to go differently, you put on your hat and walk into that office (Oval Office) and sit down, and say your speech."

On September 29, 1964, President Johnson visited Ted, who was convalescing at New England Baptist Hospital in Boston. Arriving at 1:00

a.m., after an arduous campaign swing through the Northeast, LBJ kissed the bed-bound Kennedy on his forehead.

Ted appreciated LBJ's innate compassion, and tried to steer clear of the acrimonious personal and political feud between his brother and LBJ: "Johnson was capable of kindness toward my brother, and courtesy and political support. Toward me, President Johnson was consistently solicitous and friendly. I liked him, and always got along with him very well."

President Johnson extended his generosity to other members of the Kennedy family. In February of 1964, he named Sargent Shriver (RFK's brother-in-law) as the director of the newly established governmental agency directing the *War on Poverty*. As always, LBJ had ulterior motives, knowing that the appointment of another Kennedy family member to a prime position in his administration would annoy the Attorney General.

LBJ kept in touch with the family patriarch, Joseph Kennedy, making frequent telephone calls to the Ambassador's home in Cape Cod. Disabled from a massive stroke, the elder Kennedy could only communicate with Johnson in guttural monosyllables.

On January 1, 1964, President Johnson sent RFK a telegram, hoping to improve their tense, unhappy relationship: "I know how hard the past six weeks have been for you. Under the most trying circumstances, your first thoughts have been of your country. Your brother would have been very proud of the strength you have shown. As the New Year begins, I resolve to do my best to fulfill his trust in me. I will need your counsel and support."

RFK's return telegram was polite, but non-committal. The breech between the President and Attorney General appeared impassable.

LBJ summed up his frustrations: "I'd given three years of loyal service to Jack Kennedy. During all that time, I'd willingly stayed in the background...Then, Kennedy was killed, and I became the custodian of his will. I became the President. But, none of this seemed to register with Bobby Kennedy, who acted like he was the custodian of the Kennedy dream—some kind of rightful heir to the throne."

Presidential aide, George Christian, who was an eye witness to the sharp divide, believed LBJ's efforts were sincere, and could only wonder what might have been: "Lyndon Johnson made some overtures to Bobby Kennedy. That's why I think he would have loved it if Bobby had said, 'Mr. President, you are the President, and my brother is dead. He's not here, and consequently, you have my unyielding loyalty. We're going to march on together, and carry his program out.' I don't think he did that. I believe he sat in the Attorney General's office and grieved. He couldn't bring himself to saddle up and move on."

Lady Bird Johnson, whose gracefulness rarely translated into public or private criticism, described Robert Kennedy as an *enigma:* "I respect Bobby. In many ways, I admire him. But, I feel a peculiar unease around him, which I did not feel around his brother."

Unable to establish a bond with RFK, Johnson continued to court other Kennedy family members. In late March of 1964, LBJ phoned Ted Kennedy, praising him for his performance on the *NBC News* weekly program, *Meet the Press:* "The President (JFK) would have been so proud of you; I just thought you hit a home run every time they asked you a question."

In May, LBJ telephoned Joseph P. Kennedy: "You've got so much to be proud of, because Teddy is just burning up the Senate. He's the best thing they've got up there. Bobby is doing a wonderful job with the Civil Rights Bill, and I know you must be awfully proud of the training you gave those two boys."

As time passed, Johnson's patience for nostalgia from the *New Frontier* faded. Secret Service agents and White House chauffeurs, who dared to wear JFK's *PT-109* tie clips, were subject to vicious tongue lashings by LBJ.

Against the backdrop of his unremitting feud with Robert Kennedy, Lyndon Johnson was an activist President. One of his first initiatives involved the investigation of his predecessor's death. Jack Ruby's murder of Lee Harvey Oswald, while the accused presidential assassin was in the custody of the Dallas Police Department, gave root to many conspiracy theories. The Kennedy brothers' long list of enemies soon became prime suspects in the assassination, including such diverse characters as the Mafia, the Soviet Union, Fidel Castro, J. Edgar Hoover, and rogue members of the CIA. At first, the new President resolved to allow Texas law enforcement officials to handle the investigation, but soon realized that anything less than a comprehensive effort would suggest a government directed cover-up, at a time when emotions of the American people remained on edge. LBJ was also aware that some conspiracy theorists were already their fingers directly at him, since the murder was carried out in Johnson's home state.

Within days of the assassination, the Attorney General of Texas announced plans to open his own investigation, even before the FBI had compiled its report. Both houses of Congress also talked of convening special investigative committees. FBI Director, J. Edgar Hoover, warned LBJ that the investigation was at risk of turning into a "three ring circus." Though he opposed the idea on principle, Johnson soon determined that a federal commission was necessary to coordinate a single, comprehensive investigation into JFK's murder.

On Friday November 29, 1963, exactly one week after the assassination, President Johnson announced the formation of a blue ribbon panel, headed by Chief Justice Earl Warren. The *President's Commission on the Assassination of President Kennedy,* commonly known as the *Warren Commission,* spent the next *ten* months investigating JFK's murder (on September 27, 1964, the commission released its report, concluding that Lee Harvey Oswald was the *lone* assassin).

Lyndon Johnson was much different than John F. Kennedy, both in temperament and style. While JFK compartmentalized his life and made clear distinctions between work and play, LBJ labored day and night, often inviting his aides to eat dinner in the White House family quarters. He even expected his staffers to follow him into the bathroom to continue policy discussions.

Johnson's manners were a departure from those of his urbane and sophisticated predecessor. LBJ thought nothing of belching in public or lifting his shirt to display the scar from his gall bladder surgery. At state dinners, the President sometimes helped himself to food from the plates of fellow diners. On one occasion, while conducting an outdoor press conference at the LBJ Ranch, Johnson urinated in front of the assembled reporters.

Johnson loved to present White House guests with personalized gifts. The President delightedly dispensed bowls, cigarette lighters and wristwatches, all of which proudly displayed the initials *LBJ.* Johnson was particularly fond of his monogrammed electric toothbrushes: "I give these to friends, for then I know that they will think of me first thing in the morning and the last thing at night."

In exchange for his generosity, LBJ expected unwavering loyalty. Those who demonstrated disloyalty were subjected to blistering verbal assaults or were totally ignored for an indeterminate period of time—the infamous *Johnson Freeze.*

One of LBJ's most effective weapons was the telephone. Just as he had done while serving as Senate Majority Leader, Johnson thought nothing of calling members of Congress in the middle of the night to discuss pending legislation. In characteristic fashion Johnson stroked the egos of the more formidable lawmakers, and browbeat the meeker ones.

Johnson had a love affair with instant communication, installing telephones in his bathroom, bedroom, theater, cars, boats, and planes. Special rafts, designed to accommodate telephones, floated in the swimming pools at the White House and LBJ Ranch.

While criticized for his tyrannical methods, no one ever questioned LBJ's work ethic. Beginning his day at 6:00 a.m., the President read the *Washington Post, New York Times, Baltimore Sun, and Wall Street Journal* (aides also collected articles of interest from other mainstream newspapers for his review). From early morning until around four p.m. (with a working lunch crammed into the schedule), Johnson worked from the Oval Office. From four to five p.m., he retired to his bedroom for a nap, before beginning the *second half* of his work day. LBJ often remained in the West Wing until after ten o'clock, before eating a later dinner.

Besieged by paper work, Johnson developed his own style for dealing with written correspondence. After reviewing a memorandum, the President wrote across the bottom of the page, *yes, no,* or *see me.*

At the outset of the *New Frontier* (lasting just over one thousand days, it was the sixth briefest presidency in history), John F. Kennedy had articulated a bold agenda—an increase in the minimum wage, health insurance for senior citizens, fair housing laws, a tax cut, and aid to economically depressed areas. By the time of his death, only the latter (the *Area Redevelopment Bill*) had passed Congress. A coalition of conservative Southern Democrats and minority party Republicans blocked many of JFK's liberal legislative proposals from leaving committee. During the 87th Congress, only *304* of President Kennedy's *653* bills were enacted into law.

"I can't get a Mother's Day resolution through that God damn Congress," JFK bitterly complained to an adviser.

After ascending to the presidency, Lyndon Johnson skillfully marshaled passage of many of Kennedy's stalled legislative proposals. By the end of 1964, JFK's proposed tax cut and Civil Rights bills had already been enacted into law.

Once he had fulfilled the major legislative goals of the *New Frontier,* LBJ was free to introduce his own *Great Society* (the name originated from JFK/LBJ speechwriter, Richard Goodwin; Johnson had considered calling his program *The Better Deal*), with the ambitious goals of launching a *War on Poverty,* and providing universal medical care for the elderly, disabled, and poor (*Medicare* and *Medicaid*). Other *Great Society* programs included the *Economic Opportunity Act,* the *Job Corps,* and the *National Endowments for the Arts and Humanities.* LBJ's far-reaching, liberal domestic agenda rivaled Franklin Roosevelt's *New Deal.*

The Johnson legacy began on December 17, 1963, when he signed into law the *Clean Air Act;* the first significant legislation specifically designed to combat air pollution.

On January 8, 1964, the new President delivered his first State of the Union Address, outlining a bold vision for America: "Let this session of Congress be known as the session, which did more for Civil Rights than the last hundred sessions combined; as the session that enacted the most far-reaching tax cut of our time; as the session, which declared all out war on human poverty and unemployment in these United States; as the session, which finally recognized the health needs of all of our older citizens; as the session, which reformed our tangled transportation and transit policies; as the session, which achieved the most effective, efficient foreign aid program ever; and as the session, which helped to build more homes and more schools and more libraries and more hospitals than any single session of Congress in the history of our republic."

Republican Senator, Barry Goldwater, whose ideology was fundamentally opposed to governmental expansion, was alarmed by LBJ's State of the Union Address: "He out *Roosevelted* Roosevelt."

In order to appease fiscally conservative lawmakers and secure passage of JFK's tax cut bill, President Johnson trimmed the budgets of selected agencies. The *97.9 billion* dollar budget for 1964 included spending reductions that pleased Liberals in Congress—*one billion* dollars in defense, *600 million* dollars in the space program, and *300 million* in atomic energy.

In the first year of LBJ's tax cuts, the American economy blossomed. The *Gross National Product (GNP)* increased from *569.7 billion* dollars to *631.2 billion* dollars, while unemployment dropped from *4.1 million* to *3.1 million.* At the same time, government revenues increased by *7.5 billion dollars.*

On May 22, 1964, Lyndon Johnson formally introduced the *Great Society* during a speech at the University of Michigan: "We have the opportunity to move not only toward the rich society and the powerful society, but upward to the *Great Society.* The *Great Society* rests on abundance and liberty for all...It is a challenge constantly renewed, beckoning us toward a destiny, where the meaning of our lives matches the marvelous products of our labor…Will you join in the battle to build the *Great Society*, to prove that our material progress is only the foundation on which we will build a richer life of mind and spirit?"

Throughout his life, Lyndon Johnson had witnessed the twin evils of poverty and racism, and his determination to combat those societal plagues transcended political rhetoric. In March of 1949, LBJ was one of very few Southern politicians to go on record as a supporter of equal rights: "Racial prejudice is dangerous, because it is a disease of the majority endangering minority groups…For those who keep any group in our nation in bondage; I have no sympathy or tolerance."

President Kennedy had introduced Civil Rights legislation in the summer of 1963, but the bill stalled in the Senate, where Southern Democrats had threatened to filibuster. LBJ was aware that he would ultimately be held responsible for the success or failure of the historic legislative proposal: "I had to produce a Civil Rights Bill that was even stronger than the one they'd have gotten if Kennedy had lived. Without this, I'd be dead before I could even begin."

To secure passage of the controversial bill, LBJ cobbled together a legislative coalition of Liberal, non-Southern Democrats and Republicans. The President actively pressured Republican Congressmen and Senators, telling House Minority Leader, Charles Halleck: "I'm going to lay it on the line…Now you're either for Civil Rights, or you're not…You're either the party of Lincoln or you're not…By God, put up or shut up!"

When asked if a native-born Southerner could be entrusted to navigate passage of the Civil Rights Bill, Johnson was well prepared. A correspondent for the *St. Louis Post Dispatch* posed a seemingly difficult question: "Mr. President, I don't understand. You didn't have a very sterling, progressive record on Civil Rights in the House or in the Senate, and yet here, you have thrown the full weight of your presidency behind the Civil Rights movement. Would you, please sir, explain the contradiction?"

"Well, Jim, some people get a chance, late in life, to correct the sins of their youth, and very few get a chance as big as the White House," LBJ calmly replied.

In a later interview with a Texas reporter, Johnson explained his strategy: "Now I knew that as President, I couldn't make people want to integrate their schools or open their schools to blacks, but I could make them feel guilty for not doing it, and I believed it was my moral responsibility to do precisely that—to use the moral persuasion of my office to make people feel that segregation was a curse they'd carry with them to their graves."

Temporarily putting aside their personal differences, Lyndon Johnson and Robert Kennedy managed to work together to transform the ideal of racial equality into reality. The President insisted that the Attorney General be involved in all negotiations with key legislative figures. While RFK's passion for ending segregation was not as enduring as Johnson's, he was nonetheless eager to see his late brother's Civil Rights Bill enacted into law. The combined efforts of the two sworn enemies resulted in an historic triumph.

In April, President Johnson ventured into the Deep South and courageously promoted Civil Rights. Speaking in Atlanta and Gainesville, Georgia, LBJ confronted segregationists: "Full participation in our society can no longer be denied to men because of their race or their religion or the region in which they live."

Southern lawmakers were accustomed to using the filibuster to prevent Civil Rights legislation from coming to a vote on the Senate floor. LBJ, a master Senate parliamentarian, convinced Majority Leader, Mike Mansfield, to appoint Minnesota Senator, Hubert Humphrey, to manage the Civil Rights bill. With LBJ's guiding hand, Humphrey, whose passion for Civil Rights was legendary, amassed enough votes to invoke cloture on June 10, 1964 (by a vote of *seventy-one* to *twenty-nine*) ending an *eighty-three* day filibuster (the longest in Senate history).

On June 19, 1964, one year to the day after John F. Kennedy had sent his Civil Rights Bill to Congress, the Senate passed the legislation by vote of *seventy-three* to *twenty-seven*. LBJ was justifiably proud: "This has been a year without precedent in the history of our relations between the Executive and Legislative branches of government."

The historic legislation forbade racial discrimination in places of public accommodation; authorized the Attorney General to institute suits to desegregate public facilities; banned employers, labor unions, and employment agencies from engaging in discrimination by race or sex; established the *Equal Opportunity Commission*; and prohibited discrimination by state and local government authorities utilizing federal funds.

On July 2nd, in a televised ceremony in the East Room of the White House, President Johnson signed into law the *Civil Rights Act of 1964*. LBJ passed out commemorative ink pens to key operatives. With mixed emotions, Robert Kennedy stood in the back of the room during the signing ceremony. Proud of his own efforts, RFK was resentful that his brother did not receive more credit for the historic legislation. An alert Civil Rights activist noticed that Kennedy was becoming lost in the shuffle, and led the Attorney General to the front, where President Johnson presented him with a handful of commemorative signing pens for Justice Department officials.

Lyndon Johnson had been the champion and driving force behind the groundbreaking legislation. Georgia Senator and staunch segregationist, Richard Russell, summed up the defeat: "We could have beaten Kennedy on Civil Rights, but we can't beat Lyndon."

LBJ was hailed as a hero to the Civil Rights movement. The *Congressional Quarterly* proclaimed the new bill as "the most sweeping Civil Rights measure to clear either house of Congress in the twentieth century."

While enjoying his triumph, LBJ realized the new law would create long-standing difficulties for the Democratic Party: "We may win this legislation, but we're going to lose the South for a generation."

Johnson's warning was prescient. By the late 1960s, the Republicans had established a foothold in the Deep South, and, four decades later, remains the dominant party in that region.

Lyndon Johnson's domestic policy achievements overshadowed his less successful foreign policy initiatives. With a lack of experience in foreign affairs, LBJ was heavily dependent on the guidance of military, intelligence, and State Department officials. *New York Times* writer, James Reston, surmised that Johnson was, at heart, *insecure* about his foreign policy skills.

Early in his presidency, LBJ was confronted with a serious situation in Panama. A tense confrontation erupted between native Panamanians and American citizens in the area surrounding the Canal Zone. The Johnson Administration brokered a negotiated settlement, while asserting that the United States would take full measures to defend the Panama Canal. In a style reminiscent of his days of wheeling and dealing in the Senate, LBJ intimidated the Panamanian government by suggesting that United States might seek construction of a second canal in Nicaragua.

Reluctantly, LBJ confronted the growing crisis in Southeast Asia. The Communist- backed North Vietnamese showed no signs of abandoning their quest to unite the country under totalitarian rule, while the hapless South Vietnamese government drifted through a series of corrupt, ineffective leaders. While LBJ had serious doubts that the United States would ultimately prevail in a conflict dominated by guerilla warfare, he also subscribed to the *Domino Theory,* and was fearful of the spread of communism into the Third World.

"Johnson inherited a God awful mess, eminently more dangerous that the one Kennedy had inherited from Eisenhower," Secretary of Defense, Robert McNamara, later opined.

Not surprisingly, Robert Kennedy was a major ingredient in LBJ's paranoia about Vietnam. Johnson was convinced that if he ordered American forces out of the troubled region, RFK would be "out in front, leading the fight against me, telling everyone that I had betrayed John Kennedy's commitment to Vietnam."

Throughout his presidency, Lyndon Johnson cultivated a love/hate relationship with the press. As long as reporters and columnists magnified his accomplishments, LBJ remained happy. Unlike JFK, who disarmed critics with his wry sense of humor, Johnson was enraged by critical news reports.

NBC newsman, John Chancellor, once described Johnson as a "media freak." LBJ installed a wire service Teletype machine in the Oval Office, where he continuously checked reports from *UPI, AP,* and *Reuters.* Adjacent to the news ticker, a console was constructed, containing three television sets (Johnson had an identical set up in his White House bedroom). The President's aides marveled at his ability to simultaneously watch the nightly news broadcasts from all three major networks, and keep up with what each anchor was reporting. If Johnson did not believe the early evening news reports were accurate, he would often telephone the news director and demand a retraction during the 11:00 p.m. broadcast.

NBC News anchor, David Brinkley, remembered LBJ complaining about one of his "favorite hatreds—the leaker." Johnson told Brinkley that when he was deciding on a cabinet level appointment, he would instruct the prospective appointee to keep quiet until the President made a public announcement. If Johnson read anything about the potential appointment in newspapers, he would withdraw the job offer: "If I can't trust him now, how can I trust him when he joins the government?"

CBS News anchor, Walter Cronkite, who described LBJ as "larger than life," recalled the challenges faced when covering the mercurial Johnson. During the 1960 campaign, while interviewing the vice-presidential candidate at the LBJ Ranch in Texas, Cronkite noticed that Johnson's gaze was fixated on the newsman's *Rolex* wristwatch.

"Where did you get that watch?" LBJ interrupted the questioning.

Cronkite explained that is was a gift from the President of *Rolex*.

"That son of a gun told me that he only gave those watches to heads of states, and such," Johnson indignantly complained.

On April 28, 1964, President Johnson hosted a gathering of bankers and businessmen in the Rose Garden. When his pet beagle approached, LBJ lifted the dog by his ears: "If you ever follow dogs, you like to hear them yelp…it does them good to bark."

An *Associated Press* photographer captured the scene, which was released to newspapers and television stations across the country. Dog lovers were appalled by LBJ's callous actions.

"How painful it is to any living creature to be picked up by the ears," the Director of the *Chicago Humane Society* proclaimed.

Afterwards, Johnson complained to his Press Secretary, George Reedy: "Hell, the pictures show that the dog was standing on his hind heels, and there's not anything that hurts him doing that!"

Reedy was certain the controversy would die a natural death, but LBJ could not be comforted, and inquired about the name of the reporter who wrote the story accompanying the infamous photographs: "Who was it? Doug Carnell?"

"Yes, sir," Reedy calmly replied.

"Well, I want to know what that son of a bitch looks like, and I want to give him the silent treatment for a while," Johnson, groused.

Later, Johnson raged about the incident to Senate Majority Leader, Mike Mansfield: "I stand my damned dogs up and lift them by the ears, so an *AP* photographer can get a picture, and another little guy that didn't know what he was doing—he writes a story that (says) it is cruel to dogs. Hell, I know more about hounds than he ever heard of! But, they've got every dog lover in the country raising Hell, thinking I'm burning them at the stake. It's all just a big play about nothing— because that's all they can get."

Unable to let go of the beagle story, Johnson ruminated about it during a conversation with Senator Hubert Humphrey: "All I was doing was holding the beagle up, so they could get his front in the picture, instead of his ass. They got his ass for ten days here, and I wanted to show them a good, well-formed head. And, besides, when a hound dog barks—I don't want to be in the paper on this, but that's his pleasure, that's not his hurting!"

Johnson was also annoyed by a feature story that appeared in *Time* magazine in early April of 1964. The article, entitled *Mr. President, You're Fun,* chronicled Johnson racing around the LBJ Ranch is his Lincoln Continental, at speeds up to ninety miles per hour, while sipping from a paper cup filled with beer.

Angered by the *Time* article, LBJ took his frustrations out on his Press Secretary, George Reedy: "All of our people talk too much…just whap-whap-whap-whap-whap—big hydrophobia of the mouth. We've just got to stop opening our mouths!"

Johnson advised Reedy on how to deal with the press corps: "This crowd here, you got to understand, they're not the masters of the White House. They're just the servants, and we give them what we want to give them."

LBJ carefully scripted his press conferences, and often made sure that his prepared remarks occupied at least half of the allotted time, to minimize questions from reporters. If media coverage was generally positive, Johnson might hold one or more press conferences per week. Conversely, if the President felt he was being treated unfairly, he would sometimes go several weeks between formal press conferences.

To the dismay of White House correspondents, Johnson failed to give advance notice of his press conferences; to keep the newspapers and networks from bringing in specialty reporters, who were well versed on particular topics, and might pose questions that the President could not easily answer. LBJ also refused to release his travel schedule in advance. On numerous occasions, White House correspondents were forced to scramble, at the last minute, to accompany the President on trips outside of Washington D.C.

On June 9, 1964, the *Washington Star* published a two-page article, entitled *The Johnson Money.* The story estimated LBJ's net worth at *nine million* dollars, "amassed almost entirely while Mr. Johnson was in public office." LBJ had long maintained that Lady Bird was the true manager of their radio and television stations, and was directly responsible for their enormous success. LBJ, however, was actively involved in the business operations throughout his political career. After he ascended to the presidency, Johnson adamantly refused to place his family's private holdings in a blind trust, as recommended by his legal counsel (in sharp contrast to JFK, who had donated his 100,000 dollar per year presidential salary to charity).

Since the President was responsible for appointing members to the *Federal Communications Commission (FCC)*, the potential for conflict of interest was very real. Nonetheless, Johnson was unwilling to divorce public service from private sector profiteering. As window dressing, the *LBJ Company* was renamed the *Texas Broadcasting Company* after Johnson became President.

Johnson complained that the newspaper story about his business ventures was "very vicious." LBJ angrily suggested that the article had been "planted" by friends of Robert Kennedy, who were "controlling" the newspaper—an unsubstantiated product of Johnson's vivid imagination.

In reality, the only significant error in the *Washington Star* article was an underestimation of LBJ's net worth, which was closer to the range of *fourteen* to *twenty million* dollars.

While he mostly distrusted the press, Johnson was a master at self-promotion. Following his 1964 State of the Union Address, he bragged to syndicated columnist, Drew Pearson: "I got *eighty-one* applauses in *2900* words. It was a *twenty-five* minute speech, and it took *forty-one*, because of the applauses...Did you ever hear anything like that?"

LBJ was a monumental headache for those responsible for his protection. In the wake of his predecessor's assassination, Johnson lost faith in the Secret Service, and often asked the FBI to assign an agent to accompany him on out of town trips. The President complained loudly to Secret Service Director, James Rowley: "Your damn Secret Service car stays right behind me every trip...You're going to kill more people than you save..."

During a telephone conversation with Senator Mike Mansfield, LBJ offered a less than flattering assessment of his protective detail: "Between us, the Secret Service that covers me are a fine and dedicated group, but my judgment is that they are more likely to get me killed, as they are to protect me. They're just not heavy thinkers; they're like the average cop..."

"They never do anything but endanger you; they notify everybody in town what time you're coming, how you're coming, where you're coming and how to kill you, if you want to..." Johnson complained.

The 1964 presidential election was an opportunity for Lyndon Johnson to obtain a mandate for his *Great Society*. Robert Kennedy, on the other hand, wanted out of the Johnson Administration, and contemplated running for the United States Senate. The Kennedy family maintained a legal residence in New York, providing RFK with an opportunity to run for office in a powerful state.

Many Kennedy loyalists began to actively promoted RFK for the vice-presidency. While Robert Kennedy did not relish the idea of playing second fiddle to Lyndon Johnson, he harbored remote fantasies of serving as an influential Vice-President with unprecedented powers. He also realized the vice-presidency would be an ideal launch pad for his own run at the White House in 1968 or 1972. Furthermore, as Lyndon Johnson had discovered months earlier, the Vice-President was only a heartbeat away from the presidency.

In his heart, RFK knew that LBJ wanted no part of him on the ticket, as he privately shared with Ken O'Donnell: "Let's face it, if Johnson had to choose between Ho Chi Minh and yours truly for the vice-presidential slot, he'd go with Ho Chi Minh."

Lyndon Johnson was determined to chart his own course, independent from RFK: "Every day, as soon as I opened the papers or turned on the television, there was something about Bobby Kennedy—there was some person or group talking about what a great Vice-President he'd make. Somehow, it just didn't seem fair. I'd given three years of loyal service to Jack Kennedy. During all that time, I'd willingly stayed in the background—I knew it was *his* presidency, not mine. If I disagreed with him, I did it in private, not in public. And then, Kennedy was killed and I became custodian of his will. *I* became the President. But, none of this seemed to register with Bobby Kennedy, who acted like *he* was the custodian of the Kennedy dream—some kind of rightful heir to the throne. It just didn't seem fair. I'd waited my turn. Bobby should've waited his. But, he and the Kennedy people wanted it *now*. A tidal wave of letters and memos about how great a Vice-president Bobby would be, swept over me. But, no matter what, I simply couldn't let it happen. With Bobby on the ticket, I'd never know if I would be elected on my own."

In his angrier moments, Johnson was petulant: "If they try to push Bobby down my throat for Vice-President, I'll tell them to nominate him for the presidency, and leave me out of it."

In February of 1964, Paul Corbin, a member of the Democratic National Committee and a fanatical Kennedy supporter, brought the issue of RFK's vice-presidential candidacy to the forefront. Corbin, who had converted to Catholicism, so that Bobby and Ethel Kennedy could become his Godparents, launched a write in campaign for RFK in the New Hampshire Democratic Presidential Primary. Corbin hoped that a strong showing by Kennedy in this early primary state would force LBJ to choose him as his running mate. Johnson summoned RFK to the White House, for what Bobby recalled was a "bitter, mean conversation."

Johnson ordered the Attorney General to put a stop to Corbin's write in campaign. RFK defended his protégé: "He was loyal to President Kennedy. He'll be loyal to you."

"Get him out of there. Do you understand? I want you to get rid of him," Johnson demanded.

"I don't want to have this kind of conversation with you. He was appointed by President Kennedy, who thought he was good," Kennedy replied.

"Do it. President Kennedy isn't President, anymore—I am," Johnson bluntly asserted.

"I know you're President, and don't ever talk to me again like that!' Kennedy snapped back.

Johnson reminded RFK that he had done him a *favor* by sending him to Indonesia to assist with foreign policy, suggesting that Kennedy should be more grateful and cooperative.

"A favor? I don't want you to do any more favors for me, ever," RFK declared,   before angrily exiting the Oval Office.

When he returned to his office in the Justice Department, Kennedy angrily confided to an aide: "I'll tell you one thing; this relationship can't last much longer!"

LBJ ultimately won the New Hampshire primary, but RFK received an impressive number of write in votes. Speculation about a Johnson/Kennedy ticket would not go away, even after the President had Paul Corbin fired by the Democratic National Committee.

RFK also received encouragement from individuals outside his inner circle. World War II hero, General Douglas MacArthur, actively encouraged Kennedy to seek the vice-presidency: "Take it—take it. He won't live. He gambled on your brother and won. You gamble on him, and you'll win."

Kennedy was aware of Johnson's dilemma over picking the most suitable running mate: "I think he's hysterical about how he's going to try to avoid me. That's what he spends most of his time on, from what I understand—figuring out how he's going to avoid me."

"Our President (JFK) was a gentleman and a human being...This man is not…He's mean, bitter, vicious—an animal in many ways," RFK bitterly complained to an aide.

Kennedy nonetheless remained ambivalent, and provided Johnson with an excellent opportunity to end speculation about the vice-presidency, when he volunteered to serve as Ambassador to South Vietnam.

"I just wanted to make sure you understand that if you wished me to go to Vietnam in any capacity, I would be glad to go. It is obviously the most important problem facing the United States, and if you felt I could help, I am at your service," RFK wrote the President.

RFK's offer was tempting to LBJ, as it would have removed Kennedy from the election year landscape. Johnson, however, feared if RFK served as American Ambassador to South Vietnam, he would seize the spotlight in American foreign policy. LBJ also worried about Kennedy's safety in such a volatile region of the world: "I would be accusing myself for the rest of my life, if something happened to him out there."

In the end, Johnson politely declined RFK's offer.

LBJ briefly flirted with the prospect of offering the vice-presidency to Bobby's brother-in-law, Sargent Shriver, who was already serving as LBJ's director of the *War on Poverty*. An unhappy RFK understood that if Johnson chose Shriver, he would have a "Kennedy, without having a *bad* Kennedy."

Johnson used the situation to send a veiled message to the Attorney General. LBJ explained to Shriver the hazards of lobbying for the vice-presidency: "I think that a man who runs for Vice-President is a very foolish man. The man who runs away from it is very wise. Don't you ever be a candidate, and don't let anybody else be a candidate. Tell them, whoever runs for it, never gets it."

The possibility of Shriver serving as LBJ's running mate was quickly squelched by RFK. Bobby confronted his brother-in-law during a family weekend at Cape Cod, informing him that if anyone in the Kennedy family were going to serve as Vice-President, it would *not* be Shriver.

By June of 1964, Lyndon Johnson's approval ratings were at *seventy-five* percent, and it appeared unlikely that he would *need* Robert Kennedy to win the election. On July 15th, Barry Goldwater was nominated by the Republican Party as its presidential nominee. The ultra-conservative Goldwater's tendency to *shoot from the hip* was a fatal flaw for a presidential candidate, and LBJ was poised to win nearly every Democratic vote, along with those of many moderate and liberal Republicans.

LBJ decided the time had come to end all speculation about a Johnson/

Kennedy ticket. On July 29th, the President invited RFK to meet with him in the Oval Office. LBJ sat behind his desk, in a formal manner, reading from a memo prepared by his legal counsel.

"I have concluded that it would be inadvisable for you to be the Democratic candidate for Vice-President in this year's election. I am sure that you will understand the basis of my decision, and factors that have entered into it, because President Kennedy had to make a similar decision in 1960," Johnson explained.

LBJ told Kennedy that he had a "promising future," and suggested he serve as Chairman of the Democratic National Committee. As the meeting drew to a close, a disappointed RFK told Johnson: "I could have helped you."

LBJ was glad to have the difficult confrontation behind him, and hoped Kennedy would voluntarily and publicly announce that he was no longer interested in the vice-presidency. During an off the record discussion with three White House news reporters, LBJ made the mistake of embellishing the story about his meeting with RFK. LBJ mimicked Kennedy "gulping" when he learned that he would not be offered the vice-presidency. The story soon made its way back to RFK, who defiantly refused to make a formal statement of withdrawal.

LBJ subsequently telephoned RFK and denied making any statements about their private discussion concerning the vice-presidency. Kennedy bluntly accused the President of lying. Caught in a trap of his own making, Johnson then told RFK that he had "maybe forgotten" a conversation related to the earlier meeting, but would needed to check his office records.

When Kennedy refused to take his name out of the running, a frustrated and angry LBJ was forced to issue a public statement: "In reference to the selection of a candidate for Vice-President on the Democratic ticket, I have reached the conclusion that it would be inadvisable for me to recommend any member of the Cabinet or any of those who meet regularly with the Cabinet."

The improbable notion of a Johnson/Kennedy ticket had finally been laid to rest. RFK jokingly sent telegrams to Sargent Shriver, Secretary of Defense McNamara, Secretary of Agriculture Freeman, Secretary of State Rusk, and United Nations Ambassador, Adlai Stevenson: "Sorry I took so many of you nice fellows over the side with me."

In a private discussion with a Justice Department aide, Robert Kennedy sarcastically contemplated his political future: "Now, I have to decide what to do. Ah, what the Hell, let's go form our own country."

Lyndon Johnson was finally free to build his future without any further debt to the Kennedy clan.

Chapter 13

What Lyndon wanted, Lyndon got

Lyndon Johnson was relieved to have Robert Kennedy out of the vice-presidential equation: "Now that damn albatross is off my neck."

The prospects of his election all but certain, LBJ was free to choose a loyal and subservient running mate. With Barry Goldwater as the November opponent, Johnson did not need a running mate with broad appeal. It was crucial, however, that the vice-presidential nominee be loyal; a personality trait that the President valued above all others. LBJ summarized the job requirement in simple terms: "I want his pecker in my pocket."

Johnson was determined to make 1964 a memorable presidential election year and generate a mandate for his populist agenda. In characteristic fashion, LBJ orchestrated suspense by waiting until convention time to select a running mate.

LBJ added a political feather to his cap in April of 1964, by successfully mediating a nationwide railroad strike. *New York Times* journalist, James Reston, praised the President's "tireless negotiating skill," reporting that Johnson was "one of the vital natural resources of this country."

Johnson's statesmanship contrasted sharply with Goldwater's right wing ideology. Many political pundits were predicting a Johnson landslide in November.

For political reasons, Johnson hoped to delay as many controversial decisions as possible, until after Election Day. The growing conflict in Southeast Asia, however, would not go away.

Prior to 1964, Vietnam had been an afterthought to most Americans. Post World War II, the Asian nation had been a French Indochinese colony. In 1954, the French were driven out by Vietnam's freedom-seeking natives, and the region was partitioned into two countries—North Vietnam (communist controlled) and South Vietnam (pledged to democracy and capitalism).

In 1954, President Eisenhower, who was a disciple of the *Domino Theory* of encroaching communism, sent the first American *military advisers* (approximately *200*) to South Vietnam. The advisers were charged with helping South Vietnam train its democratically controlled army.

Eisenhower's successor, John F. Kennedy, followed the recommendations of his Cold Warrior advisors, and increased the number of military advisers from *685* to *18,000* during the course of his administration. In October of 1962, JFK authorized the use of defoliants to destroy Vietnamese crops and vegetation to combat the infiltration of Viet Cong guerillas into South Vietnam.

JFK, a decorated World War II veteran, had received his political upbringing during the Cold War era, and was schooled in fervid anti-Communism. At the same time, Kennedy was a student of history and, in June of 1961, listened carefully to French President, Charles deGaulle's advice concerning Vietnam: "You will find that intervention in this area will be an endless engagement. Once a nation has been aroused, no foreign power, however strong, can impose its will upon it. You will sink into a bottomless military and political quagmire, however much you spend in men and money."

In October of that same year, the President received a similar (and eerily prophetic) warning from Undersecretary of State, George Ball: "Within five years, we'll have *300,000* men in the paddies and jungles, and never find them again. That was the French experience. Vietnam is the worst possible terrain, both from a physical and political point of view."

While JFK acknowledged the warnings from deGaulle and Ball, he was wary of the political ramifications from appearing soft against Communism. In December of 1962, Kennedy had shared his concerns with Senate Majority Leader, Mike Mansfield (an early anti-war advocate): "If I tried to pull out completely now from Vietnam, we would have another Joe McCarthy Red Scare on our hands, but I can do it after I'm reelected So, we had better make damn sure I am reelected."

On December 22, 1961, Specialist Fourth Class, James Thomas Davis, of Livingston, Tennessee became the first American to die in the jungles of South Vietnam. Three other American military advisers were killed in January of 1963, when their helicopter was shot down by Viet Cong guerillas at Ap Bac, some fifty miles from Saigon. While the first American casualties marked a turning point in the conflict in Southeast Asia, no one could yet predict that a full scale ground war was only two years in the future.

In the final weeks of his presidency, JFK appeared reluctant to escalate American military involvement in Southeast Asia. On September 2, 1963, Kennedy told *CBS News* anchor, Walter Cronkite, that the South Vietnamese ultimately controlled their own fate: "In the final analysis, it's their war. They are the ones who have to win it or lose it."

In a conversation with White House advisor, Arthur Schlesinger Jr., JFK indicated a reluctance to send combat troops to Vietnam, regardless of South Vietnam's desire for greater American involvement: "They want a force of American troops…The troops will march in; the bands will play; the crowds will cheer; and four days later everyone will have forgotten. Then, we will be told we have to send in more troops. It's like taking a drink. The effect wears off, and you have to take another."

Historian and biographer of John F. Kennedy and Lyndon Johnson, Robert Dallek, summarized the Kennedy Administration's role in Vietnam: "No one can prove, of course, what Kennedy would have done about Vietnam between 1964 and 1968. His actions and statements, however, are suggestive of a carefully managed stand down from the sort of involvement that occurred under LBJ."

On October 11, 1963, five weeks before he was assassinated, President Kennedy signed *National Security Action Memorandum 263,* authorizing the withdrawal of *1000* American advisers from Vietnam by the end of the year. Based upon this limited withdrawal order, a handful of JFK's advisers along with a cadre of historians, have concluded that he planned a total withdrawal, once re-elected in 1964. Obviously, Kennedy's true agenda will never be known, but during LBJ's presidency, Vietnam soon became a household name, as the United States stepped more deeply into a *no win* scenario in Southeast Asia.

North Vietnam was controlled by its charismatic and determined communist leader, Ho Chi Minh. Ho was the hero of the French Colonial War—a fearless leader, who had expelled foreigners. South Vietnam's President, Ngo Dinh Diem, was much less revered by his countrymen. A Catholic in a country of Buddhists, Diem was viewed by many natives as a tyrant, who had been installed by foreigners. In early November of 1963, Diem was assassinated during a military coup, and American leaders hoped the new South Vietnamese government would gain broader support from its citizens—such dreams proved illusory, as a series of corrupt and ineffectual leaders attempted to rule the country.

The Army of the Republic of Vietnam (AVRN), charged with the defense of South Vietnam, was tainted by corruption and incompetence. To complicate matters, AVRN military personnel showed little appetite for fighting their northern enemy. In the end, America's stated goal of "helping the South Vietnamese help themselves" proved fallacious.

In March of 1964, Secretary of Defense, Robert McNamara visited South Vietnam, hoping to provide President Johnson with an assessment of the ruling government. After returning home, McNamara informed LBJ that the situation in Southeast Asia was "unquestionably worse," and the country's ineffectual and corrupt post-Diem government did not enjoy the wide support of its citizens.

French President, Charles de Gaulle, advised the United States to remove its military forces from Southeast Asia, and recommended the *unification* and *neutralization* of North and South Vietnam.

By May of 1964, the CIA had informed President Johnson that if the South Vietnamese military did not improve their offensive and defensive capabilities, the capacity to control the spread of Communism was *untenable.* That same month, Robert Kennedy offered LBJ gentle, but unsolicited advice about the turmoil in Vietnam: "I would think that the war would never be won militarily. Where it's going to be won, really, is the political war."

In the summer of 1964, the crisis in Vietnam reached an important milestone, just as LBJ was preparing to accept his party's presidential nomination. On August 2nd, an American Destroyer, the *U.S.S. Maddox*, was allegedly fired on by North Vietnamese torpedo boats. The American vessel was cruising in international waters, just off the coast of North Vietnam, at the time of the supposed attack. Four American fighter jets, launched from a nearby aircraft carrier, the *Ticonderoga*, attacked and damaged the North Vietnamese torpedo boats. On August 4th, a second American ship reported that it was under torpedo attack. In retaliation, the United States launched offensive air strikes against North Vietnamese coastal targets, followed by President Johnson's now infamous declaration: "We seek no wider war."

With the escalation of hostilities in Southeast Asia, LBJ sought Congressional backing for American military action. The President wanted a broad war-making resolution: "Like grandma's nightgown—it covered everything."

On August 7, 1964, the *Gulf of Tonkin Resolution* (named for the body of water where the alleged torpedo attacks occurred) passed the House of Representatives by a vote of *416-0*, and was approved by the Senate (*ninety-eight to two*). Having debated the resolution for less than a day, Congress gave the President "all necessary measures to repel any armed attacks against the forces of the United States."

While no American ground troops had yet engaged in battle, Johnson now had blanket authorization and broad discretion to take military action against North Vietnam. He had skillfully maneuvered Congress into shared responsibility for any future war, evoking the memory of his predecessor: "I think President Kennedy felt very strongly that we should not permit Southeast Asia to fall into the hands of Communists."

Nearly five decades later, the evidence supporting a *second* torpedo attack is thin, and many analysts believe the crews aboard the American ships overreacted to the site of approaching North Vietnamese patrol boats. Some historians and military analysts now question the validity of the *first* attack, believing the Gulf of Tonkin Resolution was based on a series of *non-events*.

A month and half after the incidents in the Gulf of Tonkin, LBJ, himself, privately shared his doubts with Secretary of Defense, Robert McNamara: "When we get through with all the firing, we concluded maybe they hadn't fired at all."

Of particular note, Congress and the American public were unaware of American provocation leading up to the alleged North Vietnamese attacks. Utilizing Special Forces parachutists and frogmen, the U.S had been engaging in covert military actions (code named *34A*) against targets in North Vietnam. The enemy was keenly aware of the secret operations, and was vigilant and trigger happy in the months prior to the reported attacks on American vessels.

After the second Gulf of Tonkin incident, American aircraft attacked four enemy PT boat bases and an oil depot. During an off the record interview with a reporter, Lyndon Johnson could not contain his bellicose enthusiasm: "I didn't just screw Ho, I cut his pecker off!"

LBJ's defiance was bolstered by polling data showing *eighty-five* percent of the American public approved of the retaliatory attacks, and *seventy-two* percent approved of the President's overall performance in Vietnam.

The nomination of Lyndon Johnson at the 1964 Democratic National Convention should have been little more than a formality. LBJ, however, could not shed his paranoia, fearing Robert Kennedy would somehow *steamroll* the convention and deny him the nomination. The President was determined to keep anyone from disrupting his anticipated triumph, and ordered his FBI liaison to the White House, Cartha DeLoach, to implement a clandestine spy operation at the convention in Atlantic City.

At first, J. Edgar Hoover, was appalled at the notion of using FBI agents in such a blatant political fashion, telling Deloach: "Lyndon is way out of line on this one."

Unwilling to risk LBJ's ire, Hoover soon acquiesced to the President's demands. Hoover had enjoyed a collegial relationship with Johnson, and the two men had once been next door neighbors. After JFK's assassination, Hoover once again had direct access to the White House, without having to use Robert Kennedy as an intermediary. Bound by their mutual dislike of RFK, Hoover and Johnson grew even closer.

RFK was aware of Hoover's machinations, complaining that the FBI Director sent the President regular reports about RFK's supposed plans to *overthrow* LBJ and "take the nomination away from him."

In appreciation for Hoover's loyalty, LBJ eventually issued an Executive Order exempting the FBI Director from mandatory federal government retirement at age sixty-five, allowing him to remain in office for as long as he wanted. As a result of Johnson's intervention, Hoover remained in office until his death in 1972 (serving nearly *five* decades as FBI Director).

When asked why he granted the egomaniacal Hoover a lifetime appointment, LBJ was crudely philosophical: "Well, it's probably better to have him inside the tent pissing out, than outside pissing in."

When the Democratic National Convention opened in August, *thirty* FBI special agents were in place to "assist the Secret Service," and prevent "civil disruption." In addition to monitoring the activities of Robert Kennedy and his supporters (keep them "bottled up" were LBJ's specific orders), the FBI kept close tabs on Civil Rights organizations, fearing they might stage demonstrations to embarrass President Johnson. Using telephone taps, the FBI monitored the communications of Martin Luther King and other black leaders.

Johnson also pressured White House staffers to keep close tabs on RFK's convention activities, instructing Chief of Staff, Marvin Watson: "I want to know everything the Kennedy's are going to do. I want you watch them carefully and let me know, immediately. We are not going to let Bobby and Jackie *steal* this convention."

In what should have been his shining moment, LBJ suddenly grew morose. He was obsessed that RFK was conspiring against him, to the point of suggesting the Attorney General was responsible for the tumultuous battle between black and white Mississippians concerning formal recognition and seating of the state's convention delegation. Privately, a grim-faced LBJ threatened to withdraw from the race: "I felt a strong inclination to go back to Texas while there was still time—time to enjoy my life with my wife and daughters—to work in earnest at being a rancher on the land I loved, to slow down, to reflect, to live."

In light of his intense personal ambition, LBJ's ruminations about retirement from politics appeared disingenuous. However, Johnson went so far as to draft a hand written withdrawal statement: "Therefore, I shall carry forward with your help until the new President is sworn in next January, and then go back home, as I've wanted since the day I took this job."

In response to her husband's threats to withdraw from the presidential race, Lady Bird sent him a letter: "…To step out now would be wrong for your country, and I can see nothing but a lonely wasteland for your future. Your friends would be frozen in embarrassed silence, and your enemies jeering…"

The firm scolding from his wife, along with the resolution of the conflict among Mississippi's convention delegates, jolted LBJ back into reality. Johnson's confidence was restored, and he was determined to be elected President in his own right.

After securing a pledge of loyalty from Hubert Humphrey, Johnson selected the Minnesota Senator as his running mate. From the White House, LBJ made a dramatic show of telephoning Humphrey's wife: "Muriel, how would you like to have your husband be the vice-presidential nominee? We're going to nominate your boy."

When the Democratic National Convention opened on August 24, 1964, LBJ directed the agenda, from start to finish. Hubert Humphrey remembered Johnson's absolute control: "He wrote the music, choreographed the action, chose the stars, and virtually wrote the lines. What Lyndon wanted, Lyndon got. He accepted every cheer as adulation, and when it reached a crescendo, it seemed to erase the ghost of John Kennedy's presidency from his mind."

Secretary of Agriculture, Orville Freeman, described the scene in Atlantic City: "The end of the convention hall is decked with five pictures— three small pictures across the top—Roosevelt, Kennedy, Truman—and, on the other side, enormous Johnson pictures dominate the hall. This has been a Johnson show, beginning to end, with complete dominance by the man evident, at every hand."

Robert Kennedy was scheduled to introduce a film honoring his late brother on Tuesday of convention week. Fearing the tribute to JFK might *stampede* the emotional delegates into drafting RFK for the vice-presidency (or even the presidential nomination, itself), LBJ arranged for the film to be shown on Thursday, *after* his nomination had been secured.

On Thursday night, August 27, 1964, Lyndon Johnson and Hubert Humphrey were nominated to lead the Democratic ticket. Backstage, Robert Kennedy sat with an aide in a small dressing room, waiting for his cue. LBJ had wanted the Attorney General to make his presidential nominating speech, but Kennedy had declined, focusing exclusively on his martyred brother (earlier in the evening, Democratic Party advance man, Jeb Byrne, had encountered an emotional RFK, sitting alone on the steps of a convention hall stairwell, head in hands, weeping). As he composed himself for the task at hand, Bobby broke the tension in the cramped backstage room: "Would you check the program? We can't hear anything back here. I think Lyndon may have put us back here, with orders to forget us. They'll probably let us out the day after tomorrow."

At the appointed time, Senator Henry "Scoop" Jackson opened the tribute to President Kennedy: "It is my privilege and honor to introduce a man who stood closer to him in times of crisis and in times of fun, than anyone else—his brother Robert Kennedy."

RFK, dressed in a dark suit, shyly walked on stage amidst thunderous applause from the delegates. The teary eyed crowd continued to applaud for *twenty-two* minutes. Half-smiling and nervously brushing his hair back from his forehead; RFK tried to halt the applause on several occasions, but was drowned out by the cheering delegation. When he tried to silence the crowd by raising his hand, the applause only grew louder.

"Just let them do it, Bob. Let them get it out of their system," Senator Jackson advised.

When the crowd finally quieted, RFK delivered a brief introduction to the film honoring JFK, entitled *The Thousand Days*. After the film, Bobby concluded the tribute with a passage from Shakespeare: "When he shall die; Take him and cut him out in little stars; And he will make of heav'n so fine; That all the world will be in love with the night; And pay not worship to the garish sun."

At evening's end, many observers believed that Lyndon Johnson was Robert Kennedy's embodiment of the *garish sun*.

At the convention, LBJ assigned his running mate the task of directly attacking the Republican nominee, Barry Goldwater. In his acerbic acceptance speech, Hubert Humphrey zeroed in on Goldwater: "Now, my fellow Americans, these urgent problems demand reasoned solutions, not empty slogans. Childlike answers cannot solve man-sized problems... The American presidency is not a place for a man who is impetuous at one moment, and indecisive the next, nor is it a place for one who is violently for something one day, and violently opposed to it on the next...Most Democrats and Republicans in the Senate voted for a 11.5 billion dollar tax cut for the American citizens and American businesses. But, not Senator Goldwater! Most Democrats and Republicans in the Senate, in fact four-fifths of the members of his own party, voted for the *Civil Rights Act*. But, not Senator Goldwater! Most Democrats and Republicans in the Senate voted for the establishment of the *U.S. Arms Control and Disarmament Agency* that seeks to slow down the nuclear arms race among nations. But, not the temporary Republican spokesman! Yes, my fellow Americans, it is a fact that the temporary Republican spokesman is not in the mainstream of his party. In fact, he has not touched the shore!"

On the night of his nomination, Lyndon Johnson celebrated his fifty-seventh birthday at a *one thousand dollar* per ticket party in Atlantic City. In the ballroom of Convention Hall, LBJ basked in the limelight, and listened to Carol Channing sing *Hello Lyndon* to the tune of her timeless classic, *Hello Dolly.* In only nine months, Johnson had emerged from political obscurity to become the leader of the free world.

That same week, Robert Kennedy announced his candidacy for the United States Senate in the state of New York. RFK would never again be directly accountable to the man he so despised.

Ultimately, neither LBJ nor RFK would be able to stay out of the other's shadow for very long.

Chapter 14

Get on the Johnson, Humphrey, Kennedy team

By late summer of 1964, the election of Lyndon Johnson seemed to be a foregone conclusion. LBJ nonetheless hit the campaign trail with characteristic fervor.

Johnson directed his running mate to blitz the country in support of the Democratic ticket. Hubert Humphrey clearly remembered LBJ's marching orders: "You have to understand that this is like a marriage with no chance of divorce. I need complete and unswerving loyalty."

Johnson crudely emphasized his loyalty requirements: "I want people around me who would kiss my ass on a hot summer's day, and say it smells like roses."

LBJ barnstormed America with manic intensity. Between August 27th and Election Day, Johnson traveled just over *50,000* miles by air. In a *nineteen*-day span, LBJ visited *twenty* states and *thirty-eight* different cities.

Much to the chagrin of the Secret Service, the President waded into crowds, large and small, sometimes using a bullhorn to speak from the backseat of a convertible or the rear platform of his train. The limousine in which JFK had been assassinated had been rebuilt, with a more powerful engine, *two and a half* tons of additional steel plating, *three* inch glass windows, and bulletproof tires. The reconstructed presidential vehicle was nearly indestructible, but LBJ rarely remained inside the mobile fortress.

Johnson carefully orchestrated his campaign appearances. He insisted that his lectern be four feet tall, to accommodate his six feet three inches, and his advance team was forced to secure an adjustable speaker's stand at each campaign stop.

The LBJ campaign seemed ubiquitous; while the President was in one state, Lady Bird visited another, and Humphrey campaigned in a third. Over the course of *four* days, the First Lady travelled *1628* miles by train, visiting *eight* different Southern states, aboard the *Lady Bird Special*.

Meanwhile, Robert Kennedy launched his Senate campaign. On September 3, 1964, Kennedy scheduled an Oval Office meeting with LBJ to formally submit his letter of resignation as Attorney General.

"Do you think we ought to necessarily have a man to take pictures of me and Bobby?" a wary LBJ asked his Press Secretary, George Reedy, prior to Kennedy's arrival.

"Yes, I do," Reedy quickly answered.

"It'll be kind of hypocritical of both of us," the President protested.

"It would be sir. But, this is a case where the picture doesn't mean so much, but the *lack* of a picture becomes a story," the publicity conscious Reedy replied.

RFK's resignation letter was stilted, focusing mostly on his late brother's administration: "Under your leadership, accomplishments of the last few years have been consolidated, and the nation continues to move forward with confidence."

LBJ's return letter lacked warmth: "It is with regret that I have received your resignation. You have played a very vital role in the conduct of public affairs."

The meeting grew testy when Kennedy asked that monies raised by the National Democratic Committee in New York be shared with his senatorial campaign. LBJ quickly refused, pointing out that his national campaign was not yet adequately funded, and he was not ready to share party largess. Johnson believed there was more than enough Kennedy family money to help finance RFK's senatorial campaign, without tapping into Democratic Party funds.

Republican presidential nominee, Barry Goldwater, quickly went on the offensive, labeling LBJ as the "biggest faker in the United States," and "the phoniest individual who ever came around." Goldwater pointed out that Johnson had amassed a personal fortune while serving in Congress, suggesting financial impropriety. The Republican candidate also called into question LBJ's sincerity regarding Civil Rights.

By personally attacking Lyndon Johnson, Goldwater more than met his match. In private, LBJ raged about his opponent: "Well, we've got a bunch of goddamned thugs, here, taking us on. Now, this Goldwater talking about morality! If we wanted to deal in morality, what we could show on that guy! I've got the record in front of me, where his eighty-nine year old mother is drawing a tax deduction from the Goldwater Stores that are owned by *Associate Dry Goods,* for forty-nine hundred a year. And, she's too damned old to even get to the store!"

In an off the record conversation with the editor of the *Dallas Morning News*, LBJ accused Goldwater of mental instability: "Goldwater is a nervous man; an impulsive man; childish man...Goldwater has had two serious nervous breakdowns. He had to be taken off, out of the country, hospitalized. His wife wrote about it in full in *Good Housekeeping* (in reality, Peggy Goldwater had revealed in the magazine article that her husband had twice suffered from *nervous exhaustion*)."

Privately, Johnson summed up his opinion about Goldwater: "He's just as nutty as a fruitcake."

The Republican nominee's impulsive gaffs fed the Johnson campaign with ample ammunition to attack the Republican platform. Goldwater's image as a *trigger-happy* warrior was reinforced by his recommendation that local military commanders should be given the option to use nuclear weapons against the Soviet Union. Goldwater recklessly threatened the Russians with the prospect of nuclear attack: "Let's lob one into the men's room of the Kremlin."

During his acceptance speech at the Republican National Convention, Goldwater made a bold proclamation: "Extremism in the defense of liberty is no vice! Moderation in the pursuit of justice is no virtue."

"Well, I'd say extremism to destroy liberty is," Johnson quipped to his aide, Bill Moyers.

The Republican candidate issued controversial statements advocating the termination of Social Security and privatization of the *Tennessee Valley Authority (TVA)*. The Goldwater campaign boasted: "In your heart, you know he's right."

The Johnson camp countered with: "In your heart, you know he might. In your gut, you know he's nuts."

At a campaign stop in Dover, Delaware, Johnson contrasted himself to the seemingly unstable Goldwater: "So you are going to have to select the man whose thumbs will be close to that button. You are going to have to select the man who will answer that telephone, that 'hot line' from Moscow, when the bell starts jingling, ting-a-ling-a-ling, and they say: 'Moscow is calling!' You are going to have to select the President, and you have only one President."

An explosive television spot left its indelible mark on the 1964 presidential campaign. At 9:00 p.m., EST, on Monday September 7th, the image of a young girl sitting in a field of flowers flickered across television screens throughout the country. As she picked the petals from a daisy, the little girl melodically started counting from one to ten. Soon, a menacing male voice was heard counting down from ten to zero. When the ominous voice reached the number one, the camera focused on the little girl's eyes, and the screen briefly went black, before the image of a mushroom cloud appeared. Lyndon Johnson's voice was heard next: "These are the stakes—to make a world in which all God's children can live, or go into the dark." The political ad concluded with an apocalyptic warning: "Vote for President Johnson on November 3rd. The stakes are too high for you to stay home."

The Johnson camp had intended for the controversial spot to air only once. When the White House switchboards began to light up with calls of protest, their decision was validated.

Feigning anger and alarm, LBJ phoned his aide and campaign strategist, Bill Moyers: "What in the Hell do you mean putting on that ad? I've been swamped with calls, and the Goldwater people are calling it a low blow...You'd better get over here and tell me what you're going to do about this."

Moyers explained that the television spot had achieved its desired effect—the American voter would view Goldwater as a dangerous extremist.

Johnson chuckled: "You sure we ought to just run it *once*?"

The *Daisy Ad* was never televised again, but many American voters could not forget the uncompromising link between Barry Goldwater and the prospect of nuclear holocaust.

A small segment of the electorate helped foster the image of an unstable Goldwater. A popular news magazine polled American psychiatrists—*657* saw Goldwater as fit for office, but a solid majority (*1189*) pronounced him paranoid, and too unstable to serve as President.

Goldwater did little to counter his *trigger-happy* image. In a single *thirty* minute campaign speech, the Republican candidate mentioned nuclear weapons or nuclear war on *twenty-six* occasions. Goldwater's image as an impulsive, perhaps unstable warrior, allowed LBJ to run as the *peace candidate* in the 1964 presidential election, even though Johnson had recently ordered aerial bombardment of North Vietnam. After responding to the Gulf of Tonkin attacks, LBJ crafted an image as a *man of peace,* who was not afraid to retaliate against his enemies.

Once his senatorial candidacy was announced, Robert Kennedy established a full time residence in New York, purchasing an apartment in Manhattan's United Nations Plaza, and leasing a *twenty-five* room house in Glen Cove, Long Island, with a swimming pool and private beach.

RFK easily won the Democratic nomination, defeating Congressman, Samuel Stratton, by a margin of *86.4* to *13.7* percent. Leveraging the broad appeal of his family name, RFK began the General Election campaign against the incumbent Republican, Kenneth Keating, with a significant lead in the polls. The Kennedy campaign, however, seemed rudderless. RFK's brother-in-law, Stephen Smith, who had long managed the Kennedy financial portfolio, served as Bobby's top aide and chief adviser. Though Smith was loyal and devoted, he had little experience in the practical world of politics, and the campaign lacked the discipline and tenacity associated with past Kennedy election efforts— simply put, there was no Robert Kennedy to run the show.

RFK's friend and adviser, Kenneth O'Donnell, believed, at heart, the candidate was ambivalent about his Senate campaign: "Bobby was more interested in being Governor than Senator, but he was not constitutionally eligible to be Governor of New York. To run for Governor of New York, he would have had to have lived in the state for the preceding five years as a registered voter, which he had not. He either ran for the Senate or retired from politics."

The Keating camp accused Kennedy of being a *carpet bagger*. Early in the campaign, the incumbent Senator sent his young opponent a road map to help him negotiate his way through New York. Realizing that Keating's criticism was not without merit, RFK purchased an elementary-school geography textbook to familiarize himself with the layout of his adopted state.

Kennedy did his best to counter the carpet bagger allegation. At a campaign stop at Columbia University, RFK explained his reason for seeking election: "My father has done very well, and I could have lived off him…And, I don't need the money, and I don't need the office space… Frank as it is, and maybe it's difficult to believe this in the state of New York, I'd like to just be a good United States Senator. I'd just like to serve."

Many political pundits viewed RFK as little more than an extension of his late brother's memory. The candidate, of course, did nothing to discount his kinship with the martyred President, and utilized Jackie and seven-year old, John F. Kennedy, Jr., as campaign companions.

On occasion, RFK encountered unanticipated enemies. In October, he was invited to throw the opening pitch in the World Series game between the New York Yankees and St. Louis Cardinals. Yankee Hall of Famer, Joe DiMaggio, who remained angry over reported affairs between his deceased ex-wife, actress Marilyn Monroe, and one or both of the Kennedy brothers (JFK and RFK), refused to shake Bobby's hand. DiMaggio believed Monroe's heartbreak over her failed romances with the architects of the *New Frontier* had directly contributed to her suicide in 1962.

New York's *Daily News* headlined its sports page: "Joltin' Joe—no fan of RFK's!"

Early on, RFK was lackadaisical, and seemingly uncomfortable, in the role of candidate. Historian, Jeff Shesol, described the Kennedy campaign's dilemma: "The thought of Bobby, on his own, was a relief and terror at the same time."

Campaign adviser, Paul Corbin, tried to shake RFK out of his malaise: "Goddamn, Bob, be yourself! You're real. Your brother's dead."

Another adviser described RFK's lack of interest in the political niceties associated with being a candidate: "People would come up to Bob Kennedy to shake hands and ask him a question, and Bob would often answer with a *yes* or *no*. The person would stand there, kind of lost. People thought he was being rude, but he wasn't. He just wasn't a hail-fellow-well-met type guy. He was not a back slapper. He couldn't do it."

Eventually, the Kennedy campaign regained its lost momentum and the candidate went on the attack. Adopting a populist message, RFK criticized Keating's failure to support construction of new housing projects, as well as his opposition to funding for federal education and extension of the minimum wage law.

A week before Election Day, the *CBS News* affiliate in New York offered to broadcast a one-hour debate between the two senatorial candidates. Ultimately, the Kennedy and Keating camps were unable to agree on a format, and RFK withdrew from the debate. To embarrass his opponent, Keating purchased the first half hour of television time, announcing that he would debate the *empty chair.*

RFK countered by trying to buy the second thirty minutes, but was rebuffed by the local affiliate. Kennedy appealed to the President of *CBS,* who ordered the local station to provide RFK with the desired half hour slot.

On the night of the debate, RFK arrived at the television station three minutes before Keating's 7:30 p.m. appearance: "I'm here to debate Senator Keating."

"Senator Keating has decided against a face-to-face debate," the television station's attorney responded.

"In that case, I demand that the empty seat be removed from the set, and that Keating's remark that I refuse to debate him be struck," Kennedy countered.

Undeterred, Keating proceeded to engage in a one-man debate. However, at the conclusion of his campaign broadcast, the Republican Senator was ridiculed for literally running out of the studio, bypassing RFK and his advisers.

During his maiden campaign, RFK began to reveal his often-masked sense of humor. When campaigning in Buffalo, a city famous for its shoe-making industry, the father of eight quipped: "I can practically support this place, single handedly."

Minnesota Senator, Hubert Humphrey, who campaigned on behalf of RFK was amazed by the adoring crowds: "I'd never seen anything quite like it…They literally tore at Bobby Kennedy, and I remember women were tossing shoes into the open car, and at the end of the tour, there was this undergarment—half girdle, half garter belt—on the floor of the car, and I said to Bobby, 'How did you do that?' I'd never seen such excitement as he generated in that particular tour."

As late summer gave way to early fall, Lyndon Johnson appeared headed toward a historic landslide victory. A month before the election, polling data showed Johnson leading Goldwater by a margin of *sixty-five* to *thirty-five* percent in the state of New York, while Kennedy trailed Keating (*fifty-three* to *forty-seven* percent). A top Kennedy adviser soon urged the candidate to seek help: "It is essential that you do everything to take advantage of the fact that Johnson will probably carry the state by one and a half million votes."

"I finally realized I was in a horse race, and I wasn't necessarily the front runner," Bobby recalled.

RFK was forced to swallow his enormous pride for the sake of political survival, and asked for LBJ's help. Overnight, campaign posters in New York featured a new slogan: "Get on the Johnson, Humphrey, Kennedy team."

With mixed emotions, Lyndon Johnson traveled to New York to campaign alongside his long time nemesis. In mid October, the mismatched couple barnstormed the state for two days.

"The United States needs a young, dynamic, compassionate, fighting, liberal representing New York in the United States Senate," Johnson proclaimed.

With characteristic zeal, LBJ draped his arm around a clearly uncomfortable RFK: "I want you to elect my boy, here!"

To reinforce an image of unity, RFK was forced to engage in the hyperbole: "I think of President Johnson with affection and admiration." At one joint appearance, Kennedy went so far as to declare Johnson as "one of the great Presidents."

The *New York Times* reported that Kennedy and Johnson were "as close as twins," and acknowledged that Bobby was "riding Mr. Johnson's long coattails."

On October 31st, just two days before the election, LBJ returned to New York for a second round of joint campaigning with RFK. Johnson's passion and energy were contagious, and Bobby was amazed by the Texan's ability to temporarily cast aside their long-standing mutual contempt for one another.

After a long day of campaigning, Kennedy asked LBJ if he really enjoyed the exhausting experience.

"Of all things in life, this is what I enjoy most," Johnson immediately answered.

RFK was stunned by the answer, confiding to an aide: "Imagine saying that, of all things in life, this is what you enjoy most!"

Nevertheless, RFK eventually joined in the fun, joking with a campaign adviser: "I've got to get to a phone, so I can call *Ethel Bird*."

The LBJ juggernaut was unstoppable, even in the face of scandal. On October 7th, LBJ's long time aide and closest White House adviser, Walter Jenkins, was arrested in the men's room of the Washington D.C. YMCA, while engaging in oral sex with another man. Johnson was blindsided by the news, having once described Jenkins as "my Vice-President of Everything." Fearing the political ramifications of his indiscretion, Jenkins quickly resigned his position in the Johnson Administration.

LBJ had difficulty believing that his long-time adviser, a staunch Catholic, who was married and had fathered several children, might be bi-sexual: "I couldn't have been more shocked about Walter Jenkins, than if I'd heard that Lady Bird had killed the Pope!"

After leaving the White House in disgrace, Jenkins returned to Texas and established an accounting practice. LBJ, who demanded loyalty from friends and subordinates, graciously proved that this trait flowed in both directions, by retaining Jenkins to manage his business and personal accounts, and helping him find other clients. LBJ promised to do two things after his presidency—he was going to smoke as many cigarettes as he liked and he was going to "wrap my arms around Walter Jenkins." Johnson kept both promises during his retirement.

Barry Goldwater knew and respected Jenkins (having served in the National Guard with him), and did not exploit the scandal, refusing to make any derogatory public comments about the situation. The Johnson camp was also the beneficiary of rival stories in the national media that kept the Jenkins' affair from dominating headlines—the St. Louis Cardinals and New York Yankees were in the midst of a seven game World Series battle, and, on October 16, 1964, Communist China exploded its first nuclear device.

Privately, Barry Goldwater shook his head in disgust: "What a way to win an election—Communists and cock suckers!"

In the final weeks of his senatorial campaign, Robert Kennedy finally hit his stride. Bolstered by Lyndon Johnson's popularity, RFK's poll numbers began to rise.

Unlike his brothers, Jack and Ted, Bobby was not a natural campaigner, and his public speaking skills were slow to develop. With a staccato delivery and high-pitched voice, both of which were particularly noticeable when he was anxious, RFK was never a master orator. A close advisor described him as an "uptight campaigner." Given his lack of familiarity with the state of New York, the candidate sometimes mispronounced the names of towns and cities along the campaign trail.

Kennedy nonetheless had a boyish charisma, which was especially appealing to women, children, and minorities, who were mesmerized by his youthful idealism. Amidst youthful crowds, RFK was willing to let his guard down, revealing a hidden charm and sense of humor: "If I had my way, I'd lower the voting age to six."

Crowds often mobbed RFK, stripping his cuff links and grabbing chunks of his hair. After a day of campaigning, Bobby's hands and forearms were bloodied and bruised. Kennedy was amazed by the groupie mentality of the younger voters: "They treat me like I'm a *Beatle*."

As Election Day neared, RFK's campaign, aided in no small part by LBJ's popularity, had turned the corner.

Lyndon Johnson ended his campaign in Austin, Texas. On Election Eve, standing on the front steps of the State Capitol Building, LBJ delivered his final speech: "It was here, as a barefoot boy, around my father's desk, in that great hall of the House of Representatives, where he served for six terms, and where my grandfather served ahead of him, that I first learned that government is not an enemy of the people. It is the people."

On Tuesday, November 3, 1964, Lyndon Johnson defeated Barry Goldwater in a landslide (*43,129,084* votes to *27,178,188*). LBJ won *sixty-one* percent of the popular vote—the largest margin of victory in American presidential election history. Johnson carried *forty-four* states and the District of Columbia. Goldwater's victories were limited to *five* Deep South states (Alabama, Georgia, Mississippi, Louisiana, and South Carolina), along with his home state of Arizona. The final electoral vote count was *486* to *52* (only FDR's *523* to *8* victory over Alf Landon in 1936 eclipsed Johnson's electoral majority) The Democratic Party gained *37* seats in the House of Representatives and *two* seats in the Senate, giving them impressive majorities of *295* and *68*, respectively.

LBJ privately dismissed the loss of Deep South states, other than Georgia: I didn't care about the other southern states. Louisiana's a bunch of crooks, and Mississippi's too ignorant to know any better, and Alabama's the same way."

In New York, Robert Kennedy defeated the incumbent, Kenneth Keating by a respectable *719,673* votes, but his triumph was dwarfed by LBJ's incredible *2,500,000* vote margin of victory. Before midnight, Keating delivered a concession speech, allowing RFK to greet his supporters in front of prime time television cameras. During his victory address, Kennedy thanked the Governor, the Mayor of New York City, and his brother-in-law, Stephen Smith, among others, but never once mentioned Lyndon Johnson.

Meanwhile, in Massachusetts, the youngest Kennedy brother savored his own electoral triumph. Ted won re-election to the Senate by over *900,000* votes, resurrecting faded images of a Kennedy political dynasty.

LBJ monitored the returns in Austin, but was unable to fully enjoy his electoral triumph. Barry Goldwater refused to issue a formal concession on Election Night, denying Johnson an opportunity to make his victory statement on prime time television. Goldwater did not make a statement until the following morning, when he read from the telegram he had sent to Johnson. From his campaign headquarters in Phoenix, Goldwater vowed that the Republicans would "remain the party of opposition, when opposition is called for."

Johnson was enraged by Goldwater's delay and poor political sportsmanship: "That damn son of a bitch!"

LBJ was also hurt and angered by Robert Kennedy's ingratitude during his victory speech: "I wonder why he didn't mention me?"

A Johnson aide shared his own frustrations: "Bobby thanked the postmasters. He thanked the precinct captains. He thanked every two-bit person who helped in the campaign. But, he didn't thank the President of the United States. He just couldn't choke it out of himself."

Robert Kennedy was less than ecstatic at the prospect of serving in the United States Senate, but felt an obligation to perpetuate the Kennedy legacy, independent of Lyndon Johnson. RFK described his election victory as an "overwhelming mandate" of his brother's polices. At the same time, he was wistful for the days of the *New Frontier*: "If my brother was alive, I wouldn't be here. I'd rather have it that way."

Shortly before midnight on Election Night, Robert Kennedy and Lyndon Johnson talked by telephone.

"Listen, I pulled you through up here!" Bobby joked, making light of LBJ's massive margin of victory in New York.

Smarting from RFK's failure to publicly acknowledge his sizeable contribution, a subdued LBJ invoked JFK's memory: "Let's stay as close together as he'd want us to."

Near the end of their phone conversation, RFK *eventually* expressed gratitude for Johnson's assistance during the campaign: "Thanks, very much. Thanks for your help…It made a hell of a difference."

The day after the election, LBJ told Bill Moyers, that the Kennedy loyalists should be forever grateful for his intervention on behalf of RFK: "Because, if I'd kept my mouth shut, he'd have been beat."

Johnson complained about Kennedy's lack of appreciation: "I thought, last night, it took him a long time to get around to admitting the President had anything to do with it."

The day after the election, LBJ and RFK once again chatted over the telephone. The exchange was uncharacteristically light-hearted and humorous. Bobby had already returned to Washington, while Johnson was resting at his ranch in Texas.

"By God, you learned how to smile in this campaign," LBJ teased Bobby.

"I did what you told me to do after you came up there," Bobby joked, recalling LBJ's admonition to smile more during campaign appearances.

"You must think you're going to be running up there a long time. I saw you smiling and waving to a bunch of kids. They're not even registered!" Johnson exclaimed, referencing RFK's photographs in the morning newspapers.

"You know what I was doing? I was thinking of working with you. That made me smile," Bobby laughed.

The smile, clearly exaggerated in the glory of electoral triumph, would be the last one shared by the two bitter rivals.

Chapter 15

How many hours do I have to sit here to be a Good Senator?

Lyndon Johnson's idealism was nothing less than grandiose: "When I first became President, I realized that if only I could take the next step and become dictator of the whole world, then I could really make things happen; every hungry person would be fed, every ignorant child educated, every jobless man employed. And, then I knew I could accomplish my greatest wish—the wish for eternal peace."

The last two months of 1964 and the first two-thirds of 1965 were the high water marks for Johnson's presidency. After his landslide victory over Barry Goldwater, LBJ used the mandate to bring his *Great Society* to life.

Johnson's inauguration in January of 1965 gave notice that JFK's *New Frontier* was now just a memory. The theme for the inaugural ceremonies reflected the personality of the newly elected President: "Ya'll come and see us."

At the beginning of the New Year, Lady Bird reflected on her husband's unique position in history: "I'm probably the only living person who would attest, believe, (and) swear that he never wanted to be President. But, now that he's in, he wants history to record…a hard-working President, a 'people-loving' President, and a President who believes that man can solve his problems."

In January, President Johnson gathered his congressional liaison team, communicating a sense of urgency about implementing the *Great Society* while his popularity remained high: "I was just elected President by the biggest popular margin in the history of the country—*sixteen million* votes. Just by the way people naturally think, and because Barry Goldwater has simply scared Hell out of them, I've already lost about three of those sixteen. After a fight with Congress or something else, I'll lose another couple of million. I could be down to *eight million* in a couple of months."

Believing that he had roughly *twenty* months to pass his *Great Society* program, before his popularity waned, LBJ hit the ground running. From January to October of 1965, President Johnson sent *115* legislative recommendations to Capitol Hill. The Eighty- Ninth Congress passed *ninety* of those proposals. A Washington based reporter described the law making frenzy: "They're rolling bills out of Congress, these days, the way Detroit turns out super sleek, souped up autos off the assembly line."

Among LBJ's legislative successes were the *Higher Education Act* (providing *650 million* dollars in college scholarships for needy students), excise tax reduction, *Medicare, Medicaid,* the *Voting Rights Act,* the *Food Stamp Act,* and housing and urban development (federal assistance for construction of low rent public housing, along with funding for the *beautification* of cities).

Two additional cabinet level departments were established during the Johnson Administration. In 1966, the *Department of Housing and Urban Development (HUD)* and the *Department of Transportation* were chartered.

In September, the *Immigration Act of 1965* was passed by Congress, ending forty years of established policy. Under the new law, immigration status was changed to *first come, first serve,* regardless of one's country of origin. Preferences were granted only to immigrants with family relationships to existing U.S. citizens and to particular occupational skills.

In symbolic fashion, President Johnson signed the bill into law at Ellis Island, in the shadow of the Statute of Liberty.

Demonstrating his commitment to environmental causes, LBJ also signed the *Water Quality Act,* the *Highway Beautification Act,* and the *Wilderness Act* (the latter two were influenced by Lady Bird Johnson, who was a dedicated environmentalist). The President also promoted passage of legislation chartering the *National Foundation of the Arts and Humanities,* as well as the *Corporation for Public Broadcasting,* giving birth to the *Public Broadcasting System (PBS)* and *National Public Radio (NPR).* To promote consumer safety, Johnson signed into law the *Fair Packaging and Labeling Act* and the *Automobile Safety Act.*

The Johnson Administration established *seventeen* task forces to study a far ranging agenda of social programs. In a master stroke of political genius, LBJ asked a number of Senators and Congressmen to join these committees, figuring that partial congressional ownership of the new programs would facilitate their legislative approval. Between 1965 and 1968, 500 new social programs were created and funded by the federal government.

Time Magazine reporter, Hugh Sidey, marveled at LBJ's unparalleled influence on Capitol Hill: "Johnson would zero in on a Congressman or Senator, and get what he wanted—a good deal. I would be amazed at some of the devices he would use. He would lie, beg, cheat, steal a little, threaten, (and) intimidate. He never lost sight of the ultimate goal—his idea of the *Great Society."*

Massachusetts Congressman, Thomas "Tip" O'Neill, admired LBJ's influence on the legislative process: "When it came to politics, that man knew all the tricks."

Veteran Washington Insider, Clark Clifford, who would later become LBJ's Secretary of Defense, was a close advisor to a handful of Presidents during his lifetime. Clifford described Lyndon Johnson as simply "the greatest legislator who ever served as President." It was little wonder that the 1965 congressional session became known as the *Fabulous Eighty-Ninth.*

Running the country was not quite enough for Lyndon Johnson, who insisted on micromanaging the smallest details in his life. On one occasion, LBJ telephoned Joseph Haggar, Jr. (Chairman of the Board of the *Haggar Company*) with detailed advice concerning the tailoring of his trousers.

"You all made me some real light slacks...I need about six pairs for summer wear. I want them about a half inch larger in the waist than they were before…I vary ten or fifteen pounds per month. Make the pockets at least an inch longer—my money and my knife and everything fall out… The crotch, down w̶ere your nuts hang, is always a little too tight…Give me an inch that I can let out there, because they cut me—they're like riding a wire fence," instructed the renowned businessman.

LBJ closely monitored Robert Kennedy's every move, certain that the newly-elected junior Senator from New York would eventually use his legislative pulpit to criticize the Johnson Administration. Meanwhile, RFK's regard for LBJ remained low, as he privately confided to a friend: "He does not know how to use people's talents, to find the very best in them, and put the best to work. But, more than any other man, he knows how to ferret out and use people's weaknesses."

Johnson nonetheless attempted to cozy up to RFK and sell him on the virtues of legislative service. During a telephone conversation in late 1964, LBJ inquired: "How do you like your new job?"

"I don't know yet," Kennedy replied, "Do you think I'll like it?"

"I do," LBJ responded, "I was happier than in any job I ever had."

RFK was continually perplexed by LBJ's preoccupation with his every move: "Why does Lyndon fear me so much, for Christ's sake? He's the President of the United States, and I'm the Junior Senator from New York."

As an elected politician, RFK's words and actions required careful weighing. In spite of their profound dislike and mistrust of one another, neither LBJ nor RFK was ready to deal with the political fallout from a public break. Historian and Kennedy biographer, Arthur Schlesinger, Jr., succinctly described the tenuous relationship: "They indulged in public praise and private propitiation."

In January of 1965, standing beside his brother, Ted, Robert Kennedy was sworn into office in the United States Senate. It marked the first time since 1803 that two brothers had served together in the Senate.

Later that same day, at a reception for freshmen Senators, Bobby joked about his carpet bagger status, as he fumbled through his notes: "First of all, I want to say how delighted I am to be here representing the great state of ah, ah…"

RFK made light of his political future: "I have absolutely no presidential ambitions, and neither does my wife, *Ethel Bird*."

While Ted Kennedy savored life in the Senate, Bobby was ill suited for the role. As Attorney General, RFK was used to setting his own agenda and making independent, often split second decisions. The slow, deliberative pace of the Senate frustrated him.

"Bobby was used to taking executive action. Teddy was a legislator and Bobby was an executive—that was the real difference," the wife of a RFK adviser explained.

"Is this the way I become a good Senator—sitting here and waiting my turn? Bobby asked his brother Ted.

"Yes," Ted replied.

"How many hours do I have to sit here to be good a Senator?" Bobby continued.

"As long as necessary, Robbie," Ted replied, addressing his brother by his pet nickname.

RFK's aide, Fred Dutton, remembered briefing his boss on pending legislation: "Bob was always impatient. I would use that as one of the key half-dozen words of his personality. He'd say, 'Cut out the shit and let's get to the point!' He was not one who liked ruminations and dragged out questions."

Robert Kennedy demonstrated his impatience by waiting only *three* weeks before delivering his first speech on the floor of the Senate (advocating the *Appalachian Economic Plan* for thirteen upstate New York counties). RFK's boldness was in sharp contrast to his brothers—JFK had waited *five* months before addressing the Senate, and Edward Kennedy had not made his maiden speech until *sixteen* months after he was elected.

RFK was often unable to mask his frustration with the slow pace of the legislative process. While waiting his turn to speak during a committee hearing, Kennedy tried to interrupt, but was reprimanded by the chairman. His frustration mounted as two other Senators droned.

"Oh, forget it!" Bobby announced loudly, flinging his papers in the air, before storming out of the committee room.

RFK's restlessness aggravated his innate mood swings. A fellow Senator remembered his unpredictable personality: "One day, we'd crack jokes for an hour. The next day he'd chop you off...I'm not sure that he realized how some people were hurt by that."

"His candor made him very unpopular among many of his colleagues," another colleague recalled.

A loner at heart, Bobby did little to cultivate camaraderie among fellow lawmakers.. Senate Majority Leader, Mike Mansfield described RFK as "in the Senate, but not of it."

With shaggy hair, frayed shirt collars, and droopy socks, RFK did not look like the prototypical statesman. Kentucky Senator, Thurston Morton, offered a blunt description: "He looks like a damned beatnik."

South Carolina poet, James Dickey, remembered his initial encounter with Senator Kennedy: "I began quoting some lines from *Julius Caesar,* and I couldn't remember how they went. To my amazement, Bobby completed the passage. He wasn't like any other politician I ever met."

Ted Kennedy later summed up his brother's unusual Senatorial career: "He searched out injustices and moral causes."

By far, Ted was the more popular and effective of the Kennedy brothers on Capitol Hill. At the same time, Ted realized that Bobby was the leader of the family and next in line for political advancement. Shortly after RFK's election, when the two brothers posed together for a photograph, the cameraman asked RFK to step back, "You're casting a shadow on Ted."

"It'll be the same in Washington," Ted quipped.

RFK's Senate colleagues tolerated his moodiness, fully aware of his political potential. A fellow Senator protested to a committee chairman that RFK, as a freshman, was receiving preferential treatment.

"Oh, no, I treat him the same way I'd treat any *future President*," the chairman quickly replied.

As a newly elected Senator and brother to a martyr, Robert Kennedy enjoyed favorable news coverage. In her daily diary, Lady Bird Johnson reflected on RFK's wide acclaim: "Someone said he has the most *instantaneously obedient* portion of the press than anybody around town."

Robert Kennedy remained daring, even reckless in his personal life. In 1965, he scaled the newly named, 13,900 feet high Canadian peak, *Mount Kennedy* (named in honor of JFK). The several day climb exposed RFK to harsh elements and dangerous heights. At the end very end, Bobby scaled the last fifty yards, alone. At the top of the mountain peak, he left behind a Kennedy family flag, a *PT-109* tie clasp, and a copy of JFK's inaugural address, as a dozen helicopters and airplanes buzzed overhead, filming the conclusion of his historic quest.

During a sailing expedition off the coast of northern Maine, a wind gust blew RFK's leather bomber jacket (originally belonging to JFK) into the ocean. Impulsively, Bobby dove into the fifty-degree water to retrieve the coat.

On another occasion, while the Kennedy family sailed in Cape Cod, a Coast Guard cutter approached their vessel. Because of rough seas, the ships were unable to draw close to one another, and the Coast Guard Captain used a bullhorn to inform Bobby and Ethel that their oldest child, Kathleen, had sustained a head injury after falling from a horse. After reluctantly donning a life preserver, RFK ignored the thirty-knot gales and dove into the waves, swimming fifty yards to the Coast Guard ship.

While touring South American jungles, RFK seemed unconcerned about the dangers of the wild. On at least one occasion, he swam in a piranha-invested section of the Amazon River.

During an African safari in Kenya, Bobby departed his Range Rover and approached to within fifteen feet of a wary rhinoceros. When the mammoth beast turned and ran away, RFK merely winked.

RFK lived his life in concert with passages he underlined from Aeschylus: "Men are not made for safe havens. The fullness of life is in the hazards of life…To the heroic, desperate odds flings a challenge."

In a private notebook, RFK copied a quote from Ralph Waldo Emerson, which proved metaphorical for his lifestyle: "Do what you are afraid to do."

"It was like he was thumping his chest, like he was saying, 'Okay, death, you just try it, I dare you!'" Kennedy friend, Lem Billings, recalled.

Even though his beloved brother had been murdered by a sniper in an open motorcade, RFK continued to travel among crowds, riding in convertibles. On one occasion, when his car backfired, Bobby remarked to an anxious adviser: "Sooner or later."

As if self-imposed recklessness was not enough, RFK was confronted with dangers outside of his control. On March 1, 1967, the Supreme Court turned down Jimmy Hoffa's last appeal before he was to be imprisoned for jury tampering. Frank Chavez, head of the Teamsters Union in Puerto Rico and a Hoffa loyalist, threatened to kill RFK.

When it was rumored that Chavez was in route to Washington, D.C., armed guards were assigned to Senator Kennedy, and *Hickory Hill* was placed under surveillance. In the end, Hoffa convinced Chavez to abandon his violent vendetta.

While he could still be curt and abrasive, Robert Kennedy's personality changed in the wake of his brother's assassination. Ted Sorensen, who idolized JFK, and grew closer to RFK with the passage of time, later commented on the younger brother's transformation: "Jack's death changed Bobby. It humbled him, softened him. He became a gentler, warmer person; a change also occasioned by his growing responsibilities in public life."

Legislative aide, Fred Dutton, urged RFK to model himself after great historical figures like Gandhi, rather than noted twentieth century politicians: "Many tens of millions of people in this country, and hundreds of millions abroad, look to you as the hope of a world and a future built not just on power and the limitations of the present…"

While respecting Lyndon Johnson's commitment to Civil Rights and the *Great Society,* Ted Sorensen considered LBJ a pale comparison to RFK. Sorensen's evaluation of Johnson was less than flattering: "With all his taste for power, Johnson, as President, was paradoxically an insecure man with a massive ego, uncomfortable with his intellectual superiors."

In the early months of 1965, as LBJ enjoyed one legislative success after another, RFK was reluctant to offer public criticism of the Johnson Administration. In July of that year, LBJ signed *Medicare* into law (a federally funded insurance program for the elderly). RFK privately questioned whether the program would be cost effective, and his concerns were validated by a first year *Medicare* budget of *3.5 billion* dollars (by 1993, the annual cost had escalated to *144 billion* dollars).

Kennedy also called into question LBJ's *Elementary and Secondary Education Act,* which earmarked *one billion* dollars for poor and disadvantaged students. RFK, who visited slums and failing schools throughout the country, doubted that federal money, alone, would solve the country's education woes. While often romanticized as a classic liberal, RFK forged a separate niche, believing that "throwing money" at social problems was not enough, without appropriate manpower and supervision.

President Johnson remained wary of sharing the limelight with the brother of a martyred President. On June 23, 1965, RFK addressed the Senate, opposing the widespread proliferation of nuclear weapons. LBJ had planned to discuss reduction of nuclear testing in an upcoming speech commemorating the twentieth anniversary of the United Nations, deleted all references to the topic.

"I do not want to get into proliferation in any way, so it looks like I'm copying Bobby," Johnson told his National Security Adviser, McGeorge Bundy.

The most contentious issues between Lyndon Johnson and Robert Kennedy involved foreign policy. Bobby did not believe that LBJ's aggressive arm-twisting, which had served him so well in promoting his domestic policy, would be effective when dealing with foreign nations.

RFK's criticisms were not unwarranted. LBJ never mastered the intricacies of foreign policy in the same way that he controlled his domestic agenda. Consequently, Johnson was dependent upon the opinions of military, intelligence, and State Department *experts* on international issues.

In April of 1965, President Johnson ordered *28,000* American troops to invade the Dominican Republic, after a leftist group staged a revolt against the existing dictatorship. Exaggerating flimsy evidence, LBJ declared the coup was an attempt by "Castroites" to overtake the Latin American Country. Initiating unilateral action, Johnson totally bypassed the *Organization of American States (OAS)*, a Western Hemisphere coalition of *thirty-five* independent states (wholeheartedly supported by the Kennedy Administration).

LBJ, however, had little faith in the OAS: "It couldn't pour piss out of a boot, if the instructions were written on the heel."

In a conversation with Mike Mansfield, Johnson tried to justify his aggressive action in the Dominican Republic: "The Castro forces are really gaining control…They're going to set up a Castro Government…We begged the OAS to send somebody in last night. They won't move. They're just phantoms. They're just the damndest fraud I ever saw…"

"They're going to eat us up, if I let another Cuba come in there. They'll say: 'Why did you sit on your big fat tail?'" LBJ explained to Mansfield.

LBJ maintained that the presence of U.S. troops in the Dominican Republic would "protect American lives." For the first time in thirty-seven years, American troops were ordered to invade a Latin American country, as Johnson scrambled to establish a link between the Dominican uprising and the menace of Communism. Secretary of Defense, Robert McNamara, and presidential adviser, Bill Moyers, cautioned LBJ to temper his public statements, and avoid exaggeration. On April 30, 1965, LBJ maintained a measure of restraint: "People outside the Dominican Republic are seeking to gain control."

Two days later, however, during a live television address, LBJ declared that the "popular democratic revolution" in the Dominican Republic had been overtaken by a "band of Communist conspirators." The President vowed the United States would not "permit the establishment of another

Communist government in the Western Hemisphere." Even though American troops were withdrawn from the Dominican Republic in 1966, Johnson's blatant exaggerations gave root to the term *credibility gap* (coined by a *New York Tribune* columnist); a designation that would haunt him for the remainder of his presidency.

LBJ also absorbed criticism from from New York's junior Senator. On May 5th, Robert Kennedy spoke from the Senate floor, criticizing the President for failing to collaborate with the OAS during the crisis in the Dominican Republic.

New York Times correspondent, Max Frankel, explained the beginnings of the public's mistrust of LBJ: "Johnson was fundamentally dishonest in presenting the facts about what was happening in the Dominican Republic to the American people—pouring troops in there and telling ridiculous stories about 1500 heads rolling around the streets, and so on. Whatever the 'credibility gap' ultimately became, the combination of opposition to policy, and the horror at the government's handling and explanation of the event, is probably where it was born."

While the *credibility gap* ultimately exposed LBJ's duplicity to the world, those who observed him closely (advisers, fellow politicians, and reporters) had long been aware of his propensity to stretch the truth. Some of the lies were harmless—such as his preference for bourbon (like all good Texans), when he really drank scotch. Other falsehoods achieved *whopper* status—LBJ claimed that his uncle fought at the Alamo, and that he had earned his *Silver Star* for "helping shoot down *twenty* Zeros." Editing a speechwriter's draft, LBJ scratched out the name Socrates in a quotation, and replaced it with "my Granddaddy."

Nicholas Katzenbach, who succeeded Robert Kennedy as Attorney General, offered his own assessment of LBJ's tendency to exaggerate the truth: "When things did not work out as he had thought they would, he was able to conjure up an explanation that had little or nothing to do with fact, and that was how it happened. It was, I believe why Bobby (RFK) thought of him as consummate liar, and one of the reasons he lost credibility with the press and the general public on Vietnam."

When confronted by reports over his exaggerations, LBJ grew defensive: "God damn it, why must all those journalists be such sticklers for details?"

In the fall of 1965, Robert Kennedy visited South America to gain a better understanding of the socioeconomic and political climates in Peru,

Chile, Argentina, Brazil, and Venezuela. RFK feared that his brother's *Alliance for Progress* was in tatters because of LBJ's Latin American policy. Kennedy was concerned that the current administration favored protection of American business interests in the region, often supporting blatantly dictatorial governments that were friendly to the United States. RFK had already criticized Johnson for his failure to consult the OAS, before sending troops into the Dominican Republic.

Prior to the start of his three-week trip, Kennedy visited with Jack Hood Vaughn, the Johnson Administration's top Latin America adviser. Concerned that the public would view his South American tour as condemnation of LBJ's foreign policy, RFK hoped to gain a better understanding of Johnson's attitude toward Latin America.

The meeting with Vaughn went poorly. When Kennedy asked how best to explain American intervention in the Dominican Republic, Vaughn told him that none of the South American countries would really be interested in that issue.

"Well, you and I don't talk to the same Latin Americans, because that's all they ever ask me!" Kennedy replied, realizing that LBJ had no interest in sharing his Latin American foreign policy, and did not welcome an outsider's intervention in the region.

Prior to his departure, RFK addressed reporters, hoping to lessen speculation about his political future: "I am not thinking of running for the presidency. I have a high feeling for President Johnson. He has been very kind to me. I would support his bid for reelection in 1968, and I strongly wish to campaign for him."

Unlike many foreign dignitaries, RFK did not spend the majority of his time attending embassy receptions in South America or traveling on state sponsored tours of the affluent regions of host countries. In Peru, RFK visited the worst ghettos, encountering open sewage, ramshackle houses, and malnourished children.

He spoke directly to a group of neglected and impoverished Brazilian children, invoking his late brother's name: "The President was most fond of school. Can I ask you do a favor for him? Stay in school, study as long as you can, and then work for your city and Brazil."

Kennedy was appalled by the abject poverty: "These people are living like animals…Wouldn't you be a Communist, if you had to live here? I think I would."

In Chile, RFK traveled 1800 feet underground with coal miners to examine the hazardous and primitive work conditions. In each country,

Kennedy spent time comforting poverty stricken, malnourished children, and by day's end, his eyes were often filled with tears.

On November 20, 1965, Robert Kennedy celebrated his fortieth birthday in Sao Paulo, Brazil. When an American Diplomat gave him a battery-operated airplane as a gift, Ethel joked that the toy aircraft was "a U-2 sent by Lyndon Johnson to spy on my husband."

When a guest exploded party favors, a startled Bobby was reminded of JFK's violent death, three years earlier, and buried his face in his hands: "Oh, no. Please don't."

The press had a field day with Kennedy's South American tour, viewing it as a direct repudiation of the Johnson Administration's Latin American policy. *The Saturday Evening Post* headlined: "The Compulsive Candidate: Robert Kennedy Runs for President Every Day."

Shortly after returning from Latin America, RFK appeared on the *NBC News* weekly program, *Meet the Press*, reporting that many South Americans believed that business interests directed U.S. policy. He also counseled against American support of repressive regimes, just because they were anti-Communist: "I think it is self-defeating, and will be catastrophic."

Robert Kennedy had drawn a firm line in the sand, demarcating his own views on Latin America, which sharply contrasted with the established policies of the Johnson Administration. Very publicly, and on an international scale, RFK had violated LBJ's most sacred principle—loyalty.

The growing war in Vietnam would ultimately define the legacy of the Johnson presidency, and bring the feud between LBJ and RFK to its crescendo. In their formative years, both men had been influenced by the *Domino Theory* regarding the spread of Communism. With the passage of time, RFK began to question the validity of this Cold War mantra. In May of 1964, the Attorney General had privately shared his doubts about American military involvement in South Vietnam with LBJ.

Johnson, however, believed a show of force was necessary in Southeast Asia: "I knew history told me that if I got out of Vietnam, then I'd be doing exactly what Chamberlain did in World War II. I'd be giving a big fat reward to aggression."

LBJ clearly remembered how President Truman's post World War II popularity had plummeted, when he was blamed for allowing Communism to overtake mainland China. Johnson also doubted the sincerity of RFK's newfound dovish tendencies, reasoning that if South Vietnam collapsed,

Kennedy would quickly change his tune, and blame LBJ for not fulfilling JFK's promise to halt the spread of communism.

At 2:00 a.m. on February 6, 1965, the conflict in Indochina escalated, when Viet Cong guerillas explode thirteen satchels of explosive charges against the walls of Camp Holloway, near the South Vietnamese city of Pleiku, followed by intense mortar and rifle fire. *Eight* American soldiers were killed and another *128* were wounded.

Unwilling to allow enemy belligerence go unpunished, President Johnson ordered retaliatory air strikes. Twelve hours after the attacks at Pleiku, American aircraft bombed North Vietnamese barracks at Dong Hei, just north of the seventeenth parallel.

Four days later, Viet Cong guerillas assaulted a military installation at Qui Nohn, killing *twenty-three* Americans and wounding more than *100* (the most casualties the U.S. had suffered, to date, in a enemy attack). While RFK recommended a "negotiated settlement," President Johnson was determined to teach the belligerents a hard lesson, and initiated a massive bombing campaign. Code named *Operation Rolling Thunder,* the aerial bombardment was targeted to force the enemy to remove its regular army and guerilla forces from South Vietnam.

President Johnson explained his decision during a nationally televised address: "We love peace. We shall do all we can in order to preserve it for ourselves and mankind. But, we love liberty the more, and we shall take up any challenge; we shall answer any threat. We shall pay any price to make certain that freedom shall not perish from this earth."

On March 2, 1965, over *100* U.S. bombers attacked a North Vietnamese ammunition depot and a naval base. Over the next three years, more bombs would be dropped on North Vietnam than were dropped on Europe during the entirety of World War II. *Operation Rolling Thunder* launched more than *300,000* sorties, and dropped nearly *1,000,000* tons of bombs on North Vietnam, generating an estimated *72,000* civilian and military casualties.

Once *Rolling Thunder* was underway, President Johnson insisted upon being awakened throughout the night for updates on the bombing raids. LBJ described his close supervision with characteristic Texas swagger: "They can't even bomb an outhouse without my approval!"

Even with its raw power, *Rolling Thunder* remained a *controlled* or *limited* response to North Vietnamese aggression. Fearful of killing Soviet and Chinese military advisors in the major cities of Hanoi and

Haiphong, American bombers were not allowed to launch attacks north of the twentieth parallel.

China and the Soviet Union were both determined to position themselves as the *true* Communist powers in Asia. To avoid being upstaged by their Sino neighbors, the Soviet Union supplied North Vietnam with surface-to-air missiles, *IL-28* bombers, and *MIG* fighter jets. In turn, China deployed *17,000* troops to North Vietnam, with orders to remain on *stand-by*. The Chinese government issued a stern warning—if American ground forces crossed the seventeenth parallel, the *Red Army* would join in the fight.

American military leaders were privately unhappy with the constraints of a *limited war*. General John P. O'Connell later explained his dissatisfaction: "We went in there with limited objectives…It never was the intent to destroy the North Vietnam nation, itself. If it had been that intentional, we could have done it. We could have done it with air and naval power in six months."

American bombing strategy in Southeast Asia was flawed from the start. North Vietnam lacked the infrastructure and the World War II era industrialization of Germany and Japan, which lessened the destructive impact of aerial bombardment. Cold War era military leaders, like General Curtis Lemay, the hero of World War II firebombing raids over Japan, however, continued to lecture LBJ's civilian military advisers about the need to pulverize North Vietnam: "We will bomb them into the Stone Age."

National Security Adviser, McGeorge Bundy, who questioned the effectiveness of bombing alone, quickly replied: "Maybe they're already there."

The North Vietnamese regular army and Viet Cong guerillas used carefully hidden jungle trails to rapidly shift troops to and from South Vietnam, avoiding widespread loss of life from American bombs. The *Ho Chi Minh Trail*, a principle conduit, ran southward from North Vietnam through Laos and Cambodia, providing multiple entry points into South Vietnam. Writer, historian, and war correspondent, David Halberstam, described the enemy's war-making strategy: "North Vietnam could escalate or de-escalate the tempo by deciding how many of its men to send into battle at a given time."

Only four days after the initiation of *Rolling Thunder*, President Johnson was already bemoaning the ineffectiveness of American bombing raids. LBJ shared his frustrations with Richard Russell: "Airplanes ain't worth a damn, Dick…Hell; I had *160* of them over a barracks and *twenty-seven* buildings, and set (only) *two* on fire!"

A day later, LBJ shared his inner turmoil with Lady Bird: "I can't get out, and I can't finish it with what I have got. And, I don't know what the hell to do!"

Operation Rolling Thunder marked a point of no return in America's commitment to the war in Southeast Asia. Prior to the onset of the bombing campaign, the Joint Chiefs of Staff informed President Johnson that ground troops would eventually be needed to protect American air bases in South Vietnam.

On Capitol Hill, a pair of Democratic Senators, Idaho's Frank Church and South Dakota's George McGovern, began openly criticizing LBJ's Vietnam policy, stoking the growing nationwide *peace movement.* In 1965, however, LBJ's steely resolve still appealed to the majority of Americans, who feared the rise of Communism.

Johnson's public bravado masked an inner turmoil. Lady Bird was shocked to hear her husband tell Vice-President Humphrey: "I'm not temperamentally equipped to be Commander-in-Chief."

Johnson bemoaned the incessant pressure from military leaders to escalate the bombing: "I'm too sentimental to give the orders."

As early as February of 1965, LBJ questioned American military escalation in Vietnam. In a telephone conversation with Secretary of Defense McNamara, Johnson shared his misgivings: "Now we're off to bombing these people. We're over that hurdle. I don't think anything is going to be as bad as *losing,* but I don't see any way of *winning."*

Johnson grew frustrated with his hawkish military advisers, and worried about the political ramifications of lengthy American involvement in the war. In late February, LBJ ordered Army Chief of Staff, Harold Johnson, to travel to Vietnam and return with a firsthand report on the situation: "Bomb, bomb, bomb. That's all you know! Well, I want to know why there's nothing else. You Generals have all been educated at taxpayer's expense, and you're not giving me any ideas about any solutions for this damn little piss ant country. Now, I don't need ten Generals to come in here ten times, to tell me to bomb. I want solutions—I want some answers!"

In early March, General William Westmoreland, commander of American forces in South Vietnam, requested the deployment of ground troops to protect air bases now under attack from the Viet Cong. While such a move constituted a *major* commitment toward long-term involvement in

Southeast Asia, LBJ concluded that he must comply with Westmoreland's request.

On March 8, 1965, the first American combat troops (two Marine battalions) landed on the beaches of Da Nang. The soldiers were joyously greeted by bikini clad South Vietnamese women, unaware of the horrors that lay ahead.

Johnson telephoned his mentor, Richard Russell, to discuss the Marine deployment. A hawkish Conservative by reputation, Russell had long since concluded that a ground war in the jungles of Vietnam would be disastrous. LBJ explained the rationale for his latest decision: "We're going to send the Marines to protect the Hawk Battalion, the Hawk outfit at Da Nang; because they're afraid the security provided by the Vietnamese is not enough."

"I guess we've got no choice, but it scares the death out of me," Johnson continued, "I think everybody's going to think: 'We're landing the Marines. We're off to battle...'"

Russell listened to the President's monologue with glum resignation.

"So, it's a choice, and it's a hard one, but Westmoreland and Taylor (General Maxwell Taylor, the American Ambassador to South Vietnam) come in every day saying, *please* send them on. And, the Joint Chiefs say, *please* send them on! And McNamara and Rusk say, send them on...What do you think?" LBJ asked.

"We've gone so damn far, Mister President—it scares the life out of me. But, I don't know how to back up, now. It looks to me like we just got in this thing, and there's no way out..." Russell replied.

LBJ shared his own anxieties: "...I don't know, Dick...The great trouble I'm under—a man can fight if he can see daylight down the road, somewhere. But, there ain't no daylight in Vietnam. There's not a bit."

Russell agreed: "There's no end to the road. There's just nothing."

For all of his misgivings over escalating the American war effort, LBJ still ascribed to the *Domino Theory*. During a telephone conversation with syndicated columnist, Drew Pearson, the President explained the global ramifications of spreading Communism: "I don't believe I can walk. If I did, they'd take Thailand—they'd take Cambodia—they'd take Burma—they'd take Indonesia—they'd take India—they'd come right back take the Philippines..."

LBJ convinced himself that an American show of force would convince North Vietnam that a protracted guerilla-style war was a waste of time and manpower. On April 7, 1965, during a speech at Johns Hopkins University, the President proffered a deal—if the North Vietnamese would guarantee independence for South Vietnam, the United States would invest *one billion* dollars in the *Mekong River Delta Project,* to promote socioeconomic development of the impoverished region.

Ever the political pragmatist, Lyndon Johnson quietly viewed the Vietnam War as a *no win* proposition: "If I don't go in now and they later say I should have gone, then they'll be all over me in Congress. They won't be talking about my Civil Rights Bill, or education, or beautification. No sir. They'll push Vietnam up my ass, every time..."

At the same time, LBJ was fully aware that an enormous foreign policy failure would ultimately jeopardize his grandiose domestic agenda: "If we get into this war, I know what's going to happen. Those damn conservatives are going to sit in Congress, and they're going to use the war as a way of opposing my *Great Society* legislation."

By the spring of 1965, the anti-war movement was establishing a firm foothold across America. On Easter Sunday, a small group of protesters gathered outside the LBJ ranch in Texas. Days later, seventeen antiwar demonstrators staged a *sit in* on the White House driveway.

An enraged LBJ linked the peace movement to Communism, registering his displeasure to a *New York Tribune* columnist: "Our own people are creating doubts, and they're questioning our policies. So the kids are running up and down, parading, and most them are led by Communist groups...You can say most are led by beatniks and these left wing groups, and the few Senators that are joining and going to campuses to stir them up...And, that's a great disservice to America, and it's a great disservice to our fighting men..."

Later that same month, during a private meeting at the White House, Robert Kennedy joined the dissent. RFK urged the President to stop the bombing in North Vietnam and pursue a peaceful settlement. LBJ was non-committal, fearing that a halt in the bombing was equivalent to telling Ho Chi Mihn that "we were so eager for a settlement, we would do anything."

On May 6, 1965, RFK fired a warning shot at the Johnson Administration during a Senate floor address. Two days earlier, President Johnson had submitted a *700 million* dollar military appropriations request to Congress, in order to fund "mounting military requirements in Vietnam." LBJ explained that the measure was *not routine:* "Each member of Congress who supports this request is also voting to persist in our effort to halt Communist aggression in South Vietnam."

After the appropriation was passed by the House (*408* to *7*) and Senate (*88* to *3*), RFK warned that it was not a "blank check" for continued American intervention in Southeast Asia. For the first time, RFK was publicly advocating peaceful negotiations with North Vietnam.

Robert McNamara, who had been JFK's Secretary of Defense and continued to serve in the Johnson Administration, remained close to RFK. McNamara was in a unique position, having the ears of both LBJ and RFK, but his paradoxical behaviors were puzzling. When McNamara spoke privately with RFK and other Kennedy loyalists, he questioned the value of bombing North Vietnam and predicted that American military victory in Southeast Asia was unlikely. At the same time, in his public statements and private advice to President Johnson, McNamara advocated widening the war.

Reacting to growing anti-war opposition, President Johnson temporarily halted the bombing on May 12, 1965. LBJ was dubious about the value of such action, sarcastically referring to it as "Bobby Kennedy's pause." Over the course of the next three years, there would be a handful of temporary pauses in aerial bombardment, all of which proved unsuccessful in motivating the North Vietnamese to seek peace.

A month later, military leaders asked the President to commit an additional *150,000* American ground troops to Vietnam. LBJ realized the U.S. was headed toward full-scale war, and that he was stretching the limits of his constitutional powers. Privately, Johnson confided his concerns to an adviser: "We know, ourselves, in our own conscience, that when we asked for this Tonkin Gulf Resolution, we had no intention of committing this many ground troops."

LBJ, however, was unwilling to ask for broader war-making powers, fearing a prolonged battle with Congress, which would redirect attention and funding from his beloved social programs. As a consequence, the *defensive war* provisions of the Gulf of Tonkin Resolution became the sole justification for American military intervention during the entirety of the Vietnam War.

Johnson ultimately granted General Westmoreland's request for reinforcements, ordering further troop deployments as the year progressed. In June of 1965, *175,000* American soldiers were stationed in Vietnam. By the end of the year, the number grew to *200,000.*

LBJ's anxiety about Vietnam intensified. In July of 1965, he shared his fears with Lady Bird: "I don't want to get in a war, and I don't see any way out of it. I've got to call up *600,000* boys, and make them leave their homes and families."

While publicly supporting the troops, LBJ began second guessing the abilities of American foot soldiers. Johnson privately shared his doubts with Senator Birch Bayh: "They (the Viet Cong) hope they can wear us out. And, I really believe they'll last longer than we do. One of their boys gets down in a rut, and he stays there for two days without water, food, or anything, and never moves—waiting to ambush somebody. Now an American, he stays there about twenty minutes, and God damn, he's got to get him a cigarette!"

During a conversation with Richard Russell, LBJ voiced frustration over the stalemate in Vietnam: "I've never worked on anything as hard in my life."

Russell shared LBJ's angst: "It's just nearly driven me mad. I guess it's the only thing I've ever hit in my life that I didn't have some answer to."

The President was also troubled by the forecast of Chief of Naval Operations, Admiral David McDonald: "I believe that sooner or later, we'll force the enemy to the (peace) conference table. We *can't* win an all-out war."

In a series of meetings with Defense and State Department officials, the Joint Chiefs of Staff, and congressional leaders in July of 1965, the President carefully weighed their opinions on American military involvement in South Vietnam. With the exception of Undersecretary of State, George Ball and Senate Majority Leader, Mike Mansfield, both of whom advocated withdrawal, the President's civilian and military advisers supported escalation of the war effort. In the end, LBJ accepted the majority opinion, refusing to back down, and American troops continued to pour into Southeast Asia.

While Robert Kennedy was viewed as a voice of reason and steady proponent of a negotiated settlement with North Vietnam, he managed to court controversy in November of 1965. During a routine press conference, RFK expressed the willingness to donate blood to wounded North Vietnamese troops and civilians as a humanitarian gesture, which did not conflict with patriotism. Conservative Republican Senator (and former Republican presidential candidate), Barry Goldwater, proclaimed that Kennedy's statement was "close to treason."

Many Americans strongly disagreed with RFK, and the *New York*

Daily News harshly criticized him: "If you feel strongly enough for the enemy to give a pint of your blood every ninety days for so, then why not go for the whole hog? Why not light out for the enemy country and join its armed forces? Bobby Kennedy is young, strong, virile, and financially able to provide for his wife and children, while he is away at war."

The personal attacks did not diminish Kennedy's dovish tendencies. In December, he called for yet another bombing halt, to correspond with the Christmas season. In private, he shared his own conflicted feelings about the growing war: "I'd like to speak out more on Vietnam. I have talked again and again of my desire for negotiations. But, if I broke with the (Johnson) Administration, it might be disastrous for the country."

While the drumbeat of war threatened to wreck his presidency, Lyndon Johnson achieved remarkable success in the arena of Civil Rights. In 1964, LBJ had pushed legislation through Congress, ending racial discrimination. As pleased as he was with the passage of the Civil Rights Bill, Johnson knew there was more to be done: "…I want all those other things—buses, restaurants, all of that—but the right to vote, with no ifs, ands, or buts, that's the key. When the Negros get that, they'll have every politician, North, South, East, and West, kissing their ass, begging for support."

In the spring of 1965, on the heels of Selma's *Bloody Sunday,* when black voter registration was interrupted by the violent actions of white Alabamians, LBJ addressed a joint session of Congress. In the most eloquent speech of his political career, Johnson announced his plans to submit a *Voting Rights Bill*: "There is not a constitutional issue here. The command of the constitution is plain. There is no moral issue. It is wrong—deadly wrong—to deny any of your fellow Americans the right to vote in this country. There is no issue of states' rights or national rights. There is only the struggle for human rights…because; it is not just Negroes, but really all of us, who must overcome the crippling legacy of bigotry and injustice. And we shall overcome!"

While watching the President's historic speech, Civil Rights leader, Martin Luther King, burst into tears.

On August 6, President Johnson signed into law the *Voting Rights Act of 1965*. At a well publicized signing ceremony, LBJ hailed the new law with a rhetorical flourish: "They came in darkness and chains…today; we strike away the last major shackles of those fierce and ancient bonds."

Under the auspices of the new legislation, voter qualification tests were outlawed, and federal registrars were assigned to *seven* states (Alabama,

Georgia, Louisiana, North Carolina, South Carolina, Mississippi, and Virginia) to enforce the new federal mandates. Within *five* months, African American voter registration increased by *forty* percent across the Deep South.

Johnson explained the importance of voting rights to United Auto Workers' President Walter Reuther: "I'm not going to be President long, but while I am President, brother, I'm going to take care of voting in this country. Everybody's going to be able to vote."

"I'd like to do it at (age) eighteen. I'd like to do it for free. I don't give a damn how ignorant they are. They got enough instinct to know how to vote, because they've been voting for me all these years—a lot of ignorant people," LBJ told Reuther.

"They're just like my beagle—my beagle runs up, and he smells my ankles, and he knows this is the man, right here!" Johnson proclaimed.

Much to LBJ's chagrin, enactment of the *Voting Rights Act* did not alleviate rising racial tensions. On August 11, 1965, riots broke out in the Watts section of Los Angeles, following a confrontation between a black male and a white California highway patrolman. The siege lasted for *four* days, with widespread property destruction, arson, and looting. *Thirty four* people died during the rioting, and another *1000* were wounded. Some *4000* rioters were arrested, and property damage estimates approached *forty million dollars.*

Lyndon Johnson was shocked and angered by the lawless behavior of African Americans in the Watts rioting. As usual, LBJ personalized the conflict, and felt the rioters were displaying blatant ingratitude, in light of his efforts on their behalf. LBJ believed black rioters were making "fools" out of themselves, and their continued rioting and looting would jeopardize chances for further advances in racial equality.

While allocating millions of dollars to rehabilitate riot-ravaged Watts, Johnson issued a stern warning: "A rioter with a Molotov Cocktail in his hands is not fighting for Civil Rights any more than a Klansman with a sheet on his back and a mask on his face. They are both, more or less, what the law declares them—lawbreakers, destroyers of Constitutional rights and liberties, and ultimately destroyers of a free America. They must be exposed and they must be dealt with."

Robert Kennedy, who realized that poverty and discrimination could not be eradicated by words and money alone, identified with the underdog: "A lot of those looters are just kids in trouble. I got in trouble when I was that age."

Influenced by Emerson's ideal of *self-reliance,* RFK believed that ghetto dwellers could only improve their socioeconomic status by engaging in "dignified, hard and extracting work." He believed that federal spending was not the sole answer to inner city despair, and change could not be effected by "fiat from Washington." Kennedy feared that the problems of the ghetto (drugs, crime, and violence) would eventually spread to afflict the middle class.

Militant African Americans exploited the anger of their brethren, and in the height of the Watts rioting, adopted a new mantra: "Burn, baby, burn."

A new generation of revolutionary black leaders challenged the concept of *passive resistance,* which had long been the rallying cry of Martin Luther King, Jr. Men like Stokely Carmichael, H. Rap Brown, Bobby Seale, and Malcolm X openly criticized non-violence as an ineffective means to secure racial equality.

"Integration is subterfuge for maintenance of white supremacy," Carmichael proclaimed.

Fearful of racially motivated violence, white Americans began purchasing firearms at unprecedented rates. With rioting in the streets and mounting opposition to the war in Vietnam, LBJ's unprecedented Civil Rights achievements faded into the background.

In spite of the nation's problems, Lyndon Johnson took immense pride in the achievements of his first elective year in office. In August of 1965, historian William Leuchtenburg told the President that the recent Congress had *arguably* been the most significant, *ever.*

"No, it isn't," LBJ replied, "It isn't *arguable.*"

Congress eventually grew less enamored with Johnson's expansive goals. In September of 1965, LBJ suffered the first major legislative defeat of his presidency, when lawmakers voted down his proposal for *Home Rule* in the District of Columbia. The honeymoon between the executive and legislative branches of the federal government had officially ended.

The stress of the presidency took its toll on Lyndon Johnson. Presidential aide, Bill Moyers, was concerned enough to secretly consult a psychiatrist about LBJ's "depression and paranoia." The mental health professional was unwilling to render a diagnosis without examining the patient, but warned Moyers that Johnson's behavior might worsen, particularly if his stress level increased.

Moyers vividly recalled LBJ's state of mind in the summer of 1965: "It was a pronounced, prolonged depression. He would just go within himself, just disappear—morose, self-pitying, angry…He was a tormented man."

According to Moyers, LBJ feared that his decision to send combat troops to South Vietnam would mean "the end of his presidency."

LBJ's moods were mercurial. Notoriously thin skinned, he overreacted to any perceived slight or mild criticism. As expected, much of his paranoia was directed at Robert Kennedy, whom he suspected was plotting to *reclaim* the presidency. Anyone who maintained contact with RFK (or even spoke nicely of him) was immediately deemed *disloyal* by Johnson.

Johnson verbally accosted Moyers for maintaining a friendship with RFK: "That's the trouble with all you fellows—you're in bed with the Kennedy's."

Moyers, undeniably one of LBJ's most loyal and trusted aides, believed the Vietnam War was largely responsible for Johnson's trouble psyche: "An atrocious marriage of ego and nationhood, so that Johnson saw himself as America, involved in some sort of challenge to manhood."

On August 27, 1965, Lyndon Johnson celebrated his fifty-seventh birthday. Lady Bird surprised him with a special cake, decorated with the words: "You can have your cake and eat it, too." Additional decorations included a hypodermic needle (representing *Medicare*), tiny houses (representing the *Housing Act*) and a roadway building (representing the *Appalachian Act* for the poor).

This would be Johnson's last birthday as a popular and effectual leader. By the end of the year, the prospect of funding a long-term war in Southeast Asia threatened the very survival of the *Great Society*. With Robert Kennedy waiting in the wings, Lyndon Johnson's grasp on power grew more tenuous.

Chapter 16

You're just a do-gooder

On January 12, 1966, Lyndon Johnson delivered his third State of the Union Address, boldly declaring that the United States could prosecute the war in Vietnam, while continuing the *Great Society*—the so-called *guns and butter* theory. LBJ's lofty rhetoric echoed through the House chambers: "This nation is mighty enough, its society is healthy enough, its people are strong enough, to pursue our goals in the rest of the world, while building a 'Great Society' here at home."

Johnson asked Congress to enact his ambitious domestic proposals, including legislation for clean water projects, elimination of discriminatory practices in housing sales and rentals (as well as federal and state jury selection), and establishment of a Cabinet level Department of Transportation. *The Washington Post* headlined: "U.S. can continue the Great Society and fight in Vietnam."

While Congress passed *ninety-seven* of the *113* bills that LBJ submitted in 1966, the scope of the new legislation did not match the historic accomplishments of the previous year. Lawmakers quickly discovered that *guns and butter* could not be financed without a significant budget deficit or a sizeable tax increase, and neither choice was particularly palatable.

On December 18, 1965, President Johnson temporarily halted the bombing of North Vietnam, which proved to be another failed attempt to lure the enemy to the peace table. Not surprisingly, the Joint Chiefs of Staff soon asked the President to escalate the war effort, believing that a bombing halt was a sign of weakness. On January 31, 1966, after a *thirty-seven* day pause, LBJ reinstated the aerial bombardment. That same day, Robert Kennedy spoke on the floor of the Senate, delivering his most staunch antiwar declaration: "If we regard bombing as the answer in Vietnam, we are headed straight for disaster. In the past, bombing has not proved a decisive weapon against a rural economy or against a guerilla enemy."

The *Chicago Tribune* lampooned the widening breach between the Johnson Administration and RFK, referring to the New York Senator as "Ho Chi Kennedy." On February 4, 1966, the Senate Foreign Relations Committee opened public hearings on Vietnam. The committee chairman, Arkansas' William Fulbright, had grown skeptical of an American military victory in Southeast Asia, and his antiwar stance fractured his long-standing relationship with LBJ. Much to the President's chagrin, Fulbright declared that the war in Vietnam was morally wrong.

The news from South Vietnam proved equally disheartening. As the ground war escalated, nearly *four million* South Vietnamese (*twenty-three percent* of the country's population) were driven from their homes into refugee camps or already overcrowded cities. Many of the disaffected citizens were recruited to join ranks with the attacking Viet Cong guerillas. The United States appropriated *thirty million* dollars per year for the displaced refugees, but much of the money was stolen by corrupt South Vietnamese government officials.

While the Congressional hearings on Vietnam were getting underway, LBJ traveled to Honolulu to meet with the leaders of South Vietnam, vowing to continue joint efforts to defeat the North Vietnamese. Robert Kennedy privately characterized Johnson's trip as little more than a "public relations stunt."

Publicly, RFK joked about his differences with LBJ: "It isn't true that President Johnson and I didn't get along during the time I was Attorney General and he was the Vice-President. We began the Kennedy Administration with the best of relations—close, friendly, cordial—and then, as we were leaving the inaugural stand..."

"President Johnson and I are very courteous and correct in our correspondence, these days. I address my letters to him at the White House, and he writes to me at the Senate Office Building. Sometimes he only uses the initials," Kennedy quipped.

As the fighting in Vietnam grew fierce, Johnson frequently employed the patriotic trump card to promote hawkishness. On May 17th, LBJ addressed the war effort at a Democratic Party dinner in Chicago: "All I can say to you tonight, is that the road ahead is going to be difficult... There will be some 'Nervous Nellies' and some who will be frustrated and bothered, and break ranks under the strain, and some will turn on their leaders and on their country, and on our own fighting men. There will be times of trial and tension in the days ahead that will exact the best that is in all of us."

All the while, LBJ was experiencing a recurrent nightmare: "Robert Kennedy is out in front, leading the fight against me, telling everyone that I had betrayed John Kennedy's commitment to South Vietnam—that I let a democracy fall into the hands of Communists—that I was a coward—an unmanly man—a man without a spine. Oh, I could see it coming, all right. Every night, when I fell asleep, I would see myself tied to the ground in the middle of a long open space. In the distance, I could hear the voices of thousands of people. They were all shouting at me and running toward me: 'Coward, traitor, weakling!'"

LBJ's White House staff eventually fractured, as many aides found the work environment entirely too stressful. By the end of 1966, speechwriters Theodore Sorenson, and Richard Goodwin had resigned, reaffirming their loyalties to Robert Kennedy. Press Secretary, George Reedy, and National Security Adviser, McGeorge Bundy also departed, along with LBJ's long-time adviser, Jack Valenti. In perhaps the most stunning blow, Bill Moyers resigned from the White House staff in December of 1966.

The polished and articulate Moyers had long served as a calming influence on the bellicose Johnson. Moyers later recalled: "After you've worked with LBJ, you can work with the devil."

Throughout his tenure as Johnson's advisor, Moyers had maintained a working relationship with Robert Kennedy. On the day of Moyers's resignation from the Johnson Administration, RFK took the former aide to lunch. When the *Washington Star* featured a photograph of the two men together on its front page, LBJ was enraged. Political pundit, John Roche, described the President's angry response: "Johnson went right up the wall…It was such a set up, too. You've got to hand it to Bobby—that was a beauty. Of course, after that, nothing would ever convince Johnson that Moyers really hadn't been on the Kennedy payroll for years and years…Johnson never forgave him."

As 1966 moved slowly forward, and the casualties began to accumulate in Vietnam, LBJ found it increasingly difficult to explain the need for American involvement in the war. Consequently, his favorability rating declined to *forty-six* percent—the lowest point since Johnson had assumed office in November of 1963.

In the fall of 1965, Robert Kennedy was invited to address the anti-apartheid, *National Union of South African Students (NUSAS)*. Because Kennedy supported black independence in South Africa, the white minority controlled government stalled for five months, before granting him permission to enter their country.

When Kennedy landed at the Johannesburg Airport in June of 1966, a group of white South Africans greeted him with signs of protest: "Yankee go home," and "Chuck him out."

After the South African Prime Minister refused to meet with him, RFK dined with a group of businessmen, who explained that the United States should support the apartheid government, which shared common anti-Communist ideals. Kennedy quickly countered their argument: "What does it mean to be against Communism, if one's own system denies the value of the individual and gives all power to the government, just as Communists do?"

At the University of Cape Town, Bobby shared his idealism: "Few will have the greatness to bend history itself. But, each of us can work to change a small portion of events, and in the total of those acts, will be written the history of this generation. It is from numberless diverse acts of courage and belief that human history is shaped. Each time a man stands up for an ideal, or acts to improve the lot of others, or strikes out against injustice, he sends a tiny ripple of hope, and crossing each other from a million different centers of energy and daring, those ripples build a current which can sweep down the mightiest walls of oppression and resistance."

At Stellenbosch University, Kennedy challenged white religious leaders: "If blacks are not inferior to whites, why don't they take part in your elections? Why don't you allow them to worship in your churches? What the Hell would you do, if you found out God was black?"

While traveling in Johannesburg, RFK's car was surrounded by black crowds cheering: "Master, Master."

Embarrassed, Kennedy begged them: "Please don't use that word."

The white leadership of South Africa resented Kennedy's anti-apartheid message. *Die Transvaler*, a newspaper closely aligned with the government, offered "deepest sympathy for the American people, if Senator Kennedy becomes their future President."

After touring South Africa, RFK visited Tanzania, Kenya, and Ethiopia. On his return trip to the United States, he stopped in Rome for an audience with the Pope. RFK appealed to the Pontiff's social conscious, stressing that many black Africans were abandoning Christianity because "the Christian God hates Negros."

In only his second year as a United States Senator, Robert Kennedy's popularity was soaring. *U. S. News and World Report* wrote that RFK "receives more mail and speaking invitations than any other member of Congress."

RFK's maturation was striking to those who had long been acquainted him. A reporter described the changes, as Kennedy approached middle age: "He has graying, ginger hair now, lapped over his earlobes in the shaggy style of the alienated young. His blue eyes are now sad, rather than cold, and haunted, rather than hostile."

The same reporter described the atypical nature of Kennedy's public persona: "I liked him enormously…Kennedy was the first national politician I had met who had human reactions. He wasn't plastic. He wasn't programmed…I felt he was bright and that he saw the world from an angle I couldn't imagine."

Columnist, Stewart Alsop, wrote that RFK was a most unusual politician, with a "curious inability to talk about himself."

Bobby continued to prefer personal contact with only select individuals, rather than the traditional mixing and mingling associated with political gatherings. With stooped shoulders and a grim expression, he frequently found himself on the periphery of crowds at social functions; a byproduct of shyness and boredom, rather than presumed arrogance.

RFK consistently indentified with the underdog and remained most comfortable around children. During a political tour of Brooklyn, Bobby strayed from his colleagues, after noticing a ten-year-old girl wearing eyeglasses. Squatting down, he tenderly touched the back of the girl's neck: "Do you know something? My little girl has glasses just like yours. And, I love my little girl very much."

Bobby's *rock star* image made him popular among young Americans, particularly women. Teenagers often lined up outside Kennedy's Capitol Hill office, hoping to catch a glimpse of the famous Senator.

As he strolled through the Atlanta airport, RFK was spied by a teenage girl, talking on a pay phone. As Kennedy neared, the girl grew giddy: "Jane, Jane, you won't believe it! Bobby Kennedy is walking by—no, really, Bobby Kennedy is walking right by me! No, I swear, Jane, I swear he is walking by—he's coming along here, and he's almost here. God, he's gorgeous!"

With a shy smile, RFK took the phone from the girl: "Jane, it's me—just wanted to chat with you. How are you, anyway? Okay? It's really me. Have a good day."

As he grew more comfortable in the public eye, RFK revealed more of his dry wit. While in Long Island, Kennedy rode in a car driven by black entertainer, Sammy Davis, Jr. When Davis indicated that the automobile was low on gas, Kennedy responded with mock horror: "No, don't stop at a station. They'll think we're a bunch of Freedom Riders coming to picket."

Even though he was a widely recognized celebrity who captivated the imaginations of American youth, RFK retained a measure of Puritanism. On the streets of New York City, Kennedy was observed lecturing two boys on the evils of cigarette smoking.

As the war in Vietnam escalated, RFK grew increasingly frustrated: "The worst thing about the war is not the war itself, although that's bad enough, but all the great opportunities that are going down the drain. We had a real chance to do something about poverty, to get blacks out of ghettos, but we're paralyzed. I don't like Johnson, but he was doing some good things. Now, there's no direction."

An exasperated RFK found it difficult to utter Lyndon Johnson's name: "Can you believe what *he* is doing?"

As the casualties mounted in Vietnam, LBJ felt pressure from all sides, and continued to blame Robert Kennedy for many of his woes. Political scientist, John Roche, recalled LBJ's paranoia: "Not a sparrow fell from a tree, but what he was convinced it was the intervention of Kennedy."

Johnson's concept of absolute loyalty required that all Cabinet officers and White House advisers choose sides. Anyone who maintained a friendship with RFK was automatically viewed as a *traitor*.

RFK's criticism of LBJ's Vietnam policy particularly angered the President. Johnson believed that Kennedy was the lightning rod for the expanding anti-war protests: "Bobby gave the Communists the idea. Now, I'm not saying that he's a Communist, mind you. But, they saw how they might be able to divide the country against me. They (meaning the Kennedy clan) already control the three major networks..."

Robert Kennedy never believed government intervention was the sole remedy for societal ills. In contrast to classic liberal ideology, Kennedy questioned if welfare wasn't doing more harm than good, believing that job creation was a more worthy objective than guaranteed incomes.

Lyndon Johnson's pride and joy, the *Great Society,* was not immune to RFK's criticism: "There is not a problem for which money is not being spent. There is not a problem or a program on which dozens or hundreds or thousands of bureaucrats are not earnestly at work. But, does this represent a solution to our problems? Manifestly, it does not."

Kennedy dreamed of establishing an urban renewal program, managed locally and not entirely dependent on government funding. The Bedford Stuyvesant section of Brooklyn proved to be the ideal testing ground for this concept. The poverty stricken, crime-ridden area consisted mostly of minorities—*eighty* percent African American and *fifteen* percent Puerto Rican.

RFK's brainchild, the *Bed-Sty Corporation,* was governed by a local board of directors and received significant funding from private businesses and charities (including the *Ford* and *Astor Foundations*). *Bed-Sty* established a new model for *self-regeneration* of ghetto areas. *IBM* provided funding for the project, and also opened a factory in the oppressed neighborhood, creating quality jobs for area residents. Kennedy monitored the program closely, and the *Bed-Sty* staff remembered that he "wanted action, not explanations."At the formal dedication ceremony on December 10,

1966, RFK expressed hope that the area would become a "self-reliant community."

While *Bed-Sty* was not an unqualified success, its novel approach of local administration and significant private financing proved to be a working model for future social projects. Michael Harrington, author of *The Other America*, remembered *Bed-Sty* as a "modest success—which, in the context of so many failures, is to say a remarkable success."

Unlike many politicians who claimed to be socially conscious, Robert Kennedy did not rely on second hand accounts of poverty and oppression. Touring a migrant workers' camp in Upstate New York, RFK and his advisors encountered an ominous sign: "Anyone entering or trespassing without my permission will be shot if caught." While many in the group were intimidated by the warning, Kennedy marched on, discovering three migrant families living in a bus, with the seats torn out and cardboard covering the windows. RFK was appalled by the sight of six small children playing atop a filthy mattress, their bodies covered by running sores.

Fighting nausea from the stench, Bobby asked one of the black mothers how much she earned—the woman told him that she made one dollar per hour, picking lettuce. The armed owner soon arrived, as the warning sign had promised: "You had no right to go in there. You're just a do-gooder, trying to make some headlines."

"You are something out of the nineteenth century. I wouldn't let an animal live in these buses," Kennedy angrily replied.

"It's like camping out," the owner snidely remarked.

After his visit to the poverty stricken migrant camp, RFK demanded that the Governor of New York investigate conditions in all camps, and urged labor leaders to immediately organize unions for migrant farm workers.

The violent stalemate in Vietnam remained the overriding story of 1966. By October, there were *400,000* U.S. troops in Vietnam, and *6664* Americans had already died.

On August 8th, the *New York Times* reported the conclusions of a Pentagon study that predicted it would take *eight years* to win the war in Vietnam, unless U.S. forces were increased to *750,000* (even then, it would take a minimum of *five years*). In mid October, after returning from a fact finding mission in South Vietnam, Secretary of Defense McNamara, informed President Johnson that there was "no reasonable way to bring the war to an end, soon." At the time, McNamara, who was clearly conflicted, recommended adding *70,000* more combat troops in the coming year.

In late October, LBJ traveled to Vietnam too meet with American troops at Camranh Bay (this marked the first visit by a President to a war zone, since FDR's trip to Casablanca in 1943). Addressing the soldiers, Johnson voiced continued support for the American military effort: "We shall never let you down, nor your fighting comrades, nor the fifteen million people of Vietnam, nor the hundreds of millions of Asians who are counting on us to show here—here in Vietnam—that aggression doesn't pay, and aggression can't succeed."

The bellicose Texan urged the soldiers to "nail that coonskin on the wall." After his two and one-half hour meeting with American troops, LBJ's resolve to defeat the North Vietnamese was renewed. An emotional Johnson reported that he had "never been more moved by any group I have talked to—never in my life."

Back home, the President's popularity rating remained below *fifty* percent, as off year elections drew near. Johnson spent limited time on the campaign trail, hoping to keep the Vietnam controversy from negatively impacting congressional and gubernatorial elections.

Robert Kennedy, however, campaigned on behalf of fellow Democrats in *twenty-seven* states. In California, RFK debated Republican gubernatorial candidate, Ronald Reagan, who was waging a successful campaign to unseat the incumbent Democrat, Pat Brown. Kennedy was impressed with his opponent, in spite of their sharp differences in ideology: "Reagan is really a sharp cookie, and everyone is underestimating him. He's somebody to watch. I think he could go all the way."

On the campaign trail, Kennedy was greeted by cheering crowds. For the first time, RFK interpreted the electorate's enthusiasm in a different light: "I think they are really here for me, not just him (JFK)."

During a rare joint campaign appearance in New York with President Johnson, RFK flew aboard Air Force One. Kennedy insisted that Democratic advance man, Jerry Bruno, sit with him during the flight, such that he could avoid interacting with Johnson.

"The problem was that if Bob Kennedy didn't like someone, he couldn't fake it. He just wasn't capable," Bruno recalled.

Election Day, 1966, proved disastrous for many incumbent Democrats, as Republicans gained *forty-seven* seats in the House and *three* in the Senate. The Democratic majority in the House of Representatives was reduced from *248* to *187,* while the Senate majority dropped to *sixty-four.*

The Republicans also gained *eight* Governorships, resulting in an even split *(twenty-five each)*.

LBJ's prospects for reelection in 1968 now appeared tenuous. By the end of 1966, head-to-head polling showed Robert Kennedy pulling ahead of the incumbent President.

While RFK knew polls were fickle, he understood that voters were growing wary of LBJ. Kennedy surmised that he agreed with the President on "eighty percent of the issues," but was equally certain that the American people no longer trusted Johnson.

By the end of 1966, RFK's star was on the rise, while the President was handicapped by the heavy weight of *Lyndon Johnson's War*.

Chapter 17

Hey, hey LBJ—how many kids did you kill today?

In 1967, Lyndon Johnson's grandiose plans for *guns and butter* began to unravel. The United States Treasury simply did not have enough money to fund a costly war in Southeast Asia and support the domestic initiatives of the *Great Society*. For the first time during the Johnson presidency, social programs faced budget cuts.

LBJ tried to reassure his *Health, Education, and Welfare (HEW)* Secretary, John Gardner, that the reductions were temporary: "Don't worry, John. We're going to end this damned war, and then you'll have all the money you want for education, health, and everything else."

In his heart, Johnson knew that the war might drag on for years. LBJ grew cynical toward the recipients of his largess, who were now seemingly unappreciative of his past efforts. LBJ sarcastically complained about their ingratitude: "Do you know the difference between cannibals and liberals? Cannibals eat only their enemies."

The *Council of Economic Advisers (COEA)* informed the President that it was on longer possible to fund both the Vietnam War and the *Great Society*, without runaway inflation. Without reductions in military and/or domestic spending, the COEA warned that a tax increase was necessary. Congress was unwilling to raised taxes, but predicated that decision on inaccurate data. Secretary of Defense McNamara provided lawmakers with deliberately deflated budget estimates, masking the actual need for increased tax revenue. By 1967, balanced budgets were a thing of the past, and the United States had accumulated a *9.8 million* dollar budget deficit.

Facing war protestors and a budgetary crisis, LBJ grew morose: "The only difference between the Kennedy assassination and mine is that I'm alive, and it has been more torturous."

To ensure adequate funding for the war effort, across the board budget cuts were implemented. The reduced funding was not limited to social agencies. The space program, which had long enjoyed LBJ's unfailing support, was forced to deal with unaccustomed budgetary restrictions.

Dissatisfaction among NASA officials was widespread and vocal, and only intensified after the tragic events of January 27, 1967, when a fire swept through the *Apollo I* space capsule during a test at the Cape Kennedy launch pad. Astronauts, Roger B. Chafee, Edward H. White III, and Virgil I. Grissom were burned to death before they could escape from the spacecraft, and many blamed the tragic accident on budgetary reductions. LBJ described it as an "all time low for the space program."

In July of 1967, racial riots erupted in Detroit, and President Johnson was forced to send federal troops into the *Motor City* to control the violence and looting. The rioting lasted for a solid week, resulting in *forty-three* deaths and over *2000* injuries. Once again, LBJ could not understand why African Americans did not appreciate his hard fought efforts on their behalf.

In what became known as the *long, hot summer of 1967,* riots spread to other inner city black communities in Tampa, Buffalo, Memphis, Milwaukee, Washington, D.C., Baltimore, Newark, Youngstown, Hartford, and Fort Lauderdale. By the end of the summer, the worst rioting in American history resulted in *ninety* deaths and *400,000* injuries. Nearly *17,000* adults, mostly African Americans, were arrested.

LBJ was dismayed: "How is it possible? After all we've accomplished! How could it be?"

On July 27th, President Johnson addressed a nationwide television audience, calling for an end to violence in the streets. LBJ also announced the formation of a *National Advisory Commission on Civil Disorders,* to be headed by Illinois Governor, Otto Kerner. The so-called *Kerner Commission* examined the root causes of the widespread inner city rioting, and concluded that America consisted "two societies, one white and one black—separate but unequal."

Unhappy that the *Kerner* report did not give sufficient credit to his long-standing support of Civil Rights, Johnson refused to meet in person with commissioners. LBJ's recalcitrance troubled Robert Kennedy, who concluded that the President was "not going to do anything about the war, and he's not going to anything about the cities, either."

During the summer of 1967, RFK was greatly alarmed by the turmoil in both Vietnam and inner city America. While relaxing at his home, RFK contemplated the future. Pointing toward his children playing in the yard, Bobby complained to his friend, Lem Billings: "It doesn't seem like much of a world they're going to inherit, does it? I can't help wondering if I'm doing all I should to keep it from going down the drain."

In January of 1967, Martin Luther King, LBJ's long time ally in the march for Civil Rights, became a vocal critic of the war in Vietnam. King announced that he could "no longer remain silent about an issue that is destroying the soul of our nation."

A month later, King went a step further, equating America's intervention in Vietnam with domestic racism: "We are engaged in a war that seeks to turn the clock of history back and perpetuate white Colonialism."

When King violated LBJ's sacred principle of loyalty, the President was incredulous: "What is that God damned Nigger preacher doing to me? We gave him the Civil Rights Act of 1964. We gave him the Voting Rights Act of 1965, and we gave him the War on Poverty. What more does he want?"

As his presidency spun out of control, Lyndon Johnson maintained a façade of bravado. When asked if he could win reelection in 1968, LBJ appeared fearless: "I sure as hell can. If I decide to run for office, I will win and be right here."

In the jungles of Southeast Asia, North Vietnam showed no signs of abandoning its fight against American and South Vietnamese forces. Ho Chi Mihn was as defiant as Lyndon Johnson, and understood that an ever growing number of Americans were tiring of the war: "Our just cause enjoys strong sympathy and support from the peoples of the white world, including broad sections of the American people."

The American civilian and military leadership of the war effort proved to be a lesson in *mismanagement*. Robert McNamara, who LBJ described as the "ablest man I ever met," harbored growing doubts about the effectiveness of bombing in North Vietnam. For the majority of his tenure as Secretary of Defense, however, McNamara failed to share those concerns with Johnson, hoping that he could "shield" the President from the futility of the war. American military leaders in South Vietnam soon learned that the President loathed bad news, and often overestimated their bombing and battlefield successes. Many of the dovish members of the Johnson Administration were eased out of office to promote a seemingly unified effort in the prosecution of the war.

Perhaps the biggest fallacy originated from LBJ, himself. For the entirety of his political career, Johnson exercised raw power, whether by domination or flattery, to impose his will on others. The President mistakenly assumed such tactics would be equally effective with the North Vietnamese. By coupling power (bombing and combat troops), with potential rewards (like the proposed *MeKong Delta Development Project*), LBJ was certain that he could "find Ho's price."

For once, LBJ badly underestimated his opponent. Ho Chi Minh was a committed revolutionary with a single goal in mind—reuniting Vietnam and driving all foreigners out of the country.

In January of 1967, while touring Europe, Robert Kennedy became further embroiled in the growing controversy over the Vietnam War. Etienne Manac'h, head of the French Foreign Minister's Far East office, met with RFK, and delivered a message from North Vietnam; the enemy was willing to negotiate, if the United States would stop its relentless bombing.

RFK immediately relayed the offer to Washington, where an anonymous, "high ranking" White House source leaked the information to *Newsweek* magazine, which reported that the North Vietnamese had given Kennedy "a significant peace signal." Not surprisingly, LBJ accused his long-time nemesis of undermining American foreign policy.

French President, Charles de Gaulle, took the opportunity to meet with RFK during his European tour. Having led France during its own disastrous intervention in Vietnam, de Gaulle had long believed the divided Asian nation would have to settle its own differences: "As I told your brother, the United States is involved in a wrong course in Vietnam... South Vietnam would not allow the North to run their country. Ho Chi Minh realizes this, and would not attempt it. All of this is being destroyed by your role in Vietnam...History is the force at work in Vietnam, and the United States will not prevail against it..."

De Gaulle shared the lessons of his own past failures: "You are a young man with a brilliant political future. I am an old man, and I have lived through many battles and wear very many scars, so listen to me closely... Do not become embroiled in the difficulty in Vietnam."

The French President understood American politics, warning that those who opposed the war would be "badly hurt." He recommended RFK bide his time, and then seize upon the opportunity to "help your country regain its proper course."

RFK also discussed the war in Vietnam with German foreign minister, Willy Brandt, and French socialist leader, Francois Mitterrand. Both men told him that the war was misguided, and injurious to diplomatic relations between the United States and Europe.

While her husband was traveling in Europe, Ethel Kennedy shared the latest political news via telegram: "Sunday Gallup Poll will show Democrats, Republicans, and Independents combined—Kennedy *49,* Johnson *39,* and neither *10.* If this keeps up, you just may have to dump old Huckleberry Cornpone."

On February 8, 1967, RFK met with LBJ in the Oval Office to discuss his European tour. The President immediately accused Kennedy of disloyalty and interference with the administration's Vietnam policy.

Flustered, RFK denied any intent to publicize his discussion with Manac'h concerning North Vietnam's overtures of peace, explaining to Johnson that the *Newsweek* leak came from "your State Department."

"It's not my State Department Goddamn it—it's your State Department!" LBJ angrily replied, implying that Kennedy loyalists abounded within his administration.

LBJ also threatened retaliation: "I'll destroy you and every one of your dove friends in six months. You'll be dead, politically, in six months!"

Kennedy remained calm, and recommended that Johnson seize the opportunity to pursue a negotiated settlement.

"There just isn't a chance in Hell that I will do that—not the slightest chance," LBJ bitterly responded.

Johnson accused RFK and his minions of disloyalty, and reminded him that they would have to live with "American blood on their hands."

The bitter accusations angered Kennedy: "I don't have to take that from you!"

After the meeting, RFK spoke privately castigated LBJ: "He was shouting and seemed very unstable. I kept thinking that if he exploded like that with me, how could he ever negotiate with Hanoi?"

RFK soon took his anti-war crusade on the road. In March of 1967, while addressing a crowd of students at the University of Oklahoma, Kennedy was loudly booed, after announcing his opposition to student draft deferments.

Nonplussed, RFK asked the crowd: "How many of you favor student deferments?"

When the majority of students answered in the affirmative, Kennedy asked: "How many of you want to escalate the war?"

Once again, the crowd applauded, and RFK quickly responded: "Let me ask you one other question."

Kennedy now had the full attention of the puzzled students: "How many of you, who voted for escalation of the war, also voted for the exemption of students from the draft?"

Oklahoma Senator, Fred Harris, who was on stage with Kennedy, remembered a "giant gasp" emanating from the crowd.

Unwilling to compromise with Robert Kennedy and his followers, LBJ shared his frustrations with a group of congressional leaders: "We can't have peace crawling on our stomachs. We can't have it with a cup in our hands. We can't have it begging."

LBJ, however, could not contain the growing anti-war movement. College students, university faculty members, politicians, and business leaders publicly expressed their dissatisfaction with administration policy. On one occasion, the President was greeted with a macabre sign: "Lee Harvey Oswald, where are you now?"

A national poll, released in June of 1967, showed that *sixty-six* percent of the country had lost confidence in President Johnson's leadership. By this point in time, some *70,000* Americans had been killed or wounded in Vietnam.

Johnson's paranoia about Robert Kennedy's political ambitions intensified. LBJ was convinced that if he pulled out of Vietnam, RFK would suddenly backtrack, and accuse him of capitulating to Communism. Johnson was mistrustful of Kennedy's newly adopted antiwar rhetoric, believing that his nemesis was playing both sides against the middle. In an off the record chat with columnist, Drew Pearson, LBJ declared that Kennedy had the power to reshape history in his favor: "Bobby is going to have *twelve* (negative) books written about me and *twelve* (positive) books written about him, before the next election."

President Johnson's legislative successes became fewer and further in between. LBJ did take pleasure signing into law the *Postal and Federal Salary Act of 1967,* which specified that a public official may not appoint, employ, (or) advance a relative in an agency which he is serving over or which he exercises jurisdiction or control. The anti-nepotism legislation became known as the *Bobby Kennedy Law.*

Lyndon Johnson stubbornly insisted that there was no *stalemate* in Vietnam, and grew furious with newsmen and dovish politicians who maintained the United States was not winning the war. LBJ scoffed at RFK's three-point program to end American involvement in the war—an unconditional bombing halt, a multinational force to replace U.S. troops, and national elections (allowing *all* Vietnamese factions to participate). In defiance of Kennedy's proposal, the President authorized more bombing raids.

Robert Kennedy tried to lead by example, explaining that honest mistakes had been made in devising America's Southeastern Asian policy: "I can testify if fault is to be found, or responsibility assessed, there is enough to go around for all—including myself."

RFK viewed Johnson's recalcitrance with growing frustration. Kennedy privately confided to a legislative aide: "How can we possibly survive five more years of Lyndon Johnson; five more years of a crazy man?"

Kennedy sometimes grew shrill in his criticism of war. He once likened the destruction of South Vietnamese villages by the American military as "not very different from what Hitler did to the Jews."

Meanwhile, LBJ raged at the anti-war protestors and news media, both of whom seemed determined to wreck his presidency. Johnson complained that RFK received all of the positive press, while he was the media whipping boy: "I can prove that he is a son of a bitch, but television doesn't want that story. They (referring to the press) want me to be the son of a bitch."

The publication of William Manchester's, *Death of a President* (a detailed account of the events surrounding JFK's assassination) intensified LBJ's anger. Manchester's book was decidedly pro-Kennedy, and portrayed Lyndon Johnson as power hungry and insensitive to the Kennedy family in the immediate aftermath of the assassination.

LBJ privately denounced Manchester as a "fraud," and alleged that the author was a tool of the Kennedy family.

"He makes Bobby look like a great hero, and makes me look like a son of a bitch, and *ninety-five percent* percent of it is completely fabricated," Johnson proclaimed (while Manchester clearly favored JFK over his successor, his comprehensive, scholarly work was not fraudulent).

Ironically, the Kennedy family became embroiled in controversy over Manchester's book. After Jackie and Bobby complained that the chronology contained too many intimate details about JFK, the author rewrote several sections of his manuscript. Manchester's edits proved insufficient for Jackie Kennedy, who filed an unsuccessful law suit to block publication of the book. The widely publicized controversy helped *Death of a President* rise to bestseller status, and most Americans sided with Manchester, in a rare repudiation of the Kennedy clan.

While serving in the Senate, Robert Kennedy did not limit his focus to the conflict in Vietnam. As part of the *Labor Subcommittee on Poverty*, Kennedy joined a delegation that traveled to the Mississippi Delta, where he was appalled by the abject poverty. After visiting one squalid shack, which housed a destitute, malnourished family, RFK was horrified: "I cannot adequately communicate the horror of the place. It smelled of urine, of vomit—you couldn't breathe without gagging."

After returning from his sojourn to Mississippi, Bobby found his children around the dinner table. Still moved by the plight of poor Southerners, he challenged his offspring: "In Mississippi, a whole family lives in a shack the size of this room. The children are covered with sores and their tummies stick out because they have no food. Do you know how lucky you are? Do you know how *lucky* you are? Do something for your country!"

Kennedy soon petitioned the Secretary of Agriculture to issue free food stamps. RFK pointed out that the poorest Americans simply did not have enough money to buy coupons for groceries.

Senator Kennedy also formed an *Indian Education Subcommittee*, and visited the Blackfoot Reservation in Fort Hall, Idaho. RFK was alarmed by the high rates of poverty, alcoholism, delinquency, and suicide among Native American tribes.

"Lots of white men would come out here from Washington and get upset. But, their tears were crocodile tears. The tears in Senator Kennedy's eyes were very real," a Blackfoot leader recalled.

RFK also traveled to California to investigate the conditions of migrant farm workers. During a meeting to organize workers into a union, led by labor activist, Caesar Chavez, the local sheriff burst into the room.

"We are arresting these farm workers, while they are picketing, for their own safety," the sheriff announced.

"Excuse me, Sheriff, what did you say? You are arresting these people, why? Again, please?" RFK inquired.

"Well, Senator, we're arresting these people because we're afraid something is going to happen to them out there," the lawman replied.

Kennedy was incredulous: "Sheriff, while we are out at lunch, I suggest you read the Constitution of the United States, before we come back for the afternoon session!"

RFK aide, Peter Edelman, was visibly moved by Kennedy's resolve during the visit to California: "He was a different kind of Senator. He saw the justice of Chavez's case, and he was very taken with individual leadership. He realized he could use his position to give voice to the voiceless. It wasn't always popular, but he was willing to take the risk, and to make a difference. Isn't that what political power should be?"

More than ever, Kennedy believed that both state and federal governments were neglecting the poor and disadvantaged. And, he was certain that the Vietnam War was draining needed attention and resources from critical domestic issues.

Lyndon Johnson desperately wanted his legacy to be defined by something other than the war in Vietnam. In a further effort to promote racial equality, LBJ decided to appoint America's first African American Supreme Court Justice. Searching for the right candidate, Johnson could not ignore politics.

The President consulted with Larry Temple, an attorney and legislative aide to Texas Governor, John Connally: "I have a Supreme Court appointment coming up. I'm thinking of appointing a black. Who would you recommend?"

Temple suggested Federal Judge, Leon Higginbotham.

LBJ was unimpressed, resorting to racist vernacular, a habit which invariably tarnished his reputation as one of the staunchest Civil Rights activists of his generation: "Larry, the only two people who ever heard of Judge Higginbotham are you and his Momma. When I appoint a Nigger to the bench, I want everyone to know he's a Nigger!"

Johnson ultimately nominated United States Solicitor General, Thurgood Marshall, for the vacant Supreme Court position. On August 30, 1967, the Senate confirmed the appointee (by a vote of *sixty-nine* to *eleven*), and Marshall became the first black Supreme Court Justice in American history.

Vietnam remained the biggest story of 1967, as anti-war critics grew increasingly vocal. On April 25th, South Dakota's George McGovern (who would ultimately become the Democratic Party's 1972 presidential candidate), spoke out against the war on the floor of the Senate: "We seem bent upon saving the Vietnamese from Ho Chi Minh, even if we have to kill them and demolish their country to do it…I do not intend to remain silent in the face of what I regard as a policy of madness, which, sooner or later, will envelope my son and (our) American youth, by the millions, for years to come."

In September, Massachusetts Congressman, Thomas "Tip" O'Neill, who had previously supported the war, sent his constituents a newsletter, reporting his change of heart. The *Washington Star* headlined: "O'Neill splits with LBJ over Vietnam policy."

An angry LBJ quickly confronted O'Neill: "Tip, what kind of a son of a bitch are you? I expect something like this from those assholes like Bill Ryan (a liberal New York Congressman)…But, you? You're one of my own…Don't go running to the press or telling everybody your views on the war. You're the first member of the Democratic Establishment to oppose me on this, and I don't want you to start the snowball rolling."

In spite of their conciliatory overtures, LBJ did not believe the North Vietnamese were sincere about seeking peace: "I am unable to find any evidence—apart from hope or wishful thinking—which indicates Hanoi is ready, at this time, to talk seriously."

The President maintained that a show of force was his only viable option, and urged military commanders to "hit all military targets, short of provoking Russia and China."

In September, LBJ was jolted by the joint testimony of the Army Chief of Staff and Marine Commandant before the *Senate Preparedness Subcommittee*. The widely respected military leaders reported that the

Secretary of Defense and other civilian officials were constraining the military from waging full-fledged combat, and further advocated expansion of the war effort, to include wider bombing zones and the mining of North Vietnam's Haiphong Harbor.

An incredulous Johnson confronted the Chairman of the Joints Chiefs of Staff: "Your Generals almost destroyed us..."

As the anti-war movement intensified, bombs continued to rain down on North Vietnam. In October of 1967, *100,000* peace-loving protestors traveled to Washington D.C. The demonstrators largely refrained from civil disobedience, but were vocal in their dissent.

President Johnson viewed the protestors as nothing less than traitors: "I'm not going to let the Communists take this government, and they're doing that right now...I'm not going to let *200,000* of these people ruin everything for *2,000,000* Americans."

All the while, Johnson could hear demonstrators in Lafayette Park, chanting over and over again: "Hey, hey, LBJ. How many kids did you kill today?"

"Don't they know they're Americans?" an exasperated Johnson asked.

By the fall of 1967, the stress of the Vietnam War had taken its toll on Secretary of Defense McNamara. LBJ was alarmed to hear his most trusted Cabinet officer suddenly proclaim that the war in Southeast Asia was unwinnable. In early November, McNamara submitted a nine-page, single spaced memorandum on the current state of the Vietnam War—the Secretary of Defense concluded there was "no end" in sight.

Fearing a public split in his administration, Johnson appointed the emotionally exhausted McNamara to the presidency of the World Bank. A confused McNamara later recalled that he wasn't sure if he had "resigned or been fired."

Not surprisingly, LBJ blamed RFK for the Secretary of Defense's about face: "Bob McNamara started out being a good man, but he got worried he was on the wrong side of the war, after his Kennedy friends turned against it."

On November 26, 1967, Robert Kennedy appeared on the *CBS News* weekly program, *Face the Nation*, and criticized American military action in Southeast Asia: "We're killing South Vietnamese, we're killing women, we're killing innocent people, because we don't want to have the war fought on American soil, or because they're *12,000* miles away, and they might get *11,000* miles away."

At the same time, RFK tried to temper his criticism, lest LBJ escalate the war effort, out of spite. Many Kennedy loyalists began pushing RFK to challenge LBJ for the 1968 Democratic nomination. Those same advisers feared that if Kennedy waited until 1972 to run for President, the Vietnam War would be completely out of hand and America would be irrevocably torn asunder.

A year earlier, Allard Lowenstein, the prominent leader of *Americans for Democratic Action (ADA),* urged his organization to support a candidate other than Lyndon Johnson in the forthcoming presidential race. At its national board meeting in early 1967, the ADA issued a formal statement, criticizing the Johnson Administration's management of the Vietnam War. Predictably, LBJ accused the ADA of being little more than a "Kennedy-in-exile government."

RFK eventually sought the counsel of his sister-in-law concerning the 1968 presidential election. Jackie Kennedy urged patience, coupled with originality: "Well, there's a good deal of anti-Johnson sentiment out there. If I were you, I'd make a stand. But, I'd wait a few months before announcing. And, when you do run, you must be authentic. You must be yourself. Don't try to be Jack."

On December 10, 1967, RFK, Ted Kennedy, Ted Sorensen, Richard Goodwin, Pierre Salinger, Kenneth O'Donnell, and other Kennedy loyalists met to discuss the 1968 presidential race. While the majority of the group urged RFK to seek the nomination, the two Ted's (Kennedy and Sorensen) were fearful of the political repercussions of challenging an incumbent President; while LBJ had become widely unpopular, he was still the President—powerful, cunning, and resourceful.

RFK remained ambivalent: "We haven't decided anything, so I guess I'm *not* running…"

LBJ, on the other hand, was certain that Robert Kennedy was poised to reclaim the throne.

Chapter 18

Good Bobby and Bad Bobby

Historian, William Manchester, described 1968 as "the year everything went wrong." At the onset of that tumultuous year, Lyndon Johnson and Robert Kennedy found themselves at career crossroads. While certain LBJ was leading the country down the road to ruin, RFK was aware that mounting a challenge against an incumbent President could be political suicide.

An anxious LBJ ruminated about his health. Out loud, he wondered if he could survive the stress and strain of another presidential term: "I never saw Woodrow Wilson's picture in the Red Room of the White House, never looked at it, that I didn't think that it might happen to me, that I would end another term in bed with a stroke, and that (the) decisions of government would be taken care of by other people, and that was wrong, I didn't want that to happen."

In a draft of his State of the Union address on January 17, 1968,

Johnson went so far as to include a clause announcing his withdrawal from the upcoming presidential race. Ultimately, LBJ could not bring himself to step aside so early in the political season, but the possibility quietly lingered.

Anti-war Democrats continued to push Robert Kennedy to seek the presidential nomination. A confused RFK confided his doubts to a close friend, longing for counsel: "I wish my ailing father were able to speak, so that he could tell me what to do."

RFK also worried about public perception: "I think if I run, I will go a long way toward proving everything that everybody who doesn't like me has said about me...That I'm a selfish, ambitious, little S.O.B., that can't wait to get his hands on the White House."

There was some merit to his concerns; Kennedy's rise in the polls seemed to be tied to LBJ's unpopularity, rather than RFK's own personal appeal.

The pressure to run for President, however, would not go away. Columnist, Walter Lippman, confronted RFK: "Well, if you believe that Johnson's reelection would be a catastrophe for the country...The question you must live with is whether you did everything you could to avert this catastrophe."

While he was reluctant to challenge an incumbent President, there was little doubt that RFK wanted the job, leading to renewed speculation about a *Kennedy Dynasty*. The cover of *Esquire* magazine featured JFK, RFK, Teddy, and JFK, Jr. sitting, side by side, in rocking chairs, suggestive of a three decade Kennedy foothold in the White House.

Fearful of making the wrong choice and tarnishing the Kennedy name, RFK was truly conflicted: "It's all so complicated. I just don't know what to do."

A *Harris Poll*, taken in November of 1967, showed Americans preferred RFK to LBJ by *fifty-two* to *thirty-two* percent as the Democratic presidential nomination. While RFK struggled to make a decision, Johnson had little doubt about the final outcome: "That little runt will get in. The runt's going to run. I don't care what he says now."

While the Kennedy family generally received favorable press coverage, RFK's political ambition eventually became the target of pointed media barbs. Cartoonist, Jules Feiffer, created the *Bobby Twins,* describing the contrast between *Good Bobby* and *Bad Bobby*. The satirical cartoon captions contained kernels of truth: "The Good Bobby is a courageous reformer. The Bad Bobby makes deals. The Good Bobby sent federal troops Down

South to enforce Civil Rights. The Bad Bobby appointed racist judges Down South. The Good Bobby is a fervent civil libertarian. The Bad Bobby is a fervent wire tapper. The Good Bobby is ill at ease with Liberals. The Bad Bobby is ill at ease with grownups. If you want one Bobby to be your President, you will have to take both, because Bobbies are widely noted for their family unity."

The mere thought of another Kennedy in the Oval Office provoked occasional violent responses. An unnamed FBI official was overhead expressing his displeasure: "I hope that someone shoots and kills that son of a bitch!"

The year 1968 began with one crisis after another. During a series of engagements with the Vietcong, American combat troops inadvertently crossed into Cambodia, violating that country's neutrality. Afterwards, the Johnson Administration was forced to offer a public apology to Cambodia's Prince Sihanouk.

In the northwest corner of South Vietnam, the battle of Khe San marked the first time that American forces (*6000* Marines) were actually outnumbered by the enemy. Nearly three years after the arrival of American ground troops, the North Vietnamese showed no signs of weariness.

To add to LBJ's woes, an American *B-52* bomber, armed with nuclear weapons, crashed seven miles short of its runway in Greenland. Before atomic weapons' experts could arrive at the crash scene, the aircraft sank to the bottom of the frigid North Atlantic.

On January 23rd, an American intelligence ship, the *USS Pueblo*, cruising in international waters, was boarded by hostile North Korean military forces. The vessel, along with its *eighty-three* man crew, was forced into the North Korean port of Wonsan. After being subjected to coercive interrogation, a number of crew members signed letters of *confession*, indicating that the ship was engaged in spying operations. The *Pueblo* incident was not resolved until the end of the year, when the United States delivered a public *confession letter* to North Korea. The crew was released on December 23, 1968, and the American government quickly repudiated its forced confession.

As Robert Kennedy vacillated about whether or not to enter the presidential race, another anti-war Democrat had entered the fray. In late 1967, Minnesota Senator, Eugene McCarthy, declared his intention to challenge Lyndon Johnson for the Democratic nomination. Politically threatened by McCarthy's candidacy, RFK was still unwilling to pull the trigger: "I don't want to drive Johnson into doing something really crazy. I don't want to hurt the doves in the Senate, who are up for reelection. I don't want it to be interpreted in the press as just part of a personal vendetta."

Kennedy believed if McCarthy miraculously won a few early primaries and LBJ became viewed as a liability, Democratic Party leaders might draft him as the only *electable* presidential candidate. RFK also viewed McCarthy as lazy and self-indulgent, in direct opposition to his public image as an established intellectual. Kennedy believed much of the Minnesotan's political ambition was attributable to sour grapes over the 1960 presidential race: "He feels he should have been the first Catholic President, because he knew more St. Thomas Aquinas than my brother."

While many of his seasoned advisers, like Ted Sorensen and Arthur Schlesinger, Jr., urged caution, RFK's younger Senate staffers (Peter Edelman, Adam Walinsky, and Tom Johnson) believed Bobby was the only candidate who could end the Vietnam War. The idealism of his youthful aides was infectious; bolstering RFK's belief that a negotiated settlement could somehow be reached.

As the pressure mounted, RFK refused to tip his hand. On January 31, 1968, Kennedy addressed the *National Press Club* in New York, declaring he would not run against LBJ "under any conceivable circumstances." In spite of this pronouncement, Bobby remained torn and sought the counsel of his younger brother: "What would Jack tell me to do?"

The younger Kennedy qualified his answer, indicating that their father undoubtedly would be opposed: "As for Jack, he might have cautioned against it, as well; but, he probably would have made the run, himself, in similar circumstances."

Ethel Kennedy actively encouraged her husband to seek the presidency: "You're always talking as though people don't like you. "People do like you, and you've got to realize that."

"I don't know, Ethel. Sometimes in moments of depression, I get the idea that there are those around, who don't like me," RFK replied

During a March 2ⁿᵈ strategy session at *Hickory Hill,* Ted Sorensen once again argued against RFK entering the race. Ethel Kennedy immediately challenged JFK's devoted wordsmith: "Why, Ted! And, after all those high-flown phrases you wrote for President Kennedy!"

Adding to the drama of the meeting, RFK's children unfurled a *Kennedy for President* banner and loudly played the *Impossible Dream* from the popular musical, *Man of La Mancha* (the tune would later become

Kennedy's 1968 campaign theme song). In his private journal, Arthur Schlesinger, Jr. discussed Kennedy's tortured uncertainty: "The ordeal continues. I have never seen RFK so torn about anything…I think that he cannot bear the thought of consigning the country to four more years of LBJ, without having done something to avert this."

RFK's enormous pride was soon wounded by public criticism about his indecision. In early 1968, the Senator was greeted by an unflattering sign at Brooklyn College: "RFK—Hawk, Dove, or Chicken?"

Ultimately, the Vietnam War drove Lyndon Johnson and Robert Kennedy into making irrevocable decisions. A cascade of history-making events began on January 30, 1968, during *Tet*, the Vietnamese New Year. Vietcong guerillas, *80,000* strong, stormed into South Vietnam, launching the largest offensive of the entire war. American military leaders were caught completely by surprise, as the enemy attacked *five* of the *six* major cities in South Vietnam, as well as *thirty-four* of *forty-four* provincial capitals, and *sixty-six* of *242* district towns. Viet Cong guerillas also stormed the U.S. Embassy in Saigon, killing *five* American military personnel.

While American troops eventually repelled the assault and killed many of the invaders, the *Tet Offensive* was a devastating psychological blow. President Johnson realized that the chances for an American victory in Southeast Asia were now extremely remote, confiding to his National Security Adviser: "This could be bad. What can we do to shake them from this?"

Of greater importance, the surprise attacks shattered the confidence of the American people. *CBS News* anchorman, Walter Cronkite, shared his doubts with millions of evening news watchers on the night of February 27th: "To say we are closer to victory, today, is to believe, in the face of the evidence, the optimists who have been wrong in the past. To suggest we are on the edge of defeat is to yield to unreasonable pessimism. To say we are mired in stalemate seems the only realistic, yet unsatisfactory conclusion."

After listening to famed newsman's telecast, LBJ was devastated: "If I've lost Cronkite, I've lost middle America."

The President's *credibility gap* had finally been exposed to the entire world. A veteran journalist described LBJ's dilemma: "Tet just ripped the fig leaf right off."

Former presidential adviser, Jack Valenti, described the turmoil succinctly: "It was the Vietnam War that cut the arteries of the LBJ Administration."

On February 8th, Robert Kennedy spoke publicly about the Tet Offensive: "The time has come to take a new look at the war. The nation must rid itself of the illusion that Tet was some kind of victory…*Half a million* American soldiers, with *700,000* Vietnamese allies, with total command of the air and sea, backed by huge resources and the most modern weapons, are unable to secure even a single city from attacks of an enemy whose total strength is about *250,000*…We have misconstrued the nature of the war."

The next day's edition of the *New York Times* headlined: "Kennedy asserts that U.S. cannot win."

By late January of 1968, *493,000* American soldiers were fighting in Vietnam, and *17,000* had died; yet, the United States was no closer to winning the war. In a single week of fighting in February, *543* Americans were killed and another *2547* were wounded, marking the highest one week casualty rate of the war. Later that month, the Selective Service announced it would draft an additional *48,000* American youth, while the military asked for an additional *205,179* troops to be deployed in South Vietnam. The additional troop allocation would necessitate an additional *ten billion dollars* in the 1969 defense department budget (at that time, the entire federal budget was only *100 billion* dollars).

The Vietnam War had an irrevocable choke hold on Lyndon Johnson's presidency, with the New Hampshire Democratic Presidential Primary rapidly approaching. While a nationwide opinion poll showed that *sixty-two* percent of Americans *disapproved* of LBJ's handling of the Vietnam War, seasoned political pundits refused to believe the nomination could be wrestled away from an incumbent President. In early March, New Hampshire polling data showed Johnson leading Eugene McCarthy by an overwhelming margin of *sixty-two* to *twelve* percent.

Robert Kennedy, however, believed that McCarthy's support was deeper than the poll numbers reflected. A youthful army of college-aged volunteers campaigned door to door for McCarthy in New Hampshire. Sporting short haircuts, freshly shaved faces, and coats and ties, the young "Clean for Gene" campaign workers had flocked to a new leader. Bobby was alarmed about his political future: "God, I'm going to lose them, and I'm going to lose them forever."

On the eve of the New Hampshire Primary, Ted Sorensen, serving as

RFK's proxy, met with President Johnson. Sorensen suggested formation of a special commission to evaluate America's involvement in Vietnam; an idea originated by Chicago Mayor, Richard Daly, who in turn had passed the concept along to Robert Kennedy. Sorensen discounted RFK's role in the proposal, lest Johnson reject it, outright. Sorensen also suggested that Johnson replace Secretary of State, Dean Rusk, who was viewed by Kennedy loyalists as hawkish and ineffectual. LBJ quietly listened to Sorensen's proposals, but refused to make any sort of commitment.

On March 12, 1968, the voters of New Hampshire expressed their displeasure with the Vietnam War. Lyndon Johnson won only *49.4* percent of the vote, while Eugene McCarthy gathered an astonishing *42.2* percent. Based on New Hampshire's rather unusual Primary Election rules, McCarthy had won at least *twenty* of the state's *twenty-four* delegates to the Democratic National Convention.

After the New Hampshire ballots were tabulated, a local newspaper columnist wrote: "Dove bites hawk." LBJ's invincibility no longer seemed certain, and RFK was suddenly free to reconsider his election year strategy.

With a handful of primaries just around the corner, Kennedy had precious little time to make a final decision. Arthur Schlesinger, Jr., summed up the tense dilemma: "The transformation of McCarthy into a serious candidate made Kennedy's position even more intolerable than before. He could not endorse Johnson. His choices, now, were to endorse McCarthy, which he could not bring himself to do, to remain neutral, which he could not do, either, or enter himself."

RFK was most concerned that McCarthy was a single issue candidate. Aside from ending the war in Vietnam, McCarthy had shown little passion for domestic issues, such as poverty, inner city decay, and gun control.

In mid-March, just days after the New Hampshire Primary, Edward Kennedy flew to Green Bay, Wisconsin to meet with McCarthy. Serving as his brother's emissary, Ted tried to broker a political deal—if McCarthy would agree to speak out more about domestic problems, RFK would stay out of the presidential race.

McCarthy was none too happy to see RFK's younger brother. The Minnesota Senator was no admirer of the Kennedy family, and quickly informed Ted that he was not interested in a compromise, and would not join forces with RFK to oppose President Johnson.

In the wake of McCarthy's refusal, Arthur Schlesinger, Jr. suggested a compromise position to RFK: "Why not come out for McCarthy? Every

McCarthy delegate will be a potential Kennedy delegate. He can't possibly win, so you will be the certain inheritor of his support. In the meantime, go on speaking as much as you can."

"I can't do that. It would be too humiliating. Kennedys don't act that way," RFK retorted.

On March 14th, two days after the New Hampshire Primary, Robert Kennedy and Ted Sorensen, met with Secretary of Defense, Clark Clifford (who had succeeded Robert McNamara). RFK told Clifford he was compelled to take action to end the war in Vietnam.

"One way to correct policy would be to become a candidate for the Democratic nomination," Kennedy explained, "If elected, I could then change the policy. The other alternative is to find some way to persuade President Johnson to change the policy. Ending the bloodshed in Vietnam is far more important to me than starting a presidential campaign."

RFK proposed the establishment of a *Blue Ribbon Commission* (of which he would be a member) to advise LBJ on strategies to end American involvement in the war. Kennedy indicated such a commission would signal "a clear cut willingness to seek a wider path to peace in Vietnam, then my declaration of candidacy would no longer be necessary."

Sorensen soon entered the discussion: "If President Johnson would agree to make a public statement that his policy in Vietnam had proved to be in error, and that he was appointing a group of persons to conduct a study, in depth, of the issues, and come up with a recommended course of action, then Senator Kennedy would agree to not enter the race."

Clifford, a seasoned Washington Insider, quickly responded: "Ted, you know as well as I do that the President could not issue a statement saying this country's policy was a failure."

Sensing Clifford's loyalty to LBJ, Kennedy clarified Sorensen's politically naïve request: "The statement does not need to go that far. If the President would issue a statement that the time has come to re-evaluate, in its entirety, our policy in Vietnam, this language would be sufficient for me, if coupled with the appointment of a board consisting of persons recommended by us."

As expected, Clifford staunchly defended LBJ: "First, it is my opinion that the possibility of your being able to defeat President Johnson for the nomination is zero...Second, I urge you to consider that the situation could change between now and the time of the convention in August. There are a number of factors under the President's control—such as the decision as when to stop the bombings or get negotiations started. Finally, if by chance, you are able to gain the nomination, it will be valueless, because your efforts in displacing President Johnson would so split the party that the Republican nominee would win the election easily. I hope you consider with the greatest care, whether it is worth going through what you have to endure to gain a nomination , which in my view, would be worthless if you were to win it."

At the conclusion of the meeting, RFK informed Clifford that he *would* enter the presidential race if LBJ did not find a way to end the war. In turn, the Secretary of Defense promised to discuss the commission proposal with President Johnson.

Later that same day, Clifford met with LBJ, Vice-President Humphrey, and Supreme Court Justice, Abe Fortas (Johnson's long-time friend and legal adviser). Not surprisingly, Johnson immediately vetoed RFK's plan: "I came into the office of President to protect the prerogatives and strength of the office of the presidency, and I don't think our system ever contemplated turning over the functions of the Commander-in-Chief to a civilian commission, and to admit to the world and the enemy and his own country that he didn't believe in what he was doing."

Johnson's ego and colossal insecurity would not tolerate any criticism of administration foreign policy. Clifford contacted RFK to inform him of the President's rejection of his request. As LBJ silently listened on a telephone extension, Kennedy made a last ditch effort to avoid a direct challenge to the President, by indicating it was not necessary for his name to be among the *Blue Ribbon Commission* members. Johnson nonetheless refused to reconsider his position, viewing RFK's proposal as little more than political blackmail.

On March 16, 1968, four days after the New Hampshire Primary, Robert Kennedy entered the same Senate Caucus Room where his brother had announced his presidential candidacy, eight years earlier. Wearing his *PT-109* tie clasp, a lasting reminder of the *New Frontier,* RFK delighted the assembled Kennedy loyalists: "I am announcing, today, my candidacy for the presidency of the United States. I do not run for the presidency merely to oppose any man, but to propose new policies...My decision reflects no animosity or disagreement toward President Johnson. He served President Kennedy with the utmost loyalty, and was extremely kind to me and members of my family in the difficult months, which followed the events of November 1963. I have often commended his efforts in health, in education, in many areas, and I have the deepest sympathy for the burden that he carries today…At stake is simply not the leadership of our party or even our country—it is our right to moral leadership on this planet."

On the morning of his brother's announcement, Ted Kennedy lapsed into a period of uncharacteristic silence. When asked by a close family friend about his solemnity, Ted shared an eerie premonition: "I'm really afraid for him. I have a terrible feeling about this whole thing. I'm sure I'm wrong, and yet…"

Lyndon Johnson's awful dream had become reality: "The thing I feared most from the first day of my presidency was actually coming true. Robert Kennedy had openly announced his intention to reclaim the throne in memory of his brother. And, the American people, swayed by the magic of the name, were dancing in the streets."

Chapter 19

I shall not seek, and I will not accept

The night before RFK announced his presidential candidacy, Ted Kennedy joked about his brother's ambition to claim the White House: "Bobby's therapy is going to cost the family four million dollars."

Lyndon Johnson, however, was in no mood for joking; RFK was finally free to mount an unbridled attack on his administration. If LBJ wanted to keep his job, he would have to go on the offensive, and attempt to portray Kennedy as a manipulative opportunist.

The White House immediately leaked information to the press about RFK's *Blue Ribbon Commission* proposal. LBJ portrayed the plan as an ultimatum—Kennedy would either handpick the commission members *or* he would run for President. The *New York Times* headlined: "Kennedy made Johnson offer to forgo race."

Angry at Johnson's manipulation of the media, RFK quickly struck back: "I am surprised that the traditional rules of confidence governing

White House conversations are no longer respected by the White House, itself."

Kennedy called into question LBJ's character, describing the news leak as "an incredible distortion," and emblematic of "why the American people no longer believe the President." At a campaign stop in California, RFK accused the "national leadership" of "calling upon the darker impulses of the American spirit."

On the *NBC News* weekly program, *Meet the Press,* RFK was asked if he could support the President, if LBJ managed to win re-nomination. Kennedy answered that he would have "grave reservations," unless Johnson changed his Vietnam policy.

"I'm loyal to the Democratic Party, but I feel stronger about the United States and mankind, generally," RFK proclaimed.

Lyndon Johnson's combativeness after RFK announced his presidential bid proved short lived. To his long time friends and aides, the President looked "old, weathered, battered, and drained." Johnson later summarized his mindset during this crucial time in his presidency: "I frankly did not believe, in 1968, that I could survive another four years of the long hours and unremitting tensions I had just gone through."

On March 22nd, to the surprise of many of his hawkish advisers, the President turned down General Westmoreland's request for an additional 205,000 troops in South Vietnam. For the first time, LBJ appeared reluctant to escalate the war effort.

Six days after RFK announced his candidacy, LBJ surprised his advisor, Joseph Califano: "If I don't run, who do you think will get the nomination?"

"Kennedy," Califano answered.

"What about Hubert?" Johnson inquired.

"I don't think he can beat Kennedy," Califano replied.

Califano was stunned by LBJ's reply: "What's wrong with Bobby? He's made some nasty speeches about me, but he's never had to sit here…Bobby would keep fighting for the *Great Society* programs. And, when he sat in this chair, he might have different view on the war…"

Those familiar with Johnson's bouts of self-pity found it difficult to believe that he would go down without a fight. This time, however, LBJ made good on his threat.

A March 31, 1968 conversation between LBJ and his daughter set the tone for the day's startling events. Lynda Johnson Robb's husband,

Charles, a Marine Corps officer, was about to depart for a thirteen month deployment in Southeast Asia. Lynda, who was pregnant with the couple's first child, stunned her father: "Why do we have to go to Vietnam?"

LBJ was speechless, unable to answer his daughter's troubling question. That night, Johnson was scheduled to address the nation concerning the war. Mid-afternoon, LBJ shared the surprise ending to his speech with Vice-President Humphrey. Johnson swore Humphrey to secrecy, and explained that he would not make up his mind until he was actually on the air.

The American public was caught by surprise, when Johnson read the concluding sentences of his Oval Office address: "With our hopes and the world's hopes for peace in the balance every day, I do not believe that I should devote an hour or a day of my time to any personal partisan causes, or to any duties other than the awesome duties of this office—the presidency of your country. Accordingly, I shall not seek, and I will not accept the nomination of my party for another term as your President."

After his unexpected announcement, LBJ appeared happy for the first time in months. A close adviser remembered: "His air was that of a prisoner set free."

Lady Bird was relieved by her husband's withdrawal: "We were all fifty pounds lighter and ever so much looking forward to the future."

The next day, Sam Houston Johnson sent LBJ a congratulatory note: "Last night was the happiest moment of my life. I am proud to be your brother."

Johnson privately explained his decision: "I'm tired of feeling rejected by the American people. I'm tired of waking up in the middle of the night worrying about the war. I'm tired of all these personal attacks on me."

In the days following his withdrawal from the presidential race, LBJ basked in the limelight. Johnson earned compliments from his enemies—Senator William Fulbright described Johnson's decision as the "act of a very good patriot," and even Robert Kennedy declared it "magnanimous." The President's approval ratings rebounded to *fifty-seven* percent.

LBJ patted himself on the back: "I was never any surer of any decision I ever made in my life, and I never made any more unselfish one. I have *525,000* men whose very lives depend on what I do, and I can't worry about the primaries."

Robert Kennedy was on the campaign trail when he learned of LBJ's decision: "You're kidding. I don't know what to say."

Later in the evening, RFK mused: "I wonder if he would have done it if I hadn't come in?"

With LBJ's withdrawal from the presidential race, Kennedy could no longer direct his attacks exclusively against Lyndon Johnson's War. Eugene McCarthy, who resented RFK's late entry into the contest, offered his own assessment: "Up to now, Bobby was Jack running against Lyndon. Now, Bobby has to run against Jack."

"It's purely Greek," McCarthy quipped.

Years after the 1968 election, McCarthy remained bitter about Robert Kennedy's last minute run for the presidency: "He would rather have had Johnson re-nominated, probably re-elected, than see me as President."

At the outset of his presidential campaign, Robert Kennedy asked for a "unity meeting" with President Johnson. LBJ initially refused to meet with his long-time nemesis: "I won't bother seeing the grandstanding little runt."

After formally withdrawing from the race, LBJ changed his mind, and, on April 3, 1968, the two men met face-to face. Ted Sorensen accompanied RFK to the White House, while LBJ asked his National Security Adviser, Walt Rostow, and aide, Charlie Murphy, to attend the meeting.

Seated at the conference table in the Cabinet Room, the group conferred for *ninety* minutes. RFK graciously described the President's withdrawal speech as "magnificent," and apologized for not staying in closer touch: "It was my fault."

Johnson was conciliatory, asking Kennedy to "make suggestions" concerning Vietnam. LBJ clarified his current attitude: "I feel no bitterness or vindictiveness. I want everybody to get together to find a way to stop the killing."

Kennedy eventually shifted the conversation to politics: "Where do I stand in the campaign? Are you opposed to my effort, and will you marshal forces against me?"

LBJ explained that he did not plan to endorse *any* presidential candidate: "If I had thought I could get into the campaign and hold the country together, I would have run myself. If I campaign for someone else, it will defeat what I am trying to do."

Johnson declared that he had never felt "contempt" for RFK, reminding Bobby that he had abandoned "the best job I ever had" in order to help JFK defeat Richard Nixon in the 1960 presidential race. LBJ explained that he had *tried* to partner with Bobby after JFK's death: "Somewhere, up there, President Kennedy would agree that I've done so."

Continuing with his polite, but self-serving monologue, the President blamed the press for manufacturing the RFK/LBJ feud. Johnson gently chided Sorensen for lending credibility to the perceived conflict: "If you hadn't left the White House, maybe it never would have."

Sorensen took this opportunity to join the conversation: "Will people in your administration be free to take part in pre-convention politics and support candidates?"

"I will need to think about that," Johnson quickly replied.

"If you decide, later, to take a position, can we talk to you, prior to that?" Bobby asked.

"Yes," LBJ replied, "Unless I lose my head and pop off. I will try to honor your request."

"I wanted to know, because if I should hear reports that you are doing such and such, I want to know whether to believe them," Kennedy explained.

"If I move, you'll know," LBJ vowed.

The meeting ended amicably with seemingly genuine warmth, as Johnson told RFK that he could be a worthy presidential successor: "The next man who sits in this chair can do better."

"You are a brave and dedicated man. You are a brave and dedicated man," Bobby softly replied.

Unbeknownst to either man, Lyndon Johnson and Robert Kennedy would never again meet face-to-face.

Chapter 20

To tame the savageness of man

With Lyndon Johnson out of the picture, Vice President, Hubert Humphrey, was free to announce his candidacy for the Democratic presidential nomination. It was widely believed LBJ would ultimately endorse Humphrey as his successor, even though he had serious doubts about the Vice-President's toughness. Johnson also complained that Humphrey "talked too much."

Johnson warned Humphrey to never forget how roughly the Kennedy campaign had treated him during the 1960 West Virginia Democratic Presidential Primary, when the Minnesotan's courage and patriotism had been called into question. LBJ reminded Humphrey that 1968 would be no different, "because that is the kind of thing you'll be up against."

While LBJ was not yet ready to publicly support a particular candidate, he did not complain when members of his administration endorsed Humphrey. However, when certain Johnson Administration officials publicly voiced support for Robert Kennedy, LBJ protested, leading to protests against the apparent double standard.

As election year politics heated up during the spring of 1968, LBJ hoped to rehabilitate his tattered image by brokering peace in Vietnam. On April 3rd, Johnson's hopes were bolstered, when the North Vietnamese expressed a willingness to talk about ending the war.

Beginning on May 13th, representatives from both sides met in Paris to negotiate an end to the war. Establishing an absurd negotiating posture that would persist for years to come, North Vietnamese leaders insisted that the United States stop all bombing and pull its ground forces from the region, but refused to acknowledge the presence of nearly *100,000* of their own soldiers, who had already invaded South Vietnam.

The enemy's lack of *good faith* at the peace table left LBJ frustrated and skeptical: "There is no evidence that the North Vietnamese will negotiate seriously. They will do no more than remain in Paris to talk, rather than negotiate, until the next administration takes over."

Meanwhile, Robert Kennedy's whirlwind campaign focused on the remaining presidential primaries—Indiana and the District of Columbia on May 7th, Nebraska on May 14th, Oregon on May 28th, South Dakota and California on June 4th, and New York on June 18th. For the first two weeks after announcing his candidacy, RFK campaigned vigorously in Kansas, Alabama, Tennessee, New York, California, Oregon, Idaho, Utah, Nebraska, Colorado, Indiana, New Mexico, and Arizona.

RFK faced several formidable obstacles in his quest to become President. Over the years, Kennedy had earned more than his fair share of powerful enemies. Labor union leaders resented his relentless crusade against Jimmy Hoffa, while the majority of white voters in the Deep South resented his promotion of Civil Rights. Some business leaders remained unhappy about the former Attorney General using the FBI to strong arm the steel industry during JFK's presidency. The most impassioned of liberals maintained their long-standing distrust of RFK, dating back to his days as a counsel for Senator Joe McCarthy.

The day after he announced his candidacy, Kennedy marched in New York City's Saint Patrick's Day parade. McCarthy supporters greeted RFK with shouts of "coward and opportunist," while a handful of LBJ loyalists were more abusive: "Get a haircut, you bum!"

Liberal journalist, Mary McGrory, accused RFK of trying to lure back the youth, now supporting McCarthy, "with the ruthlessness of a Victorian father, whose daughter has fallen in love with the dustman."

Kennedy shared his own private doubts: "I didn't want to run for President. But, when he (LBJ) made it clear the war would go on, and nothing was going to change, I had no choice."

For the most part, RFK encountered enthusiastic crowds on the primary campaign trail. Overeager supporters swarmed Kennedy, shouting his name, ripping away his cufflinks, and grabbing chunks of his hair. Bodyguards were often forced to grasp the candidate by the waist, to keep the energetic mobs from pulling him out of his car or off the stage. On at least one occasion, an Indiana woman managed to yank RFK from his car, causing him to chip his tooth on the curb. In California, a young man stole Kennedy's shoes, later wearing them to his high school prom.

With a sense of déjà vu from his senatorial campaign, RFK's hands were bloodied and bruised by day's end. Historian, Theodore White, described the "frenzy of love" exhibited by the boisterous crowds.

RFK was genuinely surprised by the adulation. While energetically wading into the masses, Kennedy was also wary: "I'd rather be home, or anywhere else. That being touched all the time, I don't like it. But, people can hear everything about a candidate, and it's touching them they never forget."

On the campaign trail, RFK immediately took aim at the Vietnam War. Before a crowd of *14,500* at Kansas State University, Kennedy took shared responsibility for the early decisions that led to American involvement in Southeast Asia. The candidate quoted from the Greek classics: "All men make mistakes, but a good man yields, when he knows his course is wrong, and repairs the evil. The only sin is pride."

At the University of Kansas, RFK condemned the downward drift of modern society: "Our *Gross National Product*, now, is over *800 billion* dollars a year, but the *GNP*—if we should judge America by that— counts air pollution and cigarette advertising and ambulances to clear our highways of carnage. It counts special locks for our doors, and the jails for those who break them. It counts the destruction of our redwoods and the loss our natural wonder in chaotic sprawl. It counts napalm and the cost of nuclear warheads...Yet, the Gross National Product does not allow for the health of our children, the quality of their education, or the joy of their play. It does not include the beauty of our poetry or the strength of our marriages; the intelligence of our public debate, or the integrity of our public officials..."

In a style unlike any other politician of his era, Kennedy usually delivered a prepared speech, but allowed twice as long for interactive discussions. RFK tailored his approach to his strengths and weaknesses as an orator: "I don't come across well on set affairs. I do very well with questions and answers."

Kennedy was not afraid to venture into unfriendly territory. At the University of Alabama, in the heart of segregationist country, RFK explained his reason for journeying to the Deep South: "...Any candidate who seeks higher office this year, must go before all Americans—not just those who agree with them, but those who disagree..."

While in Alabama, RFK earned the support of the most unlikely of boosters—legendary University of Alabama football coach, Paul "Bear" Bryant. Bobby had established an almost immediate rapport with Bryant during his tenure as Attorney General (President Kennedy had been awarded an honorary Alabama football letter). The grizzled coach most certainly agreed with Kennedy's assessment of the gridiron: "Except for war, there is nothing in American life—nothing—which trains a boy better for life than football."

Journalist and Bryant biographer, Mickey Herskowitz, recalled a series of conversations with the Alabama coach: "Bryant was not a political man, at least not in the sense that politics indicates ideology. He admired Bobby Kennedy, largely for his tough stance on organized crime, and would sometimes chuckle over the way Kennedy tenaciously pursued Jimmy Hoffa. 'I sure hope he nails that bastard,' Bryant once said to me. He was prepared to shock people in Alabama by supporting Kennedy for President in 1968...There was no doubt that he was a Kennedy fan, and that included Kennedy's doggedness in integrating the University of Alabama."

On the campaign trail in California, Robert Kennedy reminded listeners of the tragic loss of life in Vietnam: "While the sun shines in our sky, men are dying on the other side of the Earth. Which of them could have come home and written a great symphony? Which of them could come home to cure cancer? Which of them might have played in the World Series or given us the gift of laughter from the stage?"

South Dakota Senator (and 1972 Democratic presidential nominee), George McGovern, was intimate with all three Kennedy brothers, and was familiar with their unique personalities. During the 1968 primary campaign season, McGovern shared his observations: "Teddy was more like Jack than Bobby. Teddy was a pragmatic politician, and Bobby would speak from his heart, and it got him in trouble. Bobby was more inclined to address things directly. Bobby was not a natural politician."

While aides fretted over his safety, Bobby joked about his need to be among the people: "Well, so many people hate me that I've got to give the people that love me a chance to get at me."

While the candidate mesmerized the crowds, his campaign team struggled with organization. In the chaotic, last-minute formation of his staff, RFK never officially named an actual campaign manager. Absent a controlling authority, Kennedy's younger advisers often clashed with the more experienced *New Frontiersmen.* To minimize conflict, younger advisers (like Frank Mankiewicz and Fred Dutton) traveled on the road with Kennedy, while the older hands (Ted Sorensen, Kennedy O'Donnell, and Arthur Schlesinger, Jr.) spent more time in RFK's Washington D.C. campaign headquarters.

"If he'd (RFK) been running this campaign, he would have fired everybody in there and started all over," a veteran aide complained.

As the Kennedy campaign chugged forward, tragic violence shocked the nation. On April 4, 1968, while campaigning in Indiana, RFK received word that Civil Rights leader, Martin Luther King, had been assassinated in Memphis. Stunned by the news, Bobby openly wept.

That same night, Kennedy was scheduled to give a speech in an Indianapolis ghetto. Disregarding the advice of his aides, and traveling without a police escort (local law enforcement officials refused to enter the predominately black area so soon after King's murder), RFK addressed a crowd of inner city African Americans.

"Do they know about Martin Luther King?" Kennedy asked a local campaign coordinator, when he arrived at the site of the rally.

"To some extent—we've left that up to you," the man replied.

On an unseasonably cold night, dressed in a dark overcoat, a shivering RFK mounted a flatbed truck, and discarded his prepared remarks, speaking extemporaneously: "I have some very sad news for all of you, and I think sad news for all of our fellow citizens, and people who love peace all over the world, and that is Martin Luther King was shot and killed tonight in Memphis, Tennessee."

A collective gasp arose from the crowd, followed by moans and angry murmurs. No one could realistically predict what might happen next. Bobby continued in an even tone, urging his listeners to refrain from violent reprisal: "You can be filled with bitterness, with hatred, with a desire for revenge, or we can make an effort, as Martin Luther King did, to understand and comprehend, and replace that violence, that stain of bloodshed that has spread across our land, with an effort to understand with compassion and love."

Kennedy gently reminded the crowd that his own brother had been murdered by a *white man*, and then quoted from Aeschylus: "In our sleep, pain which cannot forget, falls drop by drop upon the heart, until, in our own despair, against our will, comes wisdom through the awful grace of God."

"Let us dedicate ourselves to what the Greeks wrote so many years ago—to tame the savageness of man and make gentle the life of this world. Let us dedicate ourselves to that, and say a prayer for our country and for our people," he urged the stunned crowd.

At his hotel room, later that night, RFK met privately with a group of black leaders. Angered by the murder of their spiritual leader, Kennedy's guests accused him of being part of the "white establishment."

Emotionally spent, RFK responded with measured indignation: "You talk about establishment. I have to laugh. Big business is trying to defeat me because they think I am a friend of the Negro. You are down on me because you say I am a part of the *establishment*...I could sit next to my swimming pool. You know, God's been good to me, and I don't really need anything. But, I just feel that if He's been that good, I should try to put something back in. And, you all call yourself leaders; and you've been moaning and groaning about personal problems. You haven't once talked about your own people."

On the night of Martin Luther King's murder, over *100* American cities erupted with violence. Nationwide, *thirty-nine* people (mostly black) were killed and over *2500* were injured. More than *75,000* National Guardsmen and regular military personnel were forced into the streets to restore order. In Washington D.C., alone, *14,000* regular Army and National Guard troops deployed to control the rioting. Roadblocks were set up around the White House, and soldiers were stationed at the Southwest Gate, to ensure the safety of the President. General William Westmoreland, who had traveled from Vietnam for a meeting with the President and the Secretary of Defense, remarked that the streets of Washington D.C. looked "worse than Saigon did at the height of the Tet Offensive.'

In contrast, Indianapolis quietly grieved—the words of Robert Kennedy seemed to have soothed their anger and hurt. At the same time,

RFK made it clear that he equated assassins with rioters: "A sniper is only a coward, not a hero, and an uncontrolled mob is only the voice of madness, not the voice of reason."

President Johnson responded to King's assassination by declaring Sunday, April 7, 1968, a *National Day of Mourning*. LBJ sent Coretta Scott King a condolence note: "My thoughts have been with you and your children throughout this long and anguished day."

On this rare occasion, LBJ followed Secret Service recommendations, and did not attend King's funeral in Atlanta. On a deeper level, Johnson felt no moral obligation to attend the funeral services, finding it difficult to forgive King for his support of the anti-war movement. In the end, LBJ could not forgive the Civil Rights leader for betraying his sacred principle of loyalty.

Robert Kennedy, on the other hand, did everything possible to accommodate the grieving King family. RFK chartered a plane to transport the slain Civil Rights leader's body from Memphis to Atlanta, and also arranged for extra phones to be installed at the King home.

On April 8th, RFK attended a memorial service for King in Washington D.C. conducted by Civil Rights leader, Reverend Walter Fauntroy. After the service, Kennedy asked the pastor to tour the riot-scarred D.C. streets with him. During their stroll, Fauntroy was stunned to hear RFK casually remark: "I fear that a gun stands between me and the White House."

At King's funeral in Atlanta, RFK waded into the crowd, his own security nearly non-existent. Kennedy was well received by the mourners, who were ready to transfer the full weight of their damaged hopes and dreams onto the presidential candidate. Over *120 million* Americans watched the King funeral on television—the largest such viewership since John F. Kennedy's funeral in 1963.

RFK convinced a reluctant Jackie Kennedy to attend King's funeral. Less than five years after the murder of her husband, the former First Lady was overwhelmed by the country's violent atmosphere.

"America is going to the dogs. I don't know why you want to be President," she told Bobby.

Veteran Civil Rights activist, John Lewis, who bore multiple physical and psychological scars from the hands of white racists, recalled his fragile state of mind: "After the funeral of Dr. King, I felt I had lost a friend, a big brother, (and) a colleague. Somehow, I said to myself: 'Well, we still have Bobby Kennedy.' And, I just snapped out of it, and like that, I got back on the campaign trail."

Black entertainer, Sammy Davis, Jr., who walked alongside RFK during King's funeral march, was impressed by the presidential candidate's unifying presence: "No one relates to the black man like Bobby...He can talk to the Uncle Toms and the militants."

In the spring of 1968, the news from Vietnam remained grim. During the second week of May, *502* Americans were killed and more than *2000* were wounded. LBJ's withdrawal from the presidential race had yet to yield a peace dividend in Southeast Asia, and the remaining candidates used Lyndon Johnson's War as campaign fodder.

Martin Luther King's assassination raised serious concerns about Robert Kennedy's safety. In the spring of 1968, Secret Service protection had not yet been authorized for presidential candidates, and RFK's small group of mostly unarmed body guards were no match for a determined assassin.

At *JFK International Airport*, a man carrying a concealed .44 caliber handgun was arrested as he followed Kennedy to the departure gate. A right wing periodical featured the headline: "RFK must die."

In Lansing, Michigan, a man with a rifle was spotted on rooftop adjacent to RFK's hotel. When campaign adviser, Fred Dutton, closed the window blinds, Kennedy was nonchalant: "Don't close them. If they're going to shoot, they'll shoot."

Just prior to delivering a speech at the *Terrace Ballroom Hotel Utah* in Salt Lake City, Kennedy was alerted to a bomb threat. RFK informed law enforcement authorities that he would not evacuate the building, and then shared the potential threat with the assembled audience: "If you want to leave, you should leave in an orderly fashion. Be careful of the children. Anyone who wants to stay, I'll stay with you."

After no one exited the room, Kennedy quipped: "This is what I call opening the campaign with a bang. But, let me tell you, if I have to go, I can't think of anybody I would rather go with than you here, tonight."

Prior to Martin Luther King's assassination, Jackie Kennedy confided her fears: "Do you know what I think will happen to Bobby? The same thing that happened to Jack...There is so much hatred in this country, and more people hate Bobby than hated Jack...I've told Bobby this, but he isn't fatalistic like me."

Concerned about her own personal safety, the former First Lady was contemplating a move outside the United States. Greek millionaire,

Aristotle Onassis, had already asked for Jackie's hand in marriage. RFK was appalled by the political ramifications of his sister-in-law wedding the controversial Greek tycoon: "For God's sake, Jackie, this could cost me five states!"

After talking with Bobby and a host of other Kennedy family members, Jackie promised to delay any marriage plans until after the November presidential election.

The Kennedy campaign moved forward, still with minimal security. Impulsively, Bobby plunged into the crowds, shaking hands with supporters, and remained matter-of-fact about his personal safety: "If they want to kill me, they'll kill me."

On the night King's assassination, RFK was sadly philosophical: "You know that fellow Harvey Lee Oswald, whatever his name is, set something loose in this country."

In addition to safety concerns, the campaign disrupted RFK's home life. After his twelve year old son, David, was caught throwing rocks at cars, Bobby made a startling revelation to his younger brother: "Teddy, I want you to know that if I don't make it this time, I am not interested in running again. This all takes too much. I have to be there for David and the other children."

While romanticized as an anti-war candidate, RFK also focused on domestic problems. Kennedy emphatically denounced the existing welfare system: "We can't have the federal government in here, telling people what's good for them."

RFK's proposals for welfare reform caught the eye of conservative California Governor (and future President of the United States), Ronald Reagan, who quipped: "I get the feeling I've been writing some of his speeches."

Richard Nixon, who would ultimately win the 1968 Republican presidential nomination, commented on Kennedy's criticism of the welfare state: "Bobby and I have been sounding pretty much alike."

On April 27th, the dynamics of the presidential campaign changed when Vice-President Hubert Humphrey formally entered the race. As the designated heir apparent to Lyndon Johnson, Humphrey's relationships with established Democratic Party bosses were more cordial than those of Robert Kennedy. While RFK never doubted he could defeat McCarthy, Humphrey promised to be a more formidable opponent.

Hubert Humphrey entitled his campaign, the *Politics of Joy*. RFK soon took direct aim at Humphrey: "If you want to be filled with pabulum and tranquilizers, then you should vote for some other candidate."

"If you see a small black child starving to death in the Mississippi Delta, as I have, it is not the 'politics of joy,'" RFK proclaimed.

At a campaign stop in Indiana, Kennedy asked the crowd: "Do you know there are more rats in New York than people, and there are *nine million* people there?"

RFK told a group of Californians: "Decency is at the heart of this whole campaign...Poverty is indecent. Illiteracy is indecent. The death, the maiming of brave young men in the swamps of Vietnam...that is also indecent."

After he announced his candidacy, RFK had only twelve days to meet the deadline for entry in the Indiana Presidential Primary. The *Hoosier State* promised to be a stern opening test, with its large population of Teamsters, who were decidedly pro-Hoffa and anti-Kennedy. In addition, Governor Roger Branigin had long been on the ballot as a *Favorite Son* stalking horse for Lyndon Johnson (and was now considered a stand-in for Hubert Humphrey).

During an appearance at Ball State University, a student accused Kennedy of "telling jokes," and propagating "double talk." When the crowd booed, RFK silenced them: "He's perfectly entitled to disagree with me, and that's the only way we're going to make progress in this country—if people stand up and speak their minds.

At Valparaiso University, RFK confronted hecklers in the crowd: "Well, you tell me something now. How many of you spent time over the summer, or on vacations, working in a black ghetto, or in Eastern Kentucky, or on an Indian reservation? Instead of asking what the federal government is doing about starving children, I say what is your responsibility (and), what are you going to do about it? I think you people should organize yourselves, right here, and try to something about it."

Kennedy's straight-forward style ultimately produced electoral dividends. On May 7, 1968, RFK triumphed in Indiana, winning *forty-two* percent of the vote, compared to *thirty-one* percent for Branigin, and *twenty-seven* percent for Eugene McCarthy. Kennedy won *ten* of Indiana's *eleven* congressional districts, and *fifty-one* out of *ninety-two* counties. Kennedy's support was broad based—he won *seventeen* out the state's *twenty-two* predominately white southern counties. At the same time, RFK won *eighty-five* percent of the black votes in Lake County, which had one of the state's largest contingencies of African Americans.

Kennedy had bridged the dichotomy among Indiana's diverse citizenship. White voters were attracted to his *law and order* theme. At the same time, African Americans appreciated his support on their behalf: "White Americans should fulfill the simple claims of black Americans for decent jobs, and give them a sense that they are part of this country."

On same day of his triumph in Indiana, RFK won the Democratic Primary in the District of Columbia, earning *62.5* percent of the vote (compared to Hubert Humphrey's *37.5* percent). After dual triumphs, Kennedy was enthusiastic about the future of his campaign: "I've proved I can really be a leader of a broad spectrum. I can be a bridge between blacks and whites, without stepping back from my positions."

The campaign then moved to Nebraska, where Kennedy attracted a handful of unlikely supporters, who had previously supported segregationist Alabama Governor, George Wallace. When asked about his newfound support for RFK, a former Wallace booster could not precisely articulate his change of heart: "I like him. I don't know why, but I like him."

In the Cornhusker State, Kennedy captured *fifty-one* percent of the vote, compared to McCarthy's *thirty-one* percent. RFK won *eighty-eight* out of *ninety-three* counties, earning *sixty* percent of the farmer and blue collar votes.

With more than *fifty* percent of the U.S. population now under the age of *twenty-five*, RFK's electoral prospects appeared bright. Younger voters were enamored by Kennedy's youthful charisma and populist rhetoric.

The enthusiasm of the electorate energized Kennedy's advisers, as well and the working press following his campaign. While traveling aboard a chartered campaign train, RFK's aides and news reporters wrote a parody sung to the tune of *The Wabash Cannonball*:

Old Hubert's got big business, big labor, and big mouth, aboard the Maddox Special coming from the South;

Lyndon's got him preaching, so ecumincall, but soon he'll be heaving coal on the *Ruthless Cannonball*;

Now good clean Gene McCarthy came down the other track, a thousand Radcliffe dropouts all massed for the attack;

But, Bobby's bought the right-of-way from here back to St. Paul, 'cause money is no object, on the *Ruthless Cannonball*;

So here's to Ruthless Robert, may his name forever stand; to be feared and genuflected at, by pols across the land;

Old Ho Chi Minh is cheering, and it may appall;

He's whizzing to the White House on the *Ruthless Cannonball*.

As he grew more comfortable campaigning, RFK displayed a sense of humor reminiscent of his late brother: "President Johnson told me go west, young man, go west. But, I was in California at the time."

During a turbulent flight aboard his campaign plane, Bobby kidded the white knuckled reporters: You know, if we go down, you guys are all going to be in small print."

In another instance, a major thunderstorm shook his aircraft badly, generating considerable anxiety among the passengers. RFK *lightened* the moment, announcing over the plane's public address system that astronaut and fellow passenger, John Glenn, was "nervous."

During a California campaign appearance, the Mayor of Stockton told Kennedy: "I know God is on your side."

"As long as I have God, I hope I have some delegates to go with Him," RFK quipped, "or that when he gets to Chicago (the site of Democratic National Convention), He'll bring some with Him."

Kennedy made light of his campaign's *strengths,* in a conversation with Ted Sorensen: "I'm the only candidate who has ever united business and labor, Southerners, party bosses, and intellectuals. They're all against me."

Flying over South Dakota, RFK pointed out *Mount Rushmore:* "There's a still lot of room."

At a rural campaign stop in Nebraska, the candidate informed the crowd: "You may not know it, but I come from a farm state. New York is first in sour cherries."

Many of the reporters following Kennedy eventually became loyal supporters. While the journalists may not have always agreed with RFK's opinions, they appreciated his candor.

"He wouldn't give you a slick answer...He'd slowly come out with an answer that he'd really been thinking about, because he wasn't inclined to just give a pre-mixed answer to anything," *New York Times* reporter, James Stevenson, recalled.

Flying into New York's *John F. Kennedy International Airport,* a reporter was touched by RFK's wistful longing for the past, at a time when his own popularity was soaring.

"It must be quite something to land at an airport named for your brother," the newsman opined.

"I wish it was still called Idlewild," RFK softly replied.

On the campaign trail, RFK closely identified with children. Kennedy aide, Lester Hyman, was stunned when his six year old son came home from school with a black eye. Young David explained that other kids had beaten him up, because he was supporting Kennedy instead of McCarthy. The story of David Hyman's plight made its way to Bobby Kennedy, who sent the boy a handwritten letter: "Dear David: Your Daddy told me how much courage it took to stand up for me against all odds. I shall never forget you...Your friend, Bob."

David's father was embarrassed the candidate had taken time from his hectic schedule to address a seemingly trivial matter: "Why didn't you say something to me. I was so angry at you, and you do this beautiful thing for my son. Why didn't you tell me?"

"Jesus, Lester! You're not the one with the problem—your son is! Don't be such a baby. It was for your son, not you. It wasn't about you!" RFK replied.

While often lacking organization, RFK'S campaign was well financed. During his *eighty-two day* candidacy, Kennedy spent *eleven million dollars,* compared to McCarthy's *two and one-half million.* At the end of the campaign, his camp had accumulated more than *three million dollars* in debt (the Democratic National Committee paid off nearly *one million dollars* of the debt, while creditors were forced to "eat" the remainder).

The Kennedy campaign appeared invincible heading into the Oregon Presidential Primary, but a handful of RFK's seasoned advisers were wary of the impending contest. Kenneth O'Donnell sensed a disconnection between Kennedy and the local residents: "It is one big suburb, with a surprisingly high percentage of college graduates."

The population of Oregon was *ninety-eight* percent white, and Kennedy's messages about hunger, poverty, and equal rights did not resonate with the voters. Less than *one* percent of the state's voters were African American, and there were few Hispanics and Catholics. Organized labor was influential in Oregon, and RFK's past *demonization* of the Teamsters Union leadership angered many blue collar workers.

"I just can't get a foothold here in Oregon…Everyone is too comfortable here…" RFK lamented, "What's wrong with these people? They're unaware of what's going on—the campus riots, urban turmoil, (and) the Vietnam War. I don't get it."

Seeking an opportunity to discredit RFK, Eugene McCarthy trumpeted his pro-Second Amendment views, scoffing at Kennedy's desire to regulate firearm sales, in a state that prided itself on gun ownership. RFK unsuccessfully attempted to counter McCarthy's opposition to gun control: "So protect your right to keep and bear arms. The legislation doesn't stop you, unless you are a criminal. I don't think the registration of cars and the registration of drug prescriptions destroyed democracy, and I don't think the registration of guns will either."

McCarthy stepped up his personal attacks, describing Kennedy as a "spoiled rich kid, who can't run this race without Dad's money, and his astronaut (referring to Kennedy supporter and travel companion, John Glenn)." McCarthy also made fun of Freckles, RFK's canine campaign travel companion.

"I don't mind his taking issue with John Glenn or Dad's money, but let's leave Freckles out this. That Cocker Spaniel goes everywhere with me," RFK quipped.

In remarks, which would later haunt him, McCarthy criticized RFK's savvy public relations team: "I suppose that we'll also read, next, that Bobby Kennedy's people will leak a story that there's been an attempt on his life."

In Oregon, RFK made a crucial mistake by refusing to debate McCarthy. As the presumed front-runner, Kennedy did not want to give his opponent free publicity. Many Oregonians, however, interpreted RFK's decision as a manifestation of arrogance and insecurity.

On May 28, 1968, Eugene McCarthy won *44.7* percent of the Oregon vote, outdistancing RFK by nearly *six* percentage points. McCarthy's upset victory marked the first time a Kennedy had *ever* lost an election.

RFK was stunned by McCarthy's triumph, coupled with the fact that Hubert Humphrey was piling up delegates in non-primary states. With *172* delegates at stake, California became a *must win* state for Kennedy.

With only a week separating the Oregon and California primaries, RFK barnstormed the *Golden State*. Kennedy advocated an era of "new politics," where "federal spending will not solve all our problems and money cannot buy dignity, self-respect, or fellow feeling between citizens."

Kennedy promised his presidency would promote "the creation of dignified jobs, at decent pay, for all those who can and want to work." He further asserted that government assistance programs must be revised to ensure "adequate help to those who cannot work, without the indignities and random cruelties which afflict the present welfare system."

Learning from his previous mistake, Kennedy agreed to a televised debate with McCarthy. The most contentious issue raised during the subsequent debate was McCarthy's proposal to relocate poverty stricken inner city residents to less troubled areas. RFK pounced on McCarthy's recommendation, pointing out that it was wrong "to take *10,000* black people and move them into Orange County."

"To take these people out, put them in suburbs where they can't afford the housing, where their children can't keep up with the schools, and where they don't have the skills for the jobs—it is just going to be catastrophic," Kennedy asserted.

Polls taken after the June 1st debate gave the edge to Kennedy by a *two* to *one* margin. The *San Francisco Chronicle* wrote that RFK "had mopped the floor" with McCarthy.

While the crowds in California were wildly enthusiastic, a sense of foreboding loomed over the campaign, and many observers believed Kennedy was exposing himself to the masses without adequate protection. French writer, Romain Gary, made a shocking prediction during a private conversation with a Kennedy political adviser: "You know, your guy will be killed...He's too irresistible a temptation for the American paranoid personality—too much provocation, too rich, too attractive, too happy, too lucky, too successful. He arouses in every 'persecuted' type a deep sense of injustice."

On the eve of Primary Election Day, as RFK stood on the rear seat of a convertible in San Francisco's Chinatown, a string of firecrackers exploded near the vehicle. A stunned Ethel Kennedy grabbed her husband and pulled him into the seat—an eerie reminder of that tragic November day in Dallas.

Seemingly unfazed, RFK remained philosophical about his personal safety: "There's no way to protect a candidate who's stumping the country—no way at all. You've just got to give yourself to the people, and trust them. From then on, it's just that old 'bitch luck.'"

While the adoring crowds cheered, an unsuccessful misanthrope cut from the same cloth as Lee Harvey Oswald, prepared to change history.

Chapter 21

Robert Kennedy must be assassinated

Sirhan Bishara Sirhan was born on March 19, 1944 in Jerusalem. The son of Christian Palestinians who migrated to the United States when he was twelve years old, Sirhan lived briefly in New York, before moving with his family to Pasadena, California.

With a below average IQ score of *eighty-nine*, Sirhan was a mediocre student, earning mostly "C" grades. A junior high school classmate remembered him as argumentative and "attention seeking." Another student described Sirhan as "taciturn and withdrawn."

From an early age, Sirhan voiced staunch pro-Arabic, anti-Israeli rhetoric. While attending Pasadena Community College (where he was dismissed after *seventeen* months for "poor attendance"), Sirhan went to meetings of the *Organization of Arab Students*, and frequently expressed his hatred for Jews.

Sirhan's anti-Semitism was rooted in early childhood, when he observed, first hand, fierce fighting between Arabs and Israelis. At age four, after witnessing an Israeli bombing attack, Sirhan was severely traumatized and remained in a catatonic state for days after the deadly explosion.

An acquaintance later remembered the young Palestinian's militant anti-Semitism: "He hated the Jews because of their power and their material wealth—they had taken his country from his people, who were now refugees…"

After flunking out of college (he received five "F" grades during his final academic year), Sirhan drifted aimlessly from job to job. Employment as a gas station and assistant gardener ended because of dereliction of duties.

Sirhan had long dreamed of becoming a jockey, but lacked the coordination and riding skills to manage a thoroughbred racehorse. At five feet five inches and 120 pounds, Sirhan was also slightly oversized for a jockey, and instead worked as a stable hand and hot walker. When allowed to exercise horses, two of his rides ended in falls; one of the accidents resulted in a head injury, rendering him semi-conscious with stitches in his face.

Sirhan never applied for United States citizenship, clinging to his Middle Eastern identity. He defiantly proclaimed his ethnicity: "I am a Palestinian."

Like so many misanthropes, Sirhan struggled to find his spiritual identity, joining both the Baptist and Seventh Day Adventist Churches. He later joined the *Rosicrucian Order*, exploring mysticism and dabbling in the occult.

Sirhan episodically abused alcohol, while developing a fascination with guns. Intrigued by the assassination of Martin Luther King, Sirhan empathized with African Americans, asserting that the only way to achieve equal rights was through violent revolt. Sirhan's own mother described him as a "friendless young man."

In the spring of 1968, Sirhan Sirhan became obsessed Robert Kennedy. While many American political leaders were supportive of Israel, Sirhan was particularly angered by Kennedy's advocacy on behalf of his sworn enemy. Sirhan had difficulty reconciling Kennedy's support for underdogs (like the poor and minorities) and his opposition to the Vietnam War, while promoting weapons sales to Israel.

In the eyes of the emotionally troubled Palestinian, RFK was the epitome of hypocrisy. On May 18, 1968, Sirhan disjointedly wrote in his diary: "Robert Kennedy must be assassinated...My determination to eliminate RFK is becoming more the more (sic) of an unshakeable obsession."

Sirhan purchased a handgun (.22 caliber *Ivan Johnson Cadet* pistol), and practiced with the weapon at local firing ranges. He soon became adept with the pistol and its rapid fire capabilities.

During the California Democratic Presidential Primary, Sirhan began stalking RFK. On May 24th, he attended his first Kennedy rally at the Los Angeles Sports Arena. A week later, during a Kennedy rally at the Ambassador Hotel, Sirhan observed the candidate standing on an outdoor terrace, but subdued the impulse to act out his violent fantasies.

On June 4th, the night of the California Primary, Sirhan travelled to the Kennedy campaign headquarters at the Ambassador Hotel. During the course of the evening, the young Palestinian engaged in a loud argument with a RFK campaign volunteer: "Kennedy! He should never be President. You think he really wants to help the poor? Kennedy helps himself. He's just using the poor. Can't you see that?"

Mingling with the excited crowd, Sirhan openly criticized Kennedy: "Don't worry about him, if he doesn't win. That son of a bitch, he's a millionaire, and doesn't need to win. He just wants to go to the White House. But, if he wins, he's not going to do anything for you or any of the poor people."

As the clock edged toward midnight, with Kennedy's victory in sight, Sirhan Sirhan brooded and waited for a chance to put his name in the history books.

On Primary Election Eve, the Kennedy family spent the night at the beachside home of movie director, John Frankenheimer. With Bobby worn down from non-stop campaigning and Ethel in the middle stages of her eleventh pregnancy, the exhausted couple slept late on Election Day. Bobby spent much of the day playing with his children on the beach and poolside. At one point, twelve-year old David Kennedy was swept underwater by the powerful Pacific Ocean current, forcing Bobby to dive in after him. After a few tense moments, father and son emerged from the waves; David coughed up seawater, while RFK nursed an abrasion over his left eye.

Later on that windy, overcast afternoon, RFK napped beside the pool. Speechwriter and campaign adviser, Richard Goodwin, recalled his brittle emotions, after encountering the recumbent candidate: "...There was no movement. I felt a sudden spasm of fear. But, it swiftly receded. He was sleeping—only sleeping...I suppose none of us will ever get over John Kennedy."

In the early evening, Frankenheimer drove RFK to his campaign headquarters at the Ambassador Hotel. As the movie director sped down the winding roads, Kennedy jokingly cautioned him: "Hey, John. Take it slow. I want to live long enough to enjoy my impending victory."

Arriving at the hotel at a quarter past seven, Bobby waited with family and friends in his fifth floor hotel suite, monitoring the emerging vote count. At 11:00 p.m., PST, the major news organizations declared Kennedy the victor in the California Primary—the final count was *46.3* percent for Kennedy, *41.8* percent for McCarthy, with *11.9* percent going to the remaining candidates.

RFK also learned he had triumphed in South Dakota, winning over *fifty* percent of the votes. Kennedy approached a group of reporters outside his hotel suite after learning of his victory in South Dakota: "Have you heard about the Indian vote? You want me to tell you about the Indians? In one county in South Dakota, there were *858* Indian votes. I got *856*. Hubert Humphrey got *two*. McCarthy got *none*."

After RFK's twin triumphs, the revised national delegate count showed Humphrey with *561*, Kennedy with *393*, and McCarthy with *258*. The crucial undecided delegates numbered *872*, with a total of *1312* needed to secure the nomination. RFK's momentum was substantial; having won *four* of the *five* primaries he had entered.

Humphrey, who had not run in the primary contests, accumulated delegates via private, non-binding commitments with regional party bosses. RFK was fully aware he would have to curry favor with party leaders in other populous states, like New York and Illinois, to secure the nomination: "I'll have to chase Hubert's ass all over the country."

The Kennedy campaign had received encouraging news from Chicago Mayor, Richard Daley, who was arguably the most powerful party boss in the country. Daley indicated if RFK won the California Primary, he would likely lend his support to Kennedy.

Daley, who had been quite fond of John F. Kennedy, was less enamored with RFK's prickly personality. Nonetheless, Daley told a Kennedy staffer that "primaries count," and with enough victories, Democratic Party bosses *could not* deny RFK the nomination.

With Daley's potential endorsement, Kennedy was understandably enthusiastic: "Daley means the whole ball game."

Kennedy realized he needed to mend fences with his primary campaign opponent: "I've got to get free of McCarthy."

Kennedy instructed his adviser, Richard Goodwin, who maintained a solid relationship with McCarthy, to contact the Minnesota Senator: "I think we should tell him, if he withdraws now and supports me, I'll make him Secretary of State."

Robert Kennedy's confidence was on the upswing, and he truly believed voters were genuinely behind *his* candidacy, instead of merely endorsing the memory of John F. Kennedy. Nearing midnight, Bobby telephoned Kenneth O'Donnell, who was coordinating efforts from the campaign's Washington D.C. headquarters: "You know, Kenny, I feel now, for the first time, that I've shaken off the shadow of my brother."

Downstairs, as he stalked the corridors of the Ambassador Hotel, Sirhan Sirhan learned that RFK planned to address his supporters in the Embassy Ballroom. At 10:30 p.m., Sirhan asked a busboy if the candidate would pass through the kitchen pantry area in route to his victory speech. The hotel employee was noncommittal, and an anxious Sirhan continued to search for the ideal location to confront his target. At eleven o'clock, a private security officer eyed the young Palestinian suspiciously, and ordered Sirhan to exit the ballroom's backstage area.

At 11:45 p.m., Kennedy exited his hotel suite to greet a crowd of supporters in the *Embassy Ball Room*. In the upstairs corridor, RFK greeted campaign volunteer, Kristi Witker, inviting her to a post-victory party.

"It promised to be a wonderful night. Bobby was on top of the world," Witker recalled.

A reporter asked RFK about his celebratory plans. Smiling, Kennedy replied: "Have a drink—maybe three."

Armed with his revolver, Sirhan once again stationed himself inside the kitchen pantry, certain that his chance at immortality was near.

RFK stepped to the ballroom podium amid cheers from the boisterous crowd: "Kennedy power! Bobby power!"

Bobby thanked his aides, his cocker spaniel, Freckles, state party officials, and his wife, Ethel, joking that the acknowledgement was in "no particular order." He also congratulated Los Angeles Dodgers' pitcher, Don Drysdale, who, earlier in the evening, had broken the major league record for consecutive scoreless innings.

Kennedy soon moved to the heart of his brief message: "I am very grateful for the votes that I received—that all of you worked for…I think it indicates quite clearly what we can do here in the United States. The vote here, in the state of California, the votes in the state of South Dakota— here is the most urban state of any of the states of our union, and South Dakota, the most rural state of any of the states of our union. We were able to win them both."

As the crowd roared its approval, Kennedy continued: "I think we can end the divisions within the United States. What I think is quite clear is that we can work together, in the last analysis. And, despite what has been going on with the United States over the period of the last three years—the divisions, the violence, the disenchantment with our society; the divisions, whether it is between blacks and whites, between the poor and the more affluent, or between age groups, or over the war in Vietnam—we can start to work together, again. We are a great country, an unselfish country, and a compassionate country."

Balloons fell from the ceiling, as the crowd shouted and whistled, and RFK concluded his victory speech by alluding to the upcoming Democratic National Convention: "So, my thanks to all of you, and now it's on to Chicago, and let's win there."

With a shy smile, Kennedy flashed a victory sign, brushed his hair back from his forehead, and backed away from the podium. He was led from the rear of the stage toward the *Colonial Room*, where he was scheduled to meet with the press. The most direct route carried him through the hotel's kitchen pantry.

As usual, campaign security was lax; Kennedy forbade the use of police officers, and only one member of his security team was armed. Led by the hotel maitre de, Bobby entered the cramped kitchen pantry, stopping to shake hands with a group of hotel busboys. Nearly *eighty* people crowded into the narrow passageway.

At 12:15 a.m., on June 5, 1968, the one year to the day after Israel's triumphant victory over its Arab enemies in the *Six Day War*, Sirhan Sirhan, driven by fervid anti-Semitism, pulled the revolver from the waistband of his jeans and pointed it at Robert Kennedy's head.

Chapter 22

It's too horrible for words

"Kennedy," Sirhan, Sirhan shouted, "You son of a bitch!"

Then, the young Palestinian began to empty all eight chambers of his revolver.

RFK spun around and covered his face with his hands, grasping the clip-on necktie of the security guard closest to him, before falling backwards onto the floor. The terrified crowd standing behind Kennedy reflexively dropped to the floor, but several were wounded by Sirhan's merciless fusillade.

Kennedy's loyal, but untrained bodyguards, including former NFL defensive lineman, Rosey Grier, and Olympic decathlon gold medalist, Rafer Johnson, pinned the gunman to a steam tray table while he was still firing. With incredible strength, Sirhan continued to squeeze the trigger, until every shot was fired. Another Kennedy supporter jumped atop the table and stomped on Sirhan's wrist, finally managing to loosen the gunman's iron fisted grip on the pistol.

Lying on the floor in a growing pool of blood, RFK had been hit by three bullets. The most serious wound was just behind his right ear, where a hollow point .22-caliber slug entered his mastoid process and splintered, driving lead and bone fragments deep into his brain. A second bullet entered near his right armpit and exited through the front of his chest. A third shot hit Kennedy in the back, and lodged in his neck, near the sixth cervical vertebrae. A fourth bullet passed through his suit coat, without injuring him.

Five bystanders were also wounded, but none fatally. Kennedy aide, Paul Schrade, was hit in the forehead, while *ABC* newsman, William Weisel, was wounded in the abdomen. Seventeen year old, Irwin Stroll, a campaign volunteer, was shot in the left leg, while another campaign worker, nineteen year old, Ira Goldstein was shot in the right buttocks. Yet another bystander, Elizabeth Evans, was also struck in the forehead by one of the eight bullets.

Gravely wounded, Bobby Kennedy lay on his back, blood dripping from his grievous head wound.

"Get the gun! Get the gun!" a radio news commentator shouted.

"No, God, no!" a female voice screamed, "It's happened again!"

Juan Romero, an eighteen year old busboy, who had been shaking hands with RFK at the time of the attack, knelt on the floor, and cradled the wounded candidate's bleeding head. A stunned, but compassionate Romero placed his rosary beads in Kennedy's right hand.

On the wall behind RFK's supine body, an eerily worded sign, left over from a previous hotel function, read: "The once and future king."

"Is everybody all right?" Bobby murmured to Romero.

Ethel Kennedy, who had been separated from Bobby by the dense crowd, rushed to her husband's side: "Oh, my God!"

RFK made eye contact with his wife and moaned: "Ethel, Ethel."

"It's all right. It's okay," Ethel whispered.

A physician, who had been among the Kennedy supporters in the ballroom crowd, rushed to candidate's side and manually removed clots from the head wound to lessen mounting intracranial pressure. Ambulance attendants soon arrived with a stretcher.

"Oh, no, no, don't. Don't lift me, don't lift me," Kennedy moaned, before losing consciousness.

A horrified witness to the shooting remembered Sirhan Sirhan with "smirk on his face." Writer, George Plimpton, who was part of the Kennedy entourage, helped subdue the determined gunman: "Sirhan looked like the Devil—As long as I live, I shall never forget those utterly cold, utterly expressionless eyes of his."

When police officers arrested the would-be assassin they found a newspaper clipping in his pocket, referencing RFK's support for Israel. The article, dated May 26, 1968, originated from a Pasadena newspaper, and was entitled *Paradoxical Bob,* criticizing Kennedy's support of Israel, in light of this opposition to the Vietnam War.

Unconscious and stretcher bound, Kennedy was taken to a waiting ambulance. Ethel climbed in the back with her husband, before the vehicle lurched out of the parking lot. As the ambulance attendant attempted to staunch the blood flow from Bobby's head wound, Ethel grew hysterical, screaming and slapping the medic across his face: "Don't touch him!"

When the patient began struggling to breath, Ethel relented, and allowed an oxygen mask to be placed over Bobby's nose and mouth.

At 12:30 a.m., the ambulance arrived at *Central Receiving Hospital,* where Kennedy was wheeled into an emergency treatment room. The attending physician slapped Kennedy on the face and shouted his name, but could not revive him. After his heart was injected with adrenaline to treat cardiac arrest, the now-comatose patient was attached to life support machines.

A priest soon arrived and administered the last rites. One of the doctors allowed Ethel to use his stethoscope, reassuring her that Bobby's heart was still beating.

Because of the severity of his head wound, RFK was transferred to *Good Samaritan Hospital,* a few blocks away, where a team of neurosurgeons prepared to perform emergency surgery. At 3:15 a.m. a team of five surgeons began a nearly *four* hour operation, in hopes of saving Kennedy's life.

In New York City, Jackie Kennedy was awakened by a telephone call from her brother-in-law, Stas Radziwill: "Jackie? How's Bobby?"

"He's fine, terrific. You heard that he won California by (with) *fifty-three* percent, didn't you?" the former First Lady replied, having retired for the evening, after RFK was projected the winner in the primary contest.

"But Jackie, he's been shot. It happened just a few minutes ago," Radziwill informed her.

"No! It can't have happened!" Jackie exclaimed, realizing that her shocking premonitions about RFK's fate had come to fruition, "No! It can't have happened!"

At 3:30 a.m., EST (12:30 a.m. on the west coast), just fifteen minutes after Sirhan Sirhan had gunned down Robert Kennedy, National Security Adviser, Walt Rostow, awakened President Johnson with the upsetting news. For the remainder of the night, LBJ watched television replays of a wounded RFK, lying in a pool of blood.

"It's too horrible for words," LBJ softly moaned.

Chapter 23

We pray to God that he will spare Robert Kennedy

Robert Kennedy remained in a coma after surgery, connected to life support machines. Family and friends gathered at the hospital, praying for a miracle.

RFK's Press Secretary, Frank Mankiewicz, regularly updated the press, who clustered outside Good Samaritan Hospital. Bobby's older children, Kathleen, Joe, and Robert Jr. flew from Washington D.C. to California. After arriving from New York and eyeing her wounded brother-in-law, Jackie Kennedy immediately sensed that he would never recover.

Robert, Jr. sat at his father's bedside in the hospital's intensive care unit: "I held his hand. His head was bandaged and his eyes were blackened. I knew he had little or no chance."

When Ted Kennedy arrived at the hospital, he was forced to assume the mantle of family leader: "I can't let go. We have a job to do. If I let go, Ethel will let go, my mother will let go, all my sisters…"

As the hopeless vigil unfolded, Frank Mankiewicz encountered Ted in a darkened hospital bathroom: "I have never, ever, nor do I expect, ever, to see a face in more grief. It was beyond grief and agony."

At six o'clock on Wednesday morning, as RFK lay gravely wounded, White House Counsel, Devier Pierson, received a phone call from the President Johnson.

"Where's that legislation on Secret Service protection for federal candidates?" LBJ inquired.

"It's in my office," Pierson answered.

"Well, come down and get it, and bring it to my bedroom, right now," Johnson ordered.

After the assassination of Martin Luther King, LBJ had drafted legislation granting Secret Service protection to all presidential candidates. The bill had stalled on Capitol Hill, and Johnson decided to use RFK's tragic shooting to pressure Congress to act on it. In the meantime, LBJ issued an Executive Order, assigning Secret Service protective details to each of the remaining presidential candidates.

Later that same day, White House Press Secretary, George Christian, read a short statement on behalf of President Johnson: "There are no words equal to the horror of this tragedy. Our thoughts and our prayers are with Senator Kennedy, his family, and the other victims. All America prays for his recovery. We also pray that divisiveness and violence be driven from the hearts of men, everywhere."

LBJ rushed a telegram to Ethel Kennedy: "We grieve and pray with you."

Throughout the day and into the night, Johnson was obsessed with RFK's condition, and frequently asked his Secret Service agents: "Is he dead yet? I've got to know, is he dead yet?"

White House aide, Harry McPherson, described LBJ's troubled state of mind: "Johnson was terribly agitated after Kennedy's shooting…He would listen to the account from the Ambassador Hotel over and over…I don't know—he must have been filled with a hundred competing emotions."

At 10:00 p.m., Johnson addressed a national television audience: "I speak to you tonight, not only as your President, but as a fellow American, who is shocked and dismayed, as you are, by the attempt on Senator Kennedy's life…At this moment, the outcome is still in the balance. We pray to God that he will spare Robert Kennedy. Let us put an end to the violence and to the preaching of violence…We cannot, we must not, tolerate the sway of violent men among us. We must not permit men, who are filled with hatred and careless of innocent lives, to dominate our streets and fill our homes with fear."

Robert Kennedy failed to regain consciousness. Family and friends crowded inside the intensive care cubicle, praying and hoping against the worst. At one point, Ethel crawled into bed and rested her head atop Bobby's chest.

At 1:15 a.m., on June 6th, neurosurgeon, Dr. Henry Cuneo, met with Ethel, Ted, Jackie, and Bobby's sisters, Pat and Jean, explaining that the patient had no brain wave activity, and was being kept alive by a ventilator.

"Is there any chance of recovery, at all?" Ethel asked.

"None," Dr. Cuneo replied.

"Then, turn it off," Ethel said, pointing at the ventilator.

Once the respirator was disconnected, Ethel watched her husband breathe unassisted for a few minutes, and then stop—it was 1:44 a.m.—*twenty-five hours* and *twenty-nine minutes* since Sirhan Sirhan had fired his flurry of shots.

A short while later, standing outside the hospital, a teary eyed Frank Mankiewicz addressed reporters in a somber voice: "Senator Robert F. Kennedy died at 1:44 a.m., today, June 6, 1968. He was forty-two years old."

At 5:00 a.m. EST, President Johnson was informed that Robert Kennedy was dead. Later that same day, veteran newsman, Hugh Sidey, observed LBJ in the Oval Office, as the President listened to a radio newscaster discuss Kennedy's death. Sidey vividly recalled Johnson's response: "He stopped work. His head slumped way down between his knees as he listened, so low, that those in front of his desk could barely see him. When it was over, he snapped off the radio, rose from his chair, a stricken man, walked out the French doors into the Rose Garden, and stood there alone, silent."

Chapter 24

My brother need not be idealized

On the morning of June 6, 1968, President Johnson issued a public statement about RFK's death: "Our public life is diminished by his loss."

LBJ dispatched Air Force One to California to bring Kennedy's body back to New York. Johnson designated Sunday, June 9th, as an official day of mourning for RFK, and ordered all flags lowered to half-staff, in honor of the slain Senator.

LBJ, however, remained a man of many contradictions. That same day, he called Secretary of Defense, Clark Clifford, and asked if RFK "had the right" to be buried at Arlington National Cemetery, since he was not a war hero. Clifford, "stunned and dumbfounded," quickly told the President that he had the discretion to allow Kennedy to be interred at Arlington. The Secretary of Defense also advised LBJ that it would be insensitive and "politically reckless" to deny RFK burial in the national cemetery.

Unable to let go of his long-standing animosity against RFK,

Johnson refused to add *500,000* dollars to the 1968 supplemental budget, establishing a permanent grave marker for Kennedy. In the last days of his presidency (January of 1969) LBJ finally added *431,000* dollars to the 1970 supplemental budget—essentially handing the issue of RFK's gravesite funding to his successor, Richard Nixon.

In Los Angeles, an autopsy was performed on Kennedy's body, before it was flown to New York City. At La Guardia Airport, the longstanding RFK/LBJ feud once against reared its ugly head.

Bobby's brother-in-law, Sargent Shriver, who had been appointed United States Ambassador to France by President Johnson, was on hand for the arrival of RFK's body at 9:00 p.m. on Thursday night. When Shriver attempted to assist Kennedy loyalists unloading the casket from the aircraft, he was pushed aside—having accepting LBJ's appointment, Sarge had been branded a *traitor*.

For a full day and two nights, RFK's coffin lay in state in Manhattan's Saint Patrick's Cathedral. A line of mourners, *twenty-five* blocks long, waited up to *eight* hours to view the closed African mahogany casket.

Western Union telegrams were delivered to RFK's family and select friends and acquaintances: "You are invited to attend a requiem mass in memory of Robert Francis Kennedy at Saint Patrick's Cathedral in New York City, on Saturday, June 8, 1968 at 10:00 a.m. Please enter through the Fifth Avenue entrance by 9:30 a.m. Interment will be at Arlington Cemetery, Arlington, Virginia. You are welcome to travel on the funeral train from New York to Washington. Buses will leave the Fifth Avenue side of the cathedral immediately following the mass. This telegram will admit only the person or persons to whom it is addressed, and must be retained and presented for identification whenever it is requested."

During the *two* hour funeral mass, Leonard Bernstein conducted a Mahler symphony, and entertainer, Andy Williams, sang one of RFK's favorite tunes, *The Battle Hymn of the Republic*.

Edward Kennedy had asked his speechwriter, Milt Gwirtzman, to prepare a heartfelt eulogy: "Make it about love."

"I'm going to show them what they've done—what Bobby meant to this country—what they lost," Ted promised.

His voice cracking, Ted Kennedy delivered an unforgettable eulogy: "Love is not an easy feeling to put into words, nor is loyalty, or trust, or joy. But, he was all of those. He loved life and lived it intensely."

Inside the hushed cathedral, Ted continued: "A few years back, Robert

Kennedy wrote some words about his own father, and they expressed the way we in his family felt about him. He said of what his father meant to him, 'What it really adds up to is love—not love as is described with such futility in popular magazines, but the kind of love that is affection and respect, order, encouragement, and support. Our awareness of this was an incalculable source of strength, because real love is something unselfish and involves sacrifice and giving. We could not help but profit from it.'"

The last surviving Kennedy brother concluded the eulogy with a memorable tribute: "My brother need not be idealized, or enlarged in death, beyond what he was in life. Rather, he should be remembered simply as a good and decent man, who saw wrong and tried to right it, saw suffering and tried to heal it, saw war and tried to stop it. Those of us who loved him and take him to rest today, pray that what he was to us and what he wished for others, will someday come to pass for all the world. As he said many times, in many parts of this nation, to those he touched and who sought to touch him—'Some men see things as they are, and say, why? I dream things that never were, and say, why not?'"

Lyndon Johnson quietly and non-intrusively entered the church, just prior to the start of the funeral. LBJ's entrance did not go unnoticed and drew angry glares from a handful of Kennedy loyalists. Immediately after the service, Johnson flew back to Washington. Exercising rare self-restraint, LBJ did not divert attention from the grieving Kennedy clan.

Robert Kennedy's coffin was transported by train from New York City to Washington D.C. An estimated *two million* Americans lined the railroad tracks as the *twenty-car* train carried RFK back to the Capitol. Ethel Kennedy sat in the last car on a chair next to the casket, clutching a rosary. The pallbearers had precariously balanced the coffin atop chairs, so the mournful crowds could catch a glimpse through the train windows.

Civil Rights leader, John L. Lewis, was among the passengers: "All along the way, I saw people crying—mothers and fathers holding up signs that said, 'We love you Bobby.' It was one of the saddest days of my life."

Another mourner's sign read: "We have lost our last hope."

Arthur Schlesinger, Jr., who was among the *1146* passengers aboard the funeral train, commented on the enormous tribute: "What marvelous crowds."

Kenneth O'Donnell, who was perhaps Bobby Kennedy's closest friend, could not contain his anger-laden grief: "Yes, but what are they good for?"

The major television networks monitored the progress of the train. *NBC News* anchor, David Brinkley, memorialized RFK as "the only politician, left, who could talk to both races."

For the Kennedy family, politics could not entirely be eclipsed by grief. RFK's oldest son, sixteen-year old Joseph Patrick Kennedy, II, worked his way through the train cars, dressed in one of father's suits: "I'm Joe Kennedy. Thank you for coming."

Watching her oldest son greet the mourners, Ethel contemplated young Joe's political future: "He's got it! He's got it!"

RFK's nephew, Christopher Lawford, who was thirteen at the time of his uncle's death, later recalled the surreal atmosphere on the funeral train: "There was a lot of drinking and laughter—a pretty ordinary Irish wake—except the whole world was watching."

John F. Kennedy, Jr., now eight years old, had no clear memories of the similar tragedy that had visited his family five and half years before. However, he was fully aware that both his Father and Uncle Bobby were both gone. John asked his five year old cousin, Christopher (RFK's eighthborn child) if Bobby would still go to work each day.

"Oh, yes. He is in heaven in the morning and he goes to the office in the afternoon," Chris replied.

The train crept at a snail's pace, hoping to avoid striking the multitudes of trackside bystanders. Unfortunately, two people watching the mournful procession from an adjacent track were struck and killed by a northbound express train.

The *226*-mile rail trip from New York to Washington D.C. usually took *four* hours, but because of large crowds and slow speeds, the Kennedy funeral train did not arrive in the Capitol until *eight* hours after departure.

At 9:00 p.m., Lyndon Johnson waited in the shadows of the depot, before joining the procession of limousines heading to the cemetery. A tearful LBJ focused on RFK's mother, Rose: "That woman has suffered more than anyone I know. Her religious faith is what brings her through these tragedies."

The hearse paused briefly in front of the Justice Department building; a poignant tribute to the one time Attorney General. By the time the funeral procession reached Arlington National Cemetery, darkness had fully descended. An earlier rain storm had cooled the night air, and a nearly full moon reigned over the mournful ceremony. Hand held candles and television lights illuminated the route from the hearse to the grave.

It was first nighttime interment at Arlington in American history, and the pallbearers were momentarily disoriented by the poor light. Long-time presidential adviser, Averill Harriman whispered to RFK's brother-in-law, Steve Smith: "Steve, do you know where you're going?"

"Well, I'm not sure, but I distinctly heard a voice coming out of the coffin saying, 'Damn it. If you fellows put me down, I'll show you the way,'" Smith replied.

The graveside service lasted only *fifteen* minutes, highlighted by the Harvard University marching band's rendition of *America*. At the request of Ethel Kennedy, there were no soldiers or rifle salutes. At the conclusion of the ceremony, astronaut, John Glenn (a former Marine), folded the American flag that had adorned RFK's casket, and handed it to Ted Kennedy, who passed it along to Bobby's eldest son. Joe Kennedy, in turn, gave the flag to his mother.

On a gentle slope, just *thirty* yards from his brother's grave, Robert F. Kennedy was laid to rest.

Chapter 25

Profound feelings of disillusionment

At the midway point of 1968, Robert Kennedy was dead, and Lyndon Johnson's presidency was down to its final six months. Throughout the country, anti-war demonstrations were a regular piece of the social fabric. The murders of Martin Luther King and Bobby Kennedy had left many voters, particularly young adults and minorities, with profound feelings of disillusionment.

As a lame duck President, Johnson achieved little on the domestic front, and the raging war kept his popularity low. For all practical purposes, LBJ would function as a figurehead until the inauguration of his successor.

Two weeks after her husband's murder, Ethel Kennedy, who had been one of LBJ's most vocal critics, sent the President a handwritten note. Her tone was gracious and appreciative: "We shall always be grateful to you, Mr. President, for honoring Bobby by being at his funeral, by meeting the train in Washington, and by accompanying us to Arlington. I shall always remember the goodness of heart, which prompted your thoughtfulness, your kindness, and your help."

Johnson answered with his own handwritten missive: "Thank God you have so many who love you, nearby; that you have been blessed with so many fine children, and with a strong affirmative spirit in yourself. If there is anything I can do to help you or others in the future, Ethel, I hope you will let me know. So long as I have the power to help, please know that I have the desire to do so."

Without Bobby Kennedy as a target for his misplaced frustrations, LBJ was rudderless. His only real hope for resurrecting his presidential legacy was to negotiate a peaceful end to the Vietnam War.

In the summer and fall of 1968, the Paris peace talks dragged on, with little in the way of real progress. For over *sixty* days, negotiators argued over the shape of the table! The North Vietnamese remained unreasonable, demanding that the United States stop all bombing, but refusing to offer meaningful concessions of their own. To complicate matters, South Vietnam seemed disinterested in the peace process.

Secretary of Defense Clifford summarized the lack of commitment by the South Vietnamese: "The goal of the Saigon government had become utterly antithetical to the goal of the United States. One, the Saigon government did not want the war to end. Number two; they did not want the Americans to pull out. Number three; they did not want to make any settlement of any kind with Hanoi...They preferred it the way they were. With *540,000* American troops, they were in no danger, whatsoever, and if we stayed there long enough, ultimately, perhaps, we could exhaust Hanoi, and then, maybe, they wouldn't have to make any settlement, at all...In addition, when you've got *540,000* troops and *thousands* of civilians, it's just as though you had a golden pump running, and we were pumping money in there, and they certainly all liked that fine."

In the final year of his presidency, Lyndon Johnson no longer enjoyed his long-standing mastery of Congress. When Chief Justice Earl Warren submitted his retirement letter (specifying that his resignation date would be at the discretion of the President), LBJ sought to reshape the Supreme Court before his term ended. Johnson hoped to elevate his long time political and legal adviser, Justice Abe Fortas, to the position of Chief

Justice and add another long time friend, Federal Judge Homer Thornberry, to the Court.

Many judicial experts, however, considered Thornberry, a Texas Congressman prior to his appointment to the federal court, unqualified to serve on the Supreme Court. At the same time, Republican lawmakers believed that the newly elected President (who they hoped would be Richard Nixon) should be allowed to shape the future of the Supreme Court—namely appointing a conservative successor to the liberal Warren.

Many legislators were concerned about the close personal and political relationship between President Johnson and Justice Fortas, who had served as LBJ's personal lawyer prior to his judicial appointment. Since joining the high court, Fortas had continued to serve as one of Johnson's primary political advisers, with a private telephone line connecting his chambers to the Oval Office. Fortas drew even closer scrutiny, when it was discovered he had been paid *15,000* dollars to teach seminars at American University (the funds had been solicited from Fortas' past and present clients, creating the potential for conflict of interest in future Supreme Court rulings).

LBJ's plan for reshaping the Supreme Court was dealt a fatal blow, when Senate Republicans launched a filibuster against Fortas' nomination. A year later, when LBJ's successor, Richard Nixon, appointed Warren Burger to succeed Earl Warren as Chief Justice, a historic left to right shift of the Supreme Court ensued. On May 14, 1969, Abe Fortas was forced to resign from the Court secondary to *financial irregularities,* further tainting LBJ's legacy.

During the summer of 1968, both parties held their presidential nominating conventions. In Miami, the Republicans selected former Vice-President, Richard Nixon, as their nominee. Nixon chose Maryland Governor, Spiro Agnew, as his running mate. The GOP nominating process was sedate and businesslike, in sharp contrast to the chaotic Democratic National Convention.

In late August, the Democrats convened in Chicago amid tumultuous demonstrations against the Vietnam War. Chicago Mayor, Richard Daley, was determined to control rowdy anti-war and anti-establishment protesters. The convention hall was surrounded by barbed wire, with the entire area resembling a war zone. The Chicago police department, bolstered by the Illinois National Guard, forcefully subdued and arrested hundreds of protesters, as well as numerous innocent bystanders. The police were aggressive and indiscriminate, invading hotels and dragging confirmed and suspected protesters into the streets. The mayhem in Chicago was broadcast to an unbelieving national television audience. While conservative watchers criticized the bedraggled protesters, civil libertarians deplored the *Nazi-like* tactics of the law enforcement officers.

LBJ watched the convention from afar, rightfully concerned that his presence in Chicago would further inflame the protesters. At the same time, many believed Johnson was secretly hoping the delegates would draft him to run for another term. LBJ sensed voters would detect a fundamental lack of toughness in Hubert Humphrey, and tried to embolden and toughen his Vice-President: "The trouble with you, Hubert, is that you're just too damn good. Somebody comes along and kicks you to the floor, and you pat their leg. I give them nothing."

"He's a wonderful human being, but you can't be all things to all people. Humphrey doesn't like to face cold decisions. Well, neither do I. Neither does anyone…" LBJ confided to an aide.

Johnson said he would respect Humphrey more if the Minnesotan "showed he had some balls." In his more frustrated moments, LBJ threatened to support Nixon instead of Humphrey.

LBJ watched and waited as the convention got underway, perhaps hoping that he would emerge as the party's savior. Newsman, Charles Bartlett, believed Johnson really wanted to remain in power: "It's my impression that he would have accepted a draft movement…I don't think he had the feeling that Hubert Humphrey would be a strong candidate or a strong President. I do have the feeling that Lyndon Johnson sort of believed that the party, in its wisdom, would say: "Let's keep what we've got.'"

As the chaotic convention lurched forward, LBJ decided it was time for him go to Chicago, after all, to deliver an address defending his administration's policies. Johnson went so far as to have such a speech drafted, but ultimately acquiesced to his adviser's recommendations to steer clear of the nominating process.

The unpopularity of the Vietnam War and the widening *credibility gap* proved insurmountable obstacles, even for a seasoned politician like LBJ. The Democratic Party ultimately nominated Hubert Humphrey for the presidency. Humphrey offered the vice-presidency to Ted Kennedy, but last surviving Kennedy brother had no interest in the number two slot. Humphrey subsequently chose Maine Senator, Edmund S. Muskie, as his running mate.

Humphrey was immediately type cast as the *Johnson candidate,* who would promote continuation of the current administration's foreign and domestic policies. Early in the campaign, prospective voters appeared unhappy with perpetuation of the *status quo*, and Richard Nixon opened up a double digit lead in the polls.

Nixon promised an *honorable end* to the war in Vietnam, while Humphrey's association with *Lyndon Johnson's War* placed him at a distinct disadvantage. Humphrey's advisers urged him to break with LBJ, and formulate his own strategy for ending the war in Southeast Asia.

On September 30th, during a campaign speech in Salt Lake City, Humphrey finally separated himself from the Johnson Administration: "As President, I would stop the bombing of North Vietnam as an acceptable risk for peace, because I believe it could lead to success in negotiations, and thereby shorten the war."

LBJ was angered by his Vice-President's seeming betrayal. When the Humphrey arrived a bit late for a meeting with the President on October 1st (he had been delayed during a campaign stop in Maryland), LBJ refused to see him. Angered by Johnson's petulance, Humphrey shouted, within earshot of the LBJ: "You tell the President, he can cram it up his ass!"

After temporarily punishing him for disloyalty, LBJ ultimately supported Humphrey's candidacy. Johnson never considered the Democratic nominee as an ideal candidate, but realized the election of Nixon would symbolize a rejection of the *Great Society*.

In early October, Johnson and Humphrey seemed to catch a break, when the North Vietnamese indicated a renewed willingness to step up peaceful negotiations. In exchange for a bombing halt, the enemy expressed interest in "substantive talks." With Election Day only a month away, the prospect of ending the war was a boost for the Democratic candidate, and polling data indicated a tightening presidential race.

Richard Nixon sensed another election slipping away from him, and took matters into his own hands. In short order, South Vietnam balked at the idea of renewed peace talks. Nixon operatives had secretly utilized backdoor channels to contact South Vietnamese leaders, promising that postponement of the peace talks until after Election Day would allow the new Republican administration to pursue a tougher stance against North Vietnam.

President Johnson learned about the machinations of the Nixon camp through government intelligence sources: "They (the South Vietnamese) had been urged to delay going to the Paris meetings, and promised they would get a better deal from Nixon's administration than from Humphrey."

In private, LBJ accused Nixon of *treason,* realizing that his final opportunity to end the war had been sabotaged by the Republican nominee. Fearing retaliatory action, Nixon telephoned President Johnson two days before the election and denied any involvement in a plot to sabotage the Paris Peace Talks. While LBJ doubted Nixon's veracity, he chose not to publicize the Republican candidate's subterfuge.

On October 31ˢᵗ, President Johnson attempted to counter Nixon's treachery by ordering a bombing halt, hoping it would revive an interest in peace, and convince the electorate to vote for Humphrey. The bombing pause was not enough to salvage Humphrey's candidacy—on the first Tuesday in November, Richard Nixon was elected President. The margin of victory had been scant (less than *one percent* of the popular vote); a remarkable turn of events, given that Humphrey had once trailed his opponent by *twenty-two* percentage points.

The *Great Society* was nearing an end, and LBJ was sadly convinced that history would define his legacy by the failed war in Southeast Asia, rather than his noble, progressive social policies. Furthermore, Lyndon Johnson could no longer blame his woes on Robert Kennedy.

Chapter 26

It will be said that we tried

Lyndon Johnson was officially a lame duck, and rapidly approaching the end of nearly *thirty* years of public service. LBJ faced the future with a mixture of relief and trepidation.

Johnson was gracious to the President-Elect, but remained bitter about Nixon's pre-election contact with the South Vietnamese, which had shattered any hopes for ending the war during his administration. Johnson had also planned to attend a summit with Russian leaders to discuss nuclear arms control prior to the conclusion of his presidency. Once again, Nixon operatives undercut LBJ, convincing the Soviets to postpone any negotiations until the new administration took office.

An exasperated LBJ lost his cool, when Nixon transition team representative, Frank Lincoln, asked for a copy of the Johnson Administration's task force report on government reorganization: "Hell, no! And tell him I'm not going to publish my wife's love letters, either."

LBJ embraced the power of the presidency until his last day in office, extending executive privilege to family matters. At the last minute, on the evening of his final State of the Union address, the President decided his toddler grandson, Patrick Lyndon Nugent, should attend the 9:00 p.m. speech.

Lady Bird explained that the toddler was already tucked in bed: "That's the most ludicrous thing I've heard in my whole life—an eighteen-month old baby doesn't belong at a State of the Union speech."

"Bird, I'd just love to have you at the State of the Union speech, and I'd just love for you to take your daughters, if you choose to, and that includes all other relatives that you invited, if you want to, and even some of those dear, close friends. But, it's my State of the Union speech, and it's my last one, and the only person I'm inviting is Patrick Lyndon. If any of the rest of you wants to come, that's just fine, but I'm only inviting him," LBJ calmly replied.

Sitting in his mother's lap in the balcony of the House chamber, Patrick Lyndon Nugent was perhaps the youngest person to ever watch the presidential address on Capitol Hill.

"He might not remember it, but I would," LBJ explained.

The lame duck President retained a measure of his characteristic bravado. LBJ steadfastly declared his retirement was *voluntary*: "I have not the slightest doubt that, if I'd wanted to, I could have been re-elected."

"I would have won over Nixon by a substantial margin," Johnson boasted.

On January 14, 1969, Lyndon Johnson returned to Capitol Hill to deliver his last State of the Union Address. Lawmakers gave him a five minute standing ovation, as LBJ slowly walked down the aisle to the House podium, shaking hands along the way.

Johnson considered Congress his true home, and savored his final visit to the hallowed halls. Speaking slowly and deliberately, the President enumerated the accomplishments of his administration—voting rights, the *Civil Rights Bill,* fair housing, *Medicare,* the *Poverty Program,* federal aid to education, and environmental protection.

He concluded his address with a fond farewell: "Now, it is time to leave. I hope it may be said a hundred years from now, that by working together, we helped make our country more just for all its people, as well as to ensure and guarantee the blessings of liberty for all our posterity…That is what I hope, but, I believe that, at least, it will be said that we tried."

As Inauguration Day approached, LBJ warned others about his successor. Johnson cautioned his aide, Joseph Califano: "It's not enough for Nixon to win. He's going to have to put some people in jail."

LBJ advised Califano to pay an additional *500* dollars beyond what was owed on his income tax return, in anticipation of a Nixon-directed IRS audit against prominent Democrats. Johnson's predictions proved eerily prophetic. During his second term in office, Nixon was driven from office after the *Watergate* scandal exposed his corruption and chronic, cavalier abuse of power.

On his last day in office, LBJ authorized the National Park Service to establish the *Franklin Delano Roosevelt Memorial Park;* a fitting tribute to Johnson's idol and political benefactor. That night, LBJ hosted a small dinner party for the White House staff, and entertained his listeners with a multitude of colorful political anecdotes. The President grew teary eyed when his advisers serenaded him with *Hello Lyndon.*

January 20, 1969 was a cold, overcast day, as Richard Nixon recited the oath of office and became the thirty-seventh President of the United States. LBJ later recalled his conversation with the new Commander-in-Chief: "President Nixon said to me, 'How did you feel when you weren't President anymore?' And, I said, 'I don't know whether you'll understand this now, or not, but certainly will later. I sat there on that platform and waited for you to stand up and take the oath of office, and I think the most pleasant words that I ever heard—that ever came into my ears were, 'So help me God,' that you repeated after that oath. Because, at that time, I no longer had the fear that I was the man that could make the mistake of involving the world in war—that I was no longer the man that would have to carry the terrifying responsibility of protecting the lives of this country, and maybe the entire world, unleashing the horrors of some of our great power, if I felt that was required.'"

After the inaugural ceremony, outgoing Secretary of Defense, Clark Clifford, hosted a farewell luncheon for Johnson. In Clifford's front yard, a friendly crowd brandished signs: "Well done Lyndon. We still love you, Lyndon."

The now ex-President was gratified by the spontaneous gathering, and waded into the crowd to shake hands. Afterwards, LBJ grew emotional:

"They didn't come to see the President—they came to see Lyndon Johnson."

After the luncheon, LBJ was driven to Andrews Air Force Base for the flight home to Texas. Much to Johnson's surprise, fellow Texan and Republican Congressman, George H.W. Bush, and his wife, Barbara, were present at the airfield to bid him farewell. Bush, who would later become the forty-first President of the United States, explained his reason for being there: "He had been a fine President and invariably courteous to me and my people, and I thought that I belonged here to show, in a small way, how much I have appreciated him."

Later in the day, when the Johnson party landed at Bergstrom Air Force Base, just outside Austin, they were greeted by 500 grateful citizens. The University of Texas marching band serenaded Johnson with *The Eyes of Texas* and *Ruffles and Flourishes*. When the former President and First Lady arrived at the LBJ Ranch at dusk, Lady Bird was whimsical: "The coach has turned back into a pumpkin, and the mice have all run away."

On a lonely hill overlooking the Lincoln Memorial, darkness once again descended on Robert Kennedy's grave.

Chapter 27

By God, I'm going to do what I want to do

Like his brother before him, Robert Kennedy died at the height of his popularity. JFK and RFK were idolized as tragic heroes; a distinction Lyndon Johnson would not share.

In spite of being mentally and physically drained by the presidency, retirement did not come easy to a man accustomed to power and influence. Johnson's daughter, Luci, reflected on the harsh transition: "My Daddy committed political suicide for that war in Vietnam. And, since politics was his life, it was like committing actual suicide."

Johnson had hoped to be a gentleman rancher, but his *hands-on* management style challenged and frustrated his employees. LBJ installed two-way radios in all of the ranch vehicles and in most of the rooms of his house. All hours of the day and night, he would bark orders to his foreman and other ranch hands. Post-presidential aide, Tom Johnson, described LBJ's supervision of the ranch: "He approached his life in retirement much as he had approached his life in the White House. There was urgency in everything he undertook."

LBJ berated and scolded his employees, yet tried to motivate them: "I want each of you to make a solemn pledge that you will not go to bed tonight, until you are sure that every steer has everything he needs. We've got a chance of producing some of the finest beef cattle in this country, if we work at it, if we dedicate ourselves to the job. And, if we treat those hens with loving care, we should be able to produce the finest eggs in the country—really fresh. But, it will mean working every minute of every day."

Johnson delighted in speeding around the ranch in his Lincoln convertible, bragging to guests about the order and efficiency of his *500-acre* ranch. *Newsweek* journalist, Sam Shaffer, remembered LBJ skidding to a stop: "Look at that fence—just as straight as an Indian goes to shit."

LBJ sometimes use a restored fire engine to take visitors on tours of his ranch. Not surprisingly, Johnson delighted in sounding the vehicle's loud siren.

Ranch manager, Dale Malechek, grew frustrated trying to please his demanding boss: "I've never worked for a harder man in my life."

"I hope he runs again for President," Malechek privately groused.

Though harsh and demanding with his employees, LBJ was also remarkably generous, lavishing them with expensive gifts. Jewelry, clothing, and automobiles were bestowed upon lucky individuals on their birthdays and at Christmastime.

No longer bound by the rules of political correctness, LBJ cared little for the opinions of outsiders: "By God, I'm going to do what I want to do. If I want to drink a glass of whiskey, I'm going drink a glass of whiskey. And, if I want to have some bad manners, I'm going to have some bad manners. I've got to have some freedom to do what I want to do."

As a retiree, Johnson let his curly hair grow to shoulder length in the back, and drove recklessly, smoking two to three packs of cigarettes per day, while consuming generous amounts of alcohol. Binge eating and neglecting exercise, LBJ's weight ballooned to over *200* pounds. Resigned to the fatalistic theory that all Johnson men died from heart disease at a young age, the ex-President simply hastened the process.

Johnson delighted in playing with his grandchildren, spending hours on his hands and knees, indulging their every whim. A colorful story teller and excellent mimic, LBJ was always popular with children.

Johnson largely removed himself from the national and regional political scene. When Texas Governor, Preston Smith, asked for a meeting at the LBJ Ranch, the ex-President reluctantly agreed. Johnson later described the visit to an aide: "Well he came down here, brought his wife and Momma, and sat around in my living room for three hours. The son-of-bitch never said what he wanted. Maybe he wanted me to kiss his ass. If so, he should have just said so. After all, that's the business I've been in for the last forty years!"

LBJ's first formal public appearance occurred on July 17, 1969, when he travelled to Cape Canaveral to observe the launch of *Apollo 11*. A long-time supporter of space exploration, LBJ was invited to witness the beginning of America's historic mission to the Moon. Johnson's enthusiasm was negated by the oppressive Florida heat and humidity: "…My trousers stuck like cement to the back of my legs, the sweat from my hair dripping down my neck, and my stomach was upset. I knew, right then, I shouldn't have come."

When Vice-President Spiro Agnew arrived at the launch site, upstaging the ex-President, LBJ's misery intensified.

While he clearly missed the limelight, LBJ also savored the lack of responsibility afforded by retirement: "One of the things I enjoyed most was being able to go to bed after the ten o'clock news at night, and sleep until daylight the next morning. I don't remember ever having an experience like that in the *five* years I was in the White House."

Johnson reflected on the immense pressures of the presidency: "I watch people going into my birthplace, out by the ranch…The women all want their sons to grow up to be President. If they knew a little more about the job, I'm not sure they'd feel that way."

Lady Bird Johnson reminisced about her husband's presidency: "The first year or two in the White House was wine and roses. By the end, it was pure hell."

Visitors to the LBJ Ranch were often perplexed by their host's behavior. President Nixon's National Security Adviser, Henry Kissinger, met with Johnson to brief the former President on foreign policy matters. Kissinger thought LBJ was emotionally unstable, and was convinced that Johnson thought he was the "Prime Minister of Germany." Kissinger was appalled: "He got me all mixed up, and called me 'Dr. Schlesinger'…He didn't know who I was…He's crazy."

Johnson set out to complete his presidential memoirs (*The Vantage Point: Perspectives of the Presidency: 1963-1969*). Employing experienced historians, LBJ forced them to censor his earthy vernacular and dilute his colorful personality: "…For Christ's sake, get that vulgar language of mine out of there. What do you think this is? The tale of an uneducated cowboy? It's a presidential memoir, damn it! And, I've got to come out looking like a statesman, not some backwoods politician!"

On May 22, 1971, the *Lyndon Baines Johnson Presidential Library* was formally dedicated in Austin, Texas. Richard Nixon, Hubert Humphrey and Barry Goldwater were among the host of dignitaries attending the opening ceremony. Over *thirty million* pages of documents were catalogued, documenting Johnson's political career.

LBJ believed that library visitors should have access to a comprehensive overview of his presidency: "It's all here—the story of our time, with the bark off. There is no record of a mistake, nothing critical or unpleasant that is not included in the files here. We have papers from my years of public service, in one place, for friend and foe to judge—to approve or disapprove."

As a private citizen, Lyndon Johnson enlarged his already considerable personal fortune. In 1972, after the *FCC* ruled that a single individual could not own a television station and cable company in the same market, LBJ sold his television station for *nine million* dollars.

In addition to the LBJ Ranch, Johnson owned a penthouse in Austin, several telephone-equipped automobiles, a sailboat, a speedboat, and several airplanes. A special movie theater was constructed at the ranch for the former President's viewing pleasure.

Johnson did not play a significant role in the 1972 presidential election. He was less than enthusiastic about the Democratic candidate, South Dakota Senator, George McGovern. During a visit to the LBJ Ranch, the former President told McGovern that he was "crazy as hell" to advocate abrupt American withdrawal from Vietnam.

Privately, LBJ viewed McGovern as *inept:* "I didn't know they made presidential candidates that dumb."

McGovern was concerned by LBJ's physical condition: "He struck me as a man who really knew he had something terribly wrong with him, although he didn't seem to be distressed about it."

Johnson did not attend the 1972 Democratic National Convention. Party leaders were fearful of resurrecting *Lyndon Johnson's War,* and left the former President completely out of the program. Inside the convention hall, among portraits of other Democratic icons, Lyndon Johnson's picture was conspicuously absent.

Lyndon Johnson's health began to deteriorate early in his retirement. In March of 1970, he was hospitalized with chest pains at *Brooke Army Hospital* in San Antonio. LBJ's coronary artery disease was not amenable to cardiac bypass surgery, and he was forced to rely on nitroglycerin to ease painful angina attacks.

In June of 1972, while visiting his daughter in Charlottesville, Virginia, Johnson suffered a serious heart attack. Convinced that he would not survive, LBJ demanded to be discharged from the Virginia hospital.

"Bird, I'm going home to die—you can come if you want to," Johnson announced.

Ignoring the advice of his doctors, LBJ left the intensive care unit, only three days after admission, and flew to San Antonio. Miraculously, Johnson survived, but spent the next two weeks in a Texas hospital. After discharge, he never regained his stamina, and suffered from daily bouts of chest pain and shortness of breath, often utilizing a portable oxygen tank to assist his ailing heart and lungs.

At 3:49 p.m., on January 22, 1973, Lyndon Johnson phoned Secret Service headquarters at the LBJ Ranch, and asked for Special Agent, Mike Howard. Howard was out of the office, but two other agents, alarmed by Johnson's tone, rushed to the ranch house and found the former President unconscious on his bedroom floor. The agents administered CPR, but were unable to revive Johnson, and a local physician was summoned. Unresponsive to emergency treatment, LBJ was flown to San Antonio in one of his private planes. The trip was short, only *eighteen* minutes, but Johnson failed to recover, and was declared dead before his body was removed from the aircraft.

Lady Bird, who was in Austin at the time of her husband's fatal heart attack, quickly flew to San Antonio, where Agent Howard informed her of LBJ's death.

"This time, we didn't make it," Lady Bird stoically replied, "Well, we expected it."

Ironically, the day after Lyndon Johnson's death, an agreement was reached in Paris, ending the war in Vietnam.

At the Johnson Presidential Library, some *32,000* mourners passed by LBJ's coffin. Library Director, Larry Middleton, kept close count of the number of visitors: "Somewhere, sometime, President Johnson's going to ask me."

Johnson's body was flown to Washington D.C. aboard the same jet (formerly designated as *Air Force One)* that had taken him from Dallas to Washington D.C. on the day John F. Kennedy was assassinated. For two days, the ex-President lay in state in the Capitol Rotunda. Thousands of mourners filed past his casket. Observers estimated that *sixty* percent of the visitors were African American.

"People don't know it, but he did more for us than anybody, any President ever did," a black woman told her daughter, as they passed Johnson's coffin.

A small group of family friends maintained an overnight vigil, after Lady Bird reminded them: "Lyndon hated to be by himself."

On January 25, 1973, LBJ's funeral was held at Washington D.C.'s *National City Christian Church.* Longtime aide, Marvin Watson, eulogized his former boss: "He was ours, and we loved him beyond all telling of it."

After the funeral service, Johnson's body was flown back to the LBJ Ranch, where he was buried in the family cemetery. Johnson protégé and former Texas Governor, John Connally, delivered the graveside address: "Along this stream and under these trees he loved, he now rests. He first saw light here. He last felt life here. May he now find peace here."

Johnson's daughter, Luci, recalled her lasting image from the burial ceremony: "I remember a black man hobbled up. He was ninety-two years old. I tried to comfort him by telling him that my father loved him and his people."

"Ma'am, you don't have to tell me he loved me. He showed me he loved me. A tree would have had to fall over me to keep me from being here today," the old man replied.

Lyndon Johnson was sixty-four years old when he died, outliving his rival, Robert Kennedy, by less than *five* years.

The last participants in an epic feud had finally been laid to rest. Nonetheless, the *bad blood* that flowed between Lyndon B. Johnson and Robert F. Kennedy helped define a tumultuous decade, and represent an unforgettable chapter in American history.

EPILOGUE

In the wake of Robert Kennedy's assassination, the Los Angeles Police Department conducted a thorough investigation of the shooting and concluded that there was "no evidence of conspiracy."

On August 2, 1968, Sirhan Sirhan pled *not guilty* to the murder of Robert Kennedy and the attempted murders of the five others he wounded in the kitchen pantry of the Ambassador Hotel. Sirhan's attorneys formulated a *diminished capacity* defense, claiming that their client was not responsible for his actions on the night of RFK's assassination.

On February 10, 1969, prior to the start of witness testimony in Sirhan's murder trial, the prosecution and defense teams met in the chambers of presiding judge, Herbert V. Walker. The attorneys agreed to a plea bargain, whereby Sirhan would plead guilty to all charges in exchange for life imprisonment, thereby avoiding the death penalty. Judge Walker, however, vetoed the deal, citing the troubling controversy surrounding the assassination of John F. Kennedy: "I think you have got a very interested public. I don't let the public influence me, but, at the same time, there are a lot of ramifications. And they constantly point to the Oswald matter, and they just wonder what is going on, because the fellow wasn't tried... They would say that it was all fixed—it was greased. So, we will just go through with the trial."

On February 14th, the prosecution began its *twelve*-day presentation, soliciting testimony from *fifty-six* witnesses. Among the incriminating evidence presented against Sirhan were his murderous diary entries, and the assassin's premeditated declaration of his intent to kill Robert Kennedy (during a conversation with his garbage man).

The defense opened its case on February 28th, calling *twenty-eight* witnesses. A psychologist, testifying for the defense, diagnosed Sirhan with paranoid schizophrenia, and unable to control his actions, supporting the concept of *diminished capacity*. In contrast, a psychiatrist who testified on behalf of the state, opined that the assassin was sane at the time of the shooting.

Sirhan testified on his own behalf, claiming he had no memory of bringing his gun into the Ambassador Hotel or firing any shots in the kitchen pantry. He also claimed to be intoxicated on the night of the assassination, directly contradicting the observations of law enforcement agents, who testified that Sirhan appeared sober at the time of his arrest and during the subsequent interrogation.

Sirhan did little to improve his chances with the jury, when he made a startling announcement in open court on February 28th: "I, at this time, sir, withdraw my original plea of not guilty, and submit the plea of guilty as charged, on all counts."

On March 3rd, the defendant staged another outburst in front of the judge and jury, proclaiming that he murdered RFK "with twenty years of malice aforethought."

The trial ended after *fifteen* weeks, and the jury of *seven* men and *five* women deliberated for *three* days, before finding Sirhan Sirhan guilty on *one* count of first degree murder and *five* counts of assault with a deadly weapon, with intent to commit murder. On April 23, 1969, the jury recommended that the defendant be executed in California's gas chamber.

Senator Ted Kennedy sent the Los Angeles District Attorney a *five*-page, handwritten letter prior to the judge handing down his final sentence: "My brother was a man of love and sentiment and compassion. He would not have wanted his death to be a cause for the taking of another life."

Nonetheless, on May 21, 1969, Judge Walker sentenced Sirhan to punishment by death. In 1972, the California State Supreme Court (*California v. Anderson*) invalidated all death sentences imposed prior to that year, and Sirhan's punishment was commuted to life in prison. As of 2010, Sirhan has been denied parole on *thirteen* separate occasions (the last parole hearing was in March of 1986, and the next one is scheduled for 2011).

In May of 1982, Sirhan appealed to the parole board: "I sincerely believe that if Robert Kennedy were alive, today, I believe he would not countenance singling me out for this kind of treatment. I think he would be among the first to say that, however horrible the deed I committed *fourteen* years ago was, that it should not be the cause for denying me equal treatment under the laws of this country."

At the time of this writing, Sirhan Sirhan is incarcerated in the *California State Penitentiary* in Corcoran, California.

With the exception of Robert Kennedy, other *New Frontiersmen* were unsuccessful in their quest for elective office. JFK's Press Secretary, Pierre Salinger was defeated in his bid to become a U.S. Senator in California. Appointments Secretary, Kenneth O'Donnell lost his bid for the Massachusetts Governorship. Kennedy advisor and speechwriter, Ted Sorensen, was unsuccessful in his run for the United States Senate (in New York). RFK adviser, Adam Walinsky, lost his bid to become New York's Attorney General.

Over the past half century, much has been written about the supposed *Kennedy Curse*. Prior to his own murder, Robert Kennedy had endured the deaths of two brothers, a sister, and both of his wife's parents. He also witnessed his father's stroke induced invalidism. After RFK's assassination, a litany of additional misfortunes befell the Kennedy family.

"The death of Robert Kennedy was devastating. If President Kennedy represented what the family had been, Uncle Bobby represented what we would become," RFK's nephew, Christopher Lawford later wrote.

After RFK's murder, Jackie Kennedy was consumed by fear and bitterness: "I hate this country. I despise America, and I don't want my children to live here anymore. If they're killing Kennedy's, my kids are number one targets."

Jackie sought refuge in the arms of Greek business tycoon, Aristotle Onassis. Less than five months after RFK's death, the former First Lady married Onassis, finding refuge on her new husband's private island of Skorpios.

Consumed by grief, Ethel Kennedy withdrew into an emotional shell. In December of 1968, six months after her husband's murder, Ethel gave birth to the couple's *eleventh* child. Her capacity to function as a parent, however, was compromised by despair, and RFK's older children found themselves adrift, without a meaningful parental role model.

In 1973, RFK's oldest son, Joseph Kennedy, II, recklessly crashed his jeep, injuring his younger brother David, and permanently paralyzing David's girlfriend. Joe survived his reckless youth and eventually entered politics, serving *six* terms as a Massachusetts Congressman (occupying the seat formerly held by his uncle, John F. Kennedy).

Robert F. Kennedy, Jr. coped with his father's death by turning to drugs. In 1983, he was arrested for possession of heroin. Fulfilling the terms of his suspended sentence, Bobby Jr. entered drug rehabilitation and carried out his community service obligations. Making the most of his second chance, he obtained a law degree and embraced *environmentalism*.

Robert Kennedy, Jr. now serves as counsel for an environmental group and has hosted a political talk radio program.

"Gambling runs in our family, except that we play a game called *Kennedy roulette*," Bobby, Jr. explained, reflecting on the family's tragic misfortunes.

RFK's third son, David, was not as fortunate as his older siblings. Introspective and sensitive, David never seemed to recover from his father's death, drifting into a tragic pattern of drug abuse. Desperately wanting to talk about his father's death, David was rebuffed by his mother: "It's not a subject I want to discuss."

Even though he completed several substance dependence treatment programs, David invariably relapsed. In April of 1984, he was found dead in a Palm Beach, Florida hotel room; the victim of an overdose of both illicit and prescription drugs.

Yet another of RFK's sons, Michael, became a lightning rod for controversy and scandal. As a married, successful attorney, Michael Kennedy made nationwide headlines in 1997, when it was revealed that he had engaged in a long-standing sexual relationship with the family's babysitter (the affair began when the young woman was only *fourteen* years old). Kennedy avoided punishment for statutory rape, when the young woman's family declined to press charges. Michael, who was managing his older brother Joe's campaign for the Massachusetts Governorship, tried to rehabilitate his shattered image, but the scandal contributed to his brother abandoning his gubernatorial candidacy. On New Year's Eve, 1997, Michael Kennedy was killed on a ski slope in Aspen, Colorado, after crashing head first into a tree. His accidental death occurred while he recklessly played football during a high-speed descent on a dangerous slope.

The last surviving Kennedy brother, Ted, was forced to assume the family leadership role after Bobby's assassination, and, in many ways, was not emotionally equipped to handle the responsibility. For many years, Ted pursued a reckless course of infidelity and alcohol abuse. In the early months after RFK's murder, Ted feared for his own life: "They're going to shoot my ass off—the way they shot Bobby."

Ted's first wife, Joan, lost herself in alcoholism, and eventually sought a divorce. On the night of July 18, 1969, Ted Kennedy crashed his car into a canal on the island community of Chappaquiddick, Massachusetts. The Senator managed to escape the sinking automobile, but his unmarried female companion, Mary Jo Kopechne, was trapped inside and drowned.

For reasons that he never adequately explained, Kennedy neglected to report the accident until the following morning. His failure to immediately notify authorities was a death sentence for Kopechne, who was able to survive for a period of time by breathing from an air pocket in the submerged, overturned vehicle.

Ted Kennedy eventually pled guilty to *leaving the scene of an accident,* and received a suspended sentence. Many felt that the Kennedy name and the family fortune afforded him preferential treatment —the very epitome of arrogant privilege.

After Chappaquiddick, Lyndon Johnson cited the absence of leadership in the Kennedy family: "Never would have happened if Bobby was there!"

In 1980, Ted sought the Democratic presidential nomination, unsuccessfully attempting to unseat the incumbent President, Jimmy Carter. Hopelessly inarticulate during a national television news interview, Kennedy's candidacy soon floundered, as many voters doubted his commitment, while others could not forget Chappaquiddick. He never attempted another run for the presidency, but continued to serve in the United States Senate until his death (a remarkable *forty-six* consecutive years, from 1963-2009). For much of his life, Ted dealt with death threats, and many feared that a deranged assassin would attempt to murder the remaining Kennedy brother.

Seventy-seven year old Edward M. (Ted) Kennedy died from brain cancer on August 25, 2009 outliving his brothers, Jack and Bobby, by over *forty* years. He was the only Kennedy brother to live into his geriatric years, and the only one to die of natural causes. He was buried in Arlington National Cemetery, not far from his brothers, where a simple white cross marks his grave.

Ted Kennedy will be long remembered for his four plus decades of Congressional service, and his advocacy of a wide range of domestic issues, including immigration reform, the *Americans with Disabilities Act*, the *Head Start Program*, campaign finance reform, health care reform, and the abolition of the draft.

Perhaps the most shocking and widely publicized tragedy involving the Kennedy family involved JFK's son. In 1997, John F. Kennedy, Jr. crashed his private plane into the Atlantic Ocean, while in route from New Jersey to Cape Cod, during poor visibility conditions (night time haze), which far exceeded his skills as a pilot. Kennedy, along with his wife and sister-in-law were instantly killed.

Ethel Kennedy avoided romantic relationships after RFK's assassination. When asked if she would consider another marriage, Ethel was incredulous: "Oh, no. How could I could I possibly do that, with Bobby looking down from heaven? That would be adultery."

Today, Ethel lives on the Kennedy compound in Hyannisport, Massachusetts, having endured the deaths of her husband and *two* of her *eleven* children.

Closer examination of the so-called *Kennedy Curse* reveals that many of the tragic events were precipitated by a reckless disregard for safety. Impulsive and seemingly invincible, the Kennedy men have repeatedly engaged in high-risk behaviors, ignoring the negative and sometimes deadly consequences.

The unpopularity of the Vietnam War drove Lyndon Johnson from the presidency. By the time LBJ left office, *533,000* American military personnel were stationed in South Vietnam. From 1965 through 1968, the United States flew over *one million* sorties and dropped *750,000 tons* of bombs on North Vietnam. In spite of this commitment of manpower and weaponry, the United States failed to achieve military victory.

During his 1968 presidential campaign, Richard Nixon promised "peace with honor." This goal proved elusive, and American involvement in the war continued for another *five* years. Nixon's failed strategy centered on strengthening South Vietnamese military forces and equipping them to defend themselves— the so-called *Vietnamization* of the war.

In October of 1970, President Nixon announced that the United States would withdraw *40,000* troops from South Vietnam before Christmas. A year later, American military forces numbered slightly less than *200,000,* the lowest level since 1966.

The gradual withdrawal of troops continued, with less than *100,000* remaining at the beginning of 1972. On January 27, 1973, the *Paris Peace Accords* were signed, officially ending America's military involvement in Vietnam. On March 29, 1973, the last United States troops departed South Vietnam.

The Soviet Union, however, continued to supply North Vietnam with arms and military supplies. With American forces no longer in place to counterattack, the enemy was able to launch a sustained offensive. On April 30, 1975, one day after the last American civilian personnel fled Saigon, South Vietnam formally surrendered, leading to the creation of a unified Communist state—the *Socialist Republic of Vietnam.* Today, Saigon is known as *Ho Chi Minh City.*

Entire volumes have been written about the tragic course of the Vietnam War. From the time the first military advisers were dispatched in the 1950s until American troops finally departed in 1973, it was the longest war in American history. Over *2.5 million* American men and women served in Vietnam. Nearly *60,000* American lives were lost, while another *300,000* were wounded. From 1965 through 1973, the United States spent *120 billion* dollars fighting a losing war.

The war in Vietnam challenged conventional military strategy. American troops were unable to defeat an *invisible enemy* of guerilla warriors, who were elusive and mobile. The North Vietnamese fought a *small unit* war, attacking and retreating, frustrating superior American firepower. Utilizing snipers, booby traps, and mines, the enemy repeatedly employed the *terror factor,* effectively demoralizing American ground troops.

American military leaders were hampered in their tactics by diplomatic and political considerations. Unable to invade North Vietnam, Laos, or Cambodia, American soldiers could not pursue retreating Viet Cong guerillas, giving rise to the aptly named *limited war.*

The extensive bombing of enemy targets failed to halt the transfer of men and material to combat zones. Utilizing the *Ho Chi Minh* and *Sihanouk Trails* as conduits, North Vietnam's supply lines remained intact throughout the war.

Unlike previous wars, American forces were not able to measure success in terms of conquered territory. Most battles were fought at the platoon level, and the number of enemy soldiers killed (*body count*) was the only measure of victory. The enemy used local villagers as human shields, and thousands of South Vietnamese civilians, including women and children, were killed during American land and air attacks. The goal of "winning the hearts and minds" of South Vietnamese peasants was unobtainable, when the villagers found themselves under attack from both sides.

After a series of coups, with several leadership changes, the South Vietnamese government remained corrupt and ineffectual. The United States repeatedly overestimated the capability and motivation of South Vietnamese civilians and military. Even in the face of diminishing American troop levels, the South Vietnamese never stepped up and assumed responsibility for their own defense.

Lyndon Johnson's War proved a costly failure. In *Argument without End:*

In Search of Answers to the Vietnam Strategy, former Secretary of Defense, Robert McNamara, summed up the American experience in Southeast Asia: "The achievement of a military victory by United States forces in Vietnam was indeed a dangerous illusion."

LBJ sacrificed his presidency on the flawed premise that the American public would continue to support a war lacking clear cut goals or obvious successes. Writer, David Kamp, offered a clear synopsis of Vietnam's devastating impact on LBJ: "His commitment of ever greater numbers of U.S. troops to Vietnam, for a war that seemed to grow more pointless and less winnable every year of his presidency, proved to be his undoing."

History has largely judged the Johnson presidency based upon its failed policy in Vietnam, to the extent that LBJ's legacy of domestic policy is often overlooked. Lyndon Johnson's *Great Society* is remarkable for its boldness and massive social spending. While historians debate the successes and failures of its offspring (public housing, urban renewal, education programs, *Medicare, Medicaid* and antipoverty measures), many of the *Great Society's* programs, in one form or the other, remain in place, over *four decades* later.

Johnson's support of Civil Rights is inarguable. LBJ's commitment to end segregation and increase voting rights for African Americans is a credit to his compassion, and remains the crowning achievement of his presidency. Few white Americans advanced the cause of Civil Rights more than Lyndon Johnson.

Five years after Lyndon Johnson's death, former President, Richard Nixon, wrote of his enigmatic predecessor: "I think that Lyndon Johnson died of a broken heart, physically and emotionally. He was an enormously able and proud man. He desperately wanted, and expected, to be a great President. He drove himself to outdo his predecessor. After I won the election in 1968, and through the remaining years of Johnson's life, I saw what some have described as the 'better side' of his character. He was courteous, generally soft-spoken, and thoughtful in every way. He was not the pushing, prodding politician or the consummate partisan of his earlier career. Above all, Johnson wanted to be loved—to earn not only approval, but also the affection of every American. Much of his overblown rhetoric and many of his policies were rooted in this compulsive quest for approbation."

Lady Bird Johnson survived her husband by more than *thirty-four* years, and actively managed the Johnson media empire *(LBJ Holdings Company)* until she was in her eighties. The *Lady Bird Johnson Wildflower Center*, founded in 1982, became a highly respected research organization, and emblematic of the former First Lady's quest for the *beautification* of the nation's highways and cities. Ms. Johnson was a recipient of the *Presidential Medal of Freedom* and the *Congressional Gold Medal*.

Ninety-four year old Lady Bird Johnson died on July 11, 2007, and was buried next to her husband in the family cemetery at the LBJ ranch, on the banks of the Pedernales River. Two daughters, seven grandchildren, and ten great grandchildren survived her.

LBJ's son-in-law, Charles Robb, was an influential politician in the latter part of the twentieth century. Robb was as elected Virginia's Lieutenant Governor (1978-1982) and Governor (1982-1986), before serving two terms in the United States Senate (1989-2001).

In the years since his tragic death, many observers have memorialized Robert Kennedy as a liberal icon. While he sought to end the Vietnam War and combat poverty, racism, and hunger, RFK was no *ivory tower* liberal. He visited slums, migrant worker camps, and Indian reservations, instead of relying on demagoguery. Kennedy was certain government spending, alone, was not solution to help the disadvantaged.

Historian and RFK biographer, Michael Knox Beran, contrasted Robert Kennedy's political philosophy with the polar extremes of the political left and right: "There was much in Ronald Reagan's policies that he would have abhorred. And, yet he would, I think, have been no less troubled by his younger brother's defense of a welfare system that had manifestly failed."

Many historians and biographers have elevated RFK's legacy to mythic proportions, boldly declaring that Sirhan Sirhan robbed the country of its next President. In reality, Kennedy was not assured of winning the 1968 Democratic presidential nomination. Hubert Humphrey had a substantial lead in the delegate count, along with the presumed backing of many uncommitted delegates. To prevail at the Democratic National Convention, RFK would have needed the endorsement of Eugene McCarthy, which would have required significant *fence mending*. Furthermore, his arrogance and abrasiveness had earned Kennedy the enmity of many regional Democratic Party bosses, whose blessings would have been essential to winning the nomination.

Tom Wicker, journalist and seasoned political observer, assessed RFK's chances of winning the presidency: "It is a fallacy that if Bobby Kennedy hadn't been shot, the Democrats would have nominated him for President, and he would have won, and the whole history of the world would be different. I analyzed that very closely. Robert Kennedy never would have been nominated in 1968. Had he been nominated, I think he could have beaten Nixon. In other words, he would do better in the country than within the Democratic Party."

Ted Sorensen, guardian of the Kennedy legacy, outlined his own plausible, yet not unbiased, scenario: "I have no doubt that Robert Kennedy, had he lived, would have been the nominee, gathering all of the McCarthy delegates after Gene's defeat in California, and many of the Humphrey delegates, who wanted a winner in November. Bobby would have united the Democratic Party, thereby winning the presidency. What a President he would have been."

Had he secured the Democratic nomination, could Bobby have defeated Richard Nixon in the 1968 presidential election? In light of Nixon's razor thin margin of victory over the lackluster Hubert Humphrey; Kennedy's chances appeared quite good.

RFK's appeal to a broad cross-section of voters during the 1968 presidential primary season is undeniable. While his stated positions were not tailored to fit a single constituency, Kennedy cobbled together support from African Americans, Hispanics, farmers, factory workers, college students, avowed liberals, and traditional conservatives.

One small group of Kennedy converts was rather remarkable. Several days after RFK was assassinated, a *CBS News* reporter interviewed a handful of Tennesseans at a George Wallace campaign rally in Memphis, all of whom indicated they were prepared to vote for Kennedy.

"I just liked him. I thought he would have made a good President," one of the Wallace supporters explained to the newsman.

In November of 2001, RFK received an honor that he would have most assuredly treasured. The *Department of Justice* building in Washington D.C. was renamed in honor of Robert F. Kennedy. During the ceremony, the Kennedy family listened as the speakers praised RFK's tenure as Attorney General, citing his commitment to fighting crime and promotion of Civil Rights.

Lyndon Johnson and Robert Kennedy were very different men, with contrasting, combative personalities. More often than not, personal rather than policy differences, fueled their mutual contempt for one another.

Lyndon Johnson insisted upon being the center of attention, politically and socially. With his six feet three inch frame and animated hands, LBJ literally invaded the body space of his listeners, who were often intimidated by his physical presence, alone. Overbearing and tenacious, the oversized Texan utilized the *Johnson Treatment* to cajole and threaten politicians into his way of thinking.

Nearly six inches shorter than LBJ, Robert Kennedy was nonetheless a tenacious and formidable rival. Uncomfortable in the spotlight and sometimes inarticulate, RFK expected his followers to defer to his judgment, and seldom considered his causes anything less than righteous. While LBJ *demanded* loyalty, Bobby merely *expected* it.

LBJ was a *clothes horse,* immaculate in dress and appearance, and often decorated with jewelry. Bobby Kennedy seemed more comfortable with his tie loosened and the sleeves of his frayed shirt rolled past his elbows.

Johnson was loud, bombastic, impulsive, and crude. A master story teller, his vocabulary was peppered with earthy language. Easy to anger, LBJ's explosive outbursts were legendary. Paranoia often fueled his disagreements with friend and foe, alike. For the sake of political expediency, LBJ was capable of both forgiving and forgetting.

Kennedy was a shy, loner, who frequently assumed the role of *wall flower* during social gatherings. His anger was often reflexive, and grudges were not easily abandoned.

RFK possessed a wry wit. While fiercely committed to his own agenda, Kennedy's self-deprecating sense of humor often lessened the tension of the moment.

Johnson was incapable of laughing at himself. Vain and sensitive, he tolerated nothing less than loyalty and praise from his supporters.

LBJ was the consummate politician, who delighted in meeting people and shaking hands on the campaign trail. Johnson relished the deliberative legislative process, and was a master at manipulating and controlling the outcome.

RFK preferred the task of campaign management, and often found the role of candidate to be distasteful. Restless and impulsive, he had little patience for the *art* of political wheeling and dealing.

In spite of their vast differences in temperament and personal expectations, Lyndon Johnson and Robert Kennedy shared certain commonalities. Both men identified with the underdog, abhorred discrimination, and were driven by intense ambition. Thin skinned and sensitive, neither LBJ nor RFK easily suffered fools.

It is difficult to measure the successes and failures of Lyndon Johnson and Robert Kennedy on the same scale. RFK's youthful idealism and unfulfilled potential have made him an attractive subject for biographers and historians. Unlike Johnson, Kennedy never faced the unrelenting pressure and constant, critical observation imposed upon the President of the United States, which often tarnishes legends.

Lady Bird Johnson's Press Secretary, Liz Carpenter contrasted the leadership styles of the two long time foes: "Kennedy *inspired* which Johnson was not capable of doing, but Johnson *delivered*."

As President, could Robert Kennedy have ended the Vietnam War sooner? His untimely death leaves that critical question unanswered.

What would have been the outcome had Johnson and Kennedy marshaled forces and worked together? With his proven ability to embrace past political foes, LBJ might have welcomed RFK's loyalty and cooperation in the months following the assassination of President Kennedy. Had Kennedy tempered his anger and bitterness, waiting his turn, LBJ could have anointed RFK as his successor. RFK's grief over the death of his brother, coupled with his lack of regard for LBJ, doomed any such political marriage.

In his presidential memoirs, Lyndon Johnson summed up his difficulties with Robert Kennedy: "It was not so much a question of issues...Maybe it was just a matter of chemistry."

LBJ would have found it difficult to share the spotlight with Robert Kennedy. Moreover, RFK served as a convenient target for Johnson's displaced anger and frustration. LBJ's one time Press Secretary, George Reedy, bluntly described Johnson's attitude toward RFK: "Bobby couldn't do anything that would please LBJ, except commit suicide."

In the end, neither man liked or trusted the other. Kennedy considered Johnson an unprincipled usurper of the presidential throne: "This man is mean, bitter, and vicious—an animal in many ways."

Conversely, Lyndon Johnson never understood Robert Kennedy's sense of entitlement, and viewed him as a "grandstanding little runt." The pursuit of common good was overshadowed by intense personal animosity.

Author, David Camp, aptly described Lyndon Johnson as a "complicated man for complicated times." In his own words, LBJ explained his most basic motivation: "Some men want power simply to strut around the world and to hear the tune, *Hail to the Chief.* Others want it simply to build prestige, to collect antiques, and to buy pretty things. Well, I wanted power to give things to people—all sorts of things to all sorts of people, especially the poor and the blacks."

A fitting tribute to Robert Kennedy can be found in the words of his adviser, biographer, and close friend, Arthur Schlesinger, Jr.: "He lived through a time of unusual turbulence in American history, and he responded to that turbulence more directly and sensitively than any other political leader of the era…History changed him, and, had time permitted, he might have changed history…"

In the modern political world of media sound bites and pre-packaged answers to difficult questions, it is unlikely that another *non-political* presidential candidate like Robert F. Kennedy will emerge in the foreseeable future.

Perhaps Lyndon Johnson's legacy is best summarized in the words of the African American writer and intellectual, Ralph Ellison: "When all of the returns are in, Johnson will have to settle for being recognized as the greatest American President for the poor and Negros, but that, as I see it, is a very great honor, indeed.

The world will undoubtedly never encounter another statesman quite like Lyndon B. Johnson.

BIBLIOGRAPHY

Books:

Andersen, Christopher. *The Day John Died*. New York: William Morrow, 2000.

Ayton, Mel. *The Forgotten Terrorist: Sirhan Sirhan and the Assassination of Robert F. Kennedy*. Washington, D.C.: Potomac Books, Inc., 2007.

Beran, Michael Knox. *The Last Patrician: Bobby Kennedy and the End of American Aristocracy*. New York: St. Martin's Press, 1998.

Beschloss, Michael R., ed. *Taking Charge: The Johnson White House Tapes, 1963-1964*. New York: Simon & Schuster, 1997.

Beschloss, Michael R., ed. *Reaching for Glory: Lyndon Johnson's Secret Whitehouse Tapes, 1964-1965*. New York: Simon & Schuster, 2001.

Bishop, Jim. *The Day Kennedy Was Shot*. New York: Gramercy Books, 1968.

Brinkley, David. *David Brinkley: A Memoir*. New York: Alfred A. Knopf, 1995.

Brinkley, David. *Brinkley's Beat: People, Places, and Events that Shaped My Time*. New York: Alfred A. Knopf, 2003.

Brokaw, Tom. *Boom! Voices of the Sixties*. New York: Random House, 2007.

Byrne, Jeb. *Out in Front: Preparing the Way for JFK and LBJ*. Albany, New York: State University of New York Press, 2010.

Collier, Peter and David Horowitz. *The Kennedys: An American Dream.* New York: Summit Books, 1984.

Cronkite, Walter. *A Reporter's Life.* New York: Alfred A. Knopf, 1996.

Califano, Joseph A., Jr. *The Triumph and Tragedy of Lyndon Johnson: The White House Years.* New York: Simon and Schuster, 1991.

Canellas, Peter S., ed. *The Last Lion: The Fall and Rise of Ted Kennedy.* New York: Simon & Schuster, 2009.

Caro, Robert A. *The Years of Lyndon Johnson: The Path to Power.* New York: Alfred A. Knopf, 1982.

Caro, Robert A. *The Years of Lyndon Johnson: Means of Ascent.* New York: Alfred A. Knopf, 1990.

Caro, Robert A. *The Years of Lyndon Johnson: Master of the Senate.* New York: Alfred A. Knopf, 2002.

Carter, Graydon, Ed. *Vanity Fair's Presidential Profiles.* New York: Abrams, 2000.

Clarke, Thurston. *The Last Campaign: Robert F. Kennedy and 82 Days that Inspired America.* New York: Henry Holt and Company, 2008.

Clifford, Clark M., with Richard Holbrooke. *Counsel to the President: A Memoir.* New York: Random House, 1991.

Collier, Peter, and David Horowitz. *The Kennedys: An American Drama.* New York: Summit, 1984.

Connally, John, with Mickey Herkowitz. *In History's Shadow: An American Odyssey.* New York: Hyperion, 1993.

Dallek, Robert. *Lone Star Rising: Lyndon Johnson and His Times, 1908-1960.* New York: Oxford University Press, 1991.

Dallek, Robert. *Flawed Giant: Lyndon Johnson and his Times, 1961-1973.* New York: Oxford University Press, 1998.

Dallek, Robert. *An Unfinished Life: John F. Kennedy, 1917-1963.* New York: Little Brown, 2003.

Davis, John H. *The Kennedys: Dynasty and Disaster, 1848-1993.* New York: McGraw-Hill, 1984.

DeLoach, Cartha. *Hoover's FBI: The Inside Story by Hoover's Trusted Lieutenant.* Washington, D.C.: Regnery, 1995.

Dunnavant, Keith. *Coach: The Life of Paul "Bear" Bryant.* New York: Simon & Schuster, 1996.

Gillon, Steven M. *The Kennedy Assassination: 24 Hours After.* New York: Basic Books, 2009.

Goodwin, Doris Kearns. *The Fitzgeralds and the Kennedys.* New York: Simon & Schuster, 1987.

Hack, Richard. *The Puppet Master: The Secret Life of J. Edgar Hoover.* Beverly Hills: New Millennium Press, 2004.

Halberstam, David. *The Best and the Brightest.* New York: Ballentine, 1971.

Hamilton, Nigel. *JFK: Reckless Youth.* New York: Random House, 1992.

Hersh, Burton. *Bobby and Edgar: The Historic Face-off between the Kennedys and J. Edgar Hoover that Transformed America.* New York: Carroll and Graf Publishers, 2007.

Hersh, Seymour. *The Dark Side of Camelot.* Boston: Little Brown, 1997.

Heymann, C. David. *RFK: A Candid Biography of Robert F. Kennedy.* New York: Dutton, 1998.

Heymann, C. David. *Bobby and Jackie: A Love Story.* New York: Atria Books, 2009.

Hilty, James W. *Robert Kennedy: Brother Protector.* Philadelphia: Temple University Press, 1997.

Holland, Max. *The Kennedy Assassination Tapes: The White House Conversations of Lyndon B. Johnson Regarding the Assassination, the Warren Commission, and the Aftermath.* New York: Knopf, 2007.

Humphrey, Hubert. *The Education of a Public Man: My Life and Politics.* Minneapolis: University of Minnesota, 1975.

Johnson, Lady Bird. *A White House Diary.* New York: Holt, Rinehart, & Winston, 1970.

Johnson, Lyndon Baines. *The Vantage Point: Perspectives of the Presidency, 1963-1969.* New York: Holt, Rinehart, & Winston, 1976.

Karnow, Stanley. *Vietnam: A History.* New York: The Viking Press, 1983.

Katzenbach, Nicholas. *Some of it was Fun: Working with RFK and LBJ.* New York: W.W. Norton and Company, 2008.

Kearns, Doris. *Lyndon Johnson and the American Dream.* New York: Harper and Row, 1976.

Kennedy, Edward M. *True Compass: A Memoir.* New York: Twelve, 2009.

Kessler, Ronald. *In the President's Secret Service: Behind the Scenes with Agents in the Line of Fire and the Presidents They Protect.* New York: Crown Publishers, 2009.

Klein, Edward. *All Too Human: The Love Story of Jack and Jackie Kennedy.* New York: Pocket Books, 1996.

Klein, Edward. *The Kennedy Curse: Why Tragedy Has Haunted America's First Family for 150 Years.* New York: St. Martin's Press, 2003.

Lawford, Christopher Kennedy. *Symptoms of Withdrawal: A Memoir of Snapshots and Redemption.* New York: William Morrow, 2005.

Leamer, Laurence. *The Kennedy Women: The Saga of an American Family.* New York: Villard, 1994.

Leamer, Laurence. *The Kennedy Men: 1901-1963.* New York: Morrow, 2001.

Leamer, Laurence. *Sons of Camelot: The Fate of an American Dynasty.* New York: William Morrow, 2004.

Leaming, Barbara. *Jack Kennedy: The Education of a Statesman.* New York: W.W. Norton and Company, 2006.

MacNeil, Robert, ed. *The Way We Were: 1963, The Year Kennedy Was Shot.* New York: Carroll & Graf Publishers, Inc., 1988.

Manchester, William. *The Death of a President.* New York: Harper & Row, 1967.

McNamara, Robert S., with Brian VanDeMark. *In Retrospect: The Tragedy and Lessons of Vietnam.* New York: Times Books, 1995.

Miller, Merle. *Lyndon: An Oral Biography.* New York: G.P. Putnam's Sons, 1980.

Moldea, Dan E. *The Killing of Robert F. Kennedy: An Investigation of Motive, Means, and Opportunity.* New York: Norton, 1995.

O'Donnell, Helen. *A Common Good: The Friendship of Robert F. Kennedy and Kenneth P. O'Donnell.* New York: Morrow, 1998.

O'Donnell, Kenneth P. and Dave Powers. *Johnny, We Hardly Knew Ye.* Boston: Little-Brown, 1970.

Petro, Joseph. *Standing Next to History: An Agent's Life inside the Secret Service.* New York: St. Martin's Press, 2005.

Powers, Richard Gid. *Secrecy and Power: The Life of J. Edgar Hoover*. New York: Free Press, 1987.

Reeves, Richard. *President Kennedy: Profile of Power*. New York: Simon & Schuster, 1993.

Reeves, Thomas C. *A Question of Character*. New York: Free Press, 1991.

Remini, Robert V. *A Short History of the United States*. New York: Harper Collins Publishers, 2008.

Schieffer, Bob. *This Just in: What I Couldn't Tell You on TV*. New York: G. P. Putnam's Sons, 2003.

Schlesinger, Arthur M., Jr. *A Thousand Days: John F. Kennedy in the White House*. Boston: Houghton Mifflin, 1965.

Schlesinger, Arthur M., Jr. *Robert Kennedy and His Times*. Boston: Houghton Mifflin, 1978.

Schlesinger, Arthur M., Jr., ed. Andrew Schlesinger and Stephen Schlesinger. *Journals: 1952-2000*. New York: The Penguin Press, 2007.

Sheehan, Neil. *A Bright Shining Lie: John Paul Vann and America in Vietnam*. New York: Random House, 1988.

Shesol, Jeff. *Mutual Contempt: Lyndon Johnson, Robert Kennedy, and the Feud that Defined a Decade*. New York: Norton, 1997.

Sitkoff, Harvard. *King: Pilgrimage to the Mountaintop*. New York: Hill &Wang, 2008.

Smith, Jeffrey K. *Rendezvous in Dallas: The Assassination of John F. Kennedy*. AuthorHouse: 2009.

Sorenson, Theodore C. *Kennedy*. New York: Harper & Row, 1965.

Sorenson, Ted. *Counselor: A Life at the Edge of History*. New York: Harper Collins, 2005.

Stossel, Scott. *Sarge: The Life and Times of Sargent Shriver*. Washington, D.C.: Smithsonian Books, 2004.

Strober, Gerald S. and Deborah M. Strober. *Let Us Begin Anew: An Oral History of the Kennedy Presidency*. New York: Harper Collins Publishers, 1993.

Thomas, Evan. *Robert Kennedy: His Life*. New York: Simon & Schuster, 2000.

Thompson, Robert E. and Hortense Meyers. *Robert F. Kennedy: The Brother Within*. New York: Dell, 1963.

Valenti: Jack. *A Very Human President*. New York: Norton, 1975.

White, Theodore H. *The Making of a President*. New York: New American Library, 1965,

Witcover, Jules. *85 Days: The Last Campaign of Robert F. Kennedy*. New York: Quill, 1969.

Woods, Randall B. *LBJ: Architect of American Ambition*. New York: Free Press, 2007.

Youngblood, Rufus W. *Twenty Years in the Secret Service: My Life with Five Presidents*. New York: Simon & Schuster, 1973.

Web sites:

www.washingtonpost.com
www.dallasmorningnews.com
www.nytimes.com
www.look.com

www.newsweek.com
www.esquire.com
www.wsj.com
www.latimes.com
www.msnbc.com
www.usatoday.com
www.ap.com
www.upi.com
www.lbjlib.utexas.edu
www.whitehouse.gov
www.fas.org
www.vietnamwar.comarchive.org
www.historycentral.com
www.bioguide.congress.gov
www.pbs.org
www.educatetheusa.com
www.cnn.com
www.theweek.com

ACKNOWLEDGEMENTS

This book is not a comprehensive biography of Lyndon B. Johnson or Robert F. Kennedy, nor is it, by any means, a detailed chronology of the turbulent decade of the 1960s. Entire books are devoted to those subjects, and many are referenced in the Bibliography. I am grateful to those authors, living and dead, who have previously chronicled the life and times of these two political legends.

The presidency of Lyndon Johnson has been illuminated by the availability of *643* hours of audio taped conversations that were made available to the public in the early 1990s. LBJ ceded control of those recordings to his presidential library shortly before his death in 1973, with the provision that they not be made public for *fifty* years. Through the interventions of Lady Bird Johnson, Harry Middleton (Director of the *Lyndon Baines Johnson Presidential Library*), and other Johnson associates, the recordings were ultimately made available some *twenty* years after LBJ's death.

Lyndon Johnson's secret recordings captured raw history in unprecedented fashion. In contrast to Franklin Roosevelt and Dwight Eisenhower (both of whom rarely used the covert recording system, Harry Truman (who refused to use it), and John F. Kennedy (who recorded *250 hours* of meetings and *twelve hours* of telephone conversations), LBJ captured over *9500* conversations (mostly telephone calls, with a lesser number of Oval Office and Cabinet room chats). Lady Bird Johnson regularly dictated her diary into what she referred to as her "talking machine," immeasurably adding to the historical record.

Secret recordings contributed mightily to the downfall of Johnson's successor (by revealing Richard Nixon's blatant abuse of power and failed attempts to obstruct justice during the *Watergate* scandal). There is no available evidence that Gerald Ford, Jimmy Carter, Ronald Reagan, George H.W. Bush, Bill Clinton, George W. Bush, or Barak Obama have utilized this controversial method of recording living history. The aptly named *Johnson Tapes* have afforded historians a rare window into the American presidency. Researchers are indebted to historian, Michael Beschloss, who has compiled two annotated volumes of the LBJ recordings (as noted in the Bibliography).

As always, I am appreciative of the love and patience of my wife, Anne, who once again endured my absorption with the dates, personalities, and events of a particular historic era. She also reviewed this manuscript on two separate occasions. I love her very much.

My sons, Andy and Ben, who have grown up entirely too fast, remain the light of my life.

Jim Fulmer once again gave generously of his time, providing feedback about story development, and lent his considerable editing skills (this is our fourth book together). I am honored to call him my friend.

It is my sincere hope that this book was both entertaining and informative. If you have questions concerning chronology or historical accuracy, I welcome your feedback. However, when you discover typographical, spelling, and/or grammatical errors, please share those with anyone else but me. By the time you identify those mistakes, I can do little more than provide you a reference letter to support your quest to become an editor.

Thank you taking time to read *Bad Blood: Lyndon B. Johnson, Robert F. Kennedy, and the Tumultuous 1960s.*

ABOUT THE AUTHOR

Jeffrey K. Smith is a physician and writer. A native of Enterprise, Alabama, he received his undergraduate and medical degrees from the University of Alabama, and completed his residency at the William S. Hall Psychiatric Institute in Columbia, South Carolina. Since 1990, he has worked in private practice in upstate South Carolina.

Dr. Smith resides in Greer, South Carolina, along with his wife, Anne, and their two sons, Andy and Ben.

OTHER BOOKS BY JEFFREY K. SMITH

Novels:

Sudden Despair

Two Down, Two to Go

A Phantom Killer

Non-fiction:

Rendezvous in Dallas: The Assassination of John F. Kennedy

The Fighting Little Judge: The Life and Times of George C. Wallace

Fire in the Sky: The Story of the Atomic Bomb

To learn more about these books and purchase copies, please visit **www. newfrontierpublications.net.**

Lightning Source UK Ltd.
Milton Keynes UK
UKOW040058160911

178735UK00001B/124/P